COLONIZE
THIS!

COLONIZE THIS!

YOUNG WOMEN OF COLOR ON TODAY'S FEMINISM

New Edition

EDITED BY DAISY HERNÁNDEZ
AND BUSHRA REHMAN

SEAL PRESS

Seal Press
Hachette Book Group
1290 Avenue of the Americas, New York, NY 10104
www.sealpress.com

Second Edition: July 2019

Printed in the United States of America

Published by Seal Press, an imprint of Perseus Books, LLC, a subsidiary of Hachette Book Group, Inc. The Seal Press name and logo is a trademark of the Hachette Book Group.

The publisher is not responsible for websites (or their content) that are not owned by the publisher.

Print book interior design by Six Red Marbles Inc.

Library of Congress Control Number: 2018021019

ISBN: 978-1-58005-776-9 (paperback), 978-1-58005-883-4 (ebook)

LSC-C

10 9 8 7 6 5 4 3

Contents

Family and Community: A Litany for Survival

Talking Back, Taking Back

Foreword

"The War Path of Greater Empowerment"

CHERRÍE L. MORAGA

Colonize This! is a collection of writings by young women of color that testifies to the movement—political and physical—of a new generation of global citizens, activists, and artists. It is a portrait of the changing landscape of US women of color identity, one that guarantees no loyalties to the borders that attempt to contain it. As immigrant, native-born, and survivor-of-slavery daughters, these women are the female children of those "refugees from a world on fire" described in the 1983 edition of *This Bridge Called My Back*.[1] They are women who have come of age with the living memory of disappearance in Colombia and Argentina and the daily reality of war "always a phone call away." They are young sisters (our daughters) who didn't "grow up to be statistics" (Taigi Smith), who have read and been schooled by the feminist writings and works of the women of color who preceded them, and as such are free to ask questions of feminism more deeply than we could have imagined twenty years ago.

The feminism portrayed in *Colonize This!* reflects what in the 1980s we understood as "theory in the flesh," a strategy for women's liberation which is wrought from the living example of female labor and woman acts of loving. These narratives reflect consciousness born out of what their (our) mothers "knew first-hand: the interlocking system of racism, poverty, and sexism" (Siobhan Brooks). In *Colonize This!*, mothers serve as mirrors of choices made and unmade. They are the reflection of sacrifice, survival, and sabiduría.

They are Cecilia Ballí's mother, who each evening wiped off the dining room table after dinner to "double as a desk" for her two daughters;[2] they are she who had no more than seven years of school buying encyclopedias from the grocery store on the installment plan.

They are Ena from British Guiana, who used her sexiness to "'get' things," like "money, kerosene to light the lamps, and food for her children" (Paula Austin). They are Tanmeet Sethi's mother, who advised, "You have to make home wherever you are." And this is what she did—coming to the United States with a stranger who was her new husband. They are Siobhan Brooks's mother, who was once placed in a mental hospital for infanticide, and who, in spite of her "mental state,...paid the bills on time, shopped for food, and refused the free bread-and-butter services the government offered."

They are models of resistance from whom their daughters, through fierce loyalty to them, wield weapons of theory and practice.

In *Colonize This!*, editors Bushra Rehman and Daisy Hernández have created an expanded vocabulary to describe an expanded feminism profoundly altered by massive immigration to the United States from North Africa, South and West Asia, and Central and South America. An echoing theme in this collection is the impact of the US experience in introducing the critical questions of inequalities in relation to gender. Similarly echoed is the profound disappointment in white feminist theory to truly respond to the specific cultural and class-constructed conditions of women of color lives. As Ijeoma A. describes it, consciousness about sexism assumed language and impetus in the United States, but it was born in the "kitchens" of her native Nigeria.[3] *Colonize This!* draws a complex map of feminism, one that fights sexism and colonialism at once and recognizes genocide as a present and daily threat to our blood-nations. The feminism articulated in this collection requires cultural tradition and invention, negotiating multiple worlds; it is a theory and freedom practice which "allow[s] women to retain their culture, to have pride in their traditions, and to still vocalize the gender issues of their community" (Susan Muaddi Darraj). As Tanmeet Sethi writes, she is happy to "wear the weight of [her] culture." She speaks of the gold jewelry inherited from family, but more so, she speaks of the profound preciousness of culture: "It is heavy but not a burden."

As a new generation of women of color, these writers carry a new language to describe their passions, their política, their prayer, and their problems. In these narratives, Black feminism finds resonance in hip hop. Racism is now called "driving while black" and "walking while brown" (Pandora Leong) in the middle-class neighborhoods of Oregon.[4] White male entitlement assumes a twenty-first-century look in blond dread-locked Indophiles studying Buddhism and "getting down with the people" (Bhavana Mody). Here, sexuality and pleasure are unabashedly integrated in a feminist of color analysis of survival and liberation, and "queer familia" is neither a question nor the subject of debate.

> **" As a new generation of women of color, these writers carry a new language to describe their passions, their política, their prayer, and their problems. "**

Still, some things haven't changed. Stereotyping does not change, as Alaska-born Asian-American Pandora Leong reminds us: "I do not read Chinese or know anything about acupuncture."

Women of color still suffer the same assaults against our bodies, the artillery of misogyny ever inventive. Patricia Justine Tumang testifies to the "living nightmare" of the RU-486 "abortion" pill;[5] and Stella Luna recounts her own struggle for self-reclamation as a mother with HIV, writing:

> I realized that I was imprisoned not only by a disease but also by a culture that had trained me to be as clean and untouched in soul and body as the Virgen de Guadalupe....If I chose to live my life according to this structure, maybe I should just give up and die.

This is the real work of woman of color feminism: to resist acquiescence to fatality and guilt, to become warriors of conscience and action who resist death in all its myriad manifestations: poverty, cultural assimilation, child abuse, motherless mothering, gentrification, mental illness, welfare cuts, the prison system, racial profiling, immigrant and queer bashing, and invasion and imperialism at home and at war.

To fight any kind of war, Kahente Horn-Miller writes, quoting her elder, "the biggest single requirement is FIGHTING SPIRIT." I thought much of this as I read *Colonize This!*, since this collection appears in print at a time of escalating worldwide war—in Colombia, Afghanistan, Palestine. But is there ever a time of no-war for women of color? Is there ever a time when our home (our body, our land of origin) is not subject to violent occupation, violent invasion? If I retain any image to hold the heart-intention of this book, it is found in what Horn-Miller calls the necessity of "the war dance." This book is one rite of passage, one ceremony of preparedness on the road to consciousness, on the the war path of greater empowerment.

May 14, 2002
Oakland, California

Introduction to the Second Edition

DAISY HERNÁNDEZ

I became a feminist because of an index card.

It was my junior year of college, and I found myself one afternoon in a room at the student center that had a very low ceiling and thin carpeting. I had shown up not because the event was organized by the Feminist Collective, but because it had been advertised as a workshop on sexuality. Being the daughter of Cuban and Colombian immigrants who had worked in factories, I thought of sex as taboo. Now here was the word on a flier like an invitation.

That is how I ended up sitting in a stiff chair in a circle of mostly white girls, all of us with index cards and pens in our hands. On one side of the card, we noted our best sexual encounters, and on the back our worst. We were giddy, pensive, nervous. We glanced at each other, then at the cards. Some of us wrote too quickly. Others tapped the edges of the cards. I already knew my answers. I wrote swiftly.

The moderator collected the cards and began reading aloud from them. They were anonymous, of course, and she read the good ones first: multiple orgasms, the pleasures of receiving oral sex, hearing "I love you" after sex. I grinned like I knew what that was all about, but in reality I'd only read about most of these sexual joys in *Cosmo*. Here though were real women (my age!) confirming that sex could be good.

Then the moderator flipped the index cards and began reading the other side. Out came short lines about the boyfriend who wouldn't take no for an answer, the friend who demanded sex, the family member who forced himself. We fell silent. I fell silent. I don't remember now whether I wrote about the family member who had molested me as a child, but I do remember thinking: it wasn't just us.

"Us" was me and the girls I had known over the years who had also been abused. I had thought sexual violence only happened to me and my friends. I had thought it had to do with the way we looked, the length of our legs, our dark hair. Now here was a stack of index cards from girls I had never met before, and the index cards were telling me that my experiences as a Latina girl in one corner of Jersey belonged to a much larger story of violence against mujeres.

Later, I learned that in the early 1970s, the writer Jane O'Reilly had called this the "click"—that moment when you realize that what happens to you because you're a woman is happening to other women, too. A new awareness snaps into place. I was ready to call myself a feminist.

There was only one problem. My father.

When I was in my early twenties, academics were theorizing about the "voice" of the teenage girl—how it develops, and how she loses it—but for as long as I could remember I had used my girl voice to speak for my Cuban father, who is only fluent in Spanish. I interpreted for him at the factory where he worked and also at unemployment agencies and banks. It didn't matter whether I was twelve or twenty-two. I was Papi's voice. At home, he terrorized me and the women in our family with his rage and alcohol abuse, but out in the world, he relied on me.

Feminism for me had to address not only my experiences of gender but also of race, multilingualism, citizenship, class, and diaspora. By the time I left college and was harboring crushes on women and gender-nonconforming people, I realized that feminism had to also be about queerness. Was that a tall order? I didn't think so. It was my life and the lives of the women I knew.

After college, I discovered that black feminists—Barbara Smith, for example—had been arguing since the 1970s that feminism had to tackle how black women experience gender in combination with race and class. Smith and her feminist comadres penned this argument in the now-famous Combahee River Collective Statement, and in 1980 Gloria Anzaldúa and Cherríe Moraga published the anthology *This Bridge Called My Back*, bringing together women of color to talk about feminism, raza y más. In that book, Cherríe wrote exactly what I was thinking about two decades later: "I want a movement that helps me make some sense of the trip from Watertown to Roxbury, from white to Black. I love women the entire way, beyond a doubt."

I, too, needed a feminism that helped me make sense of the bus rides I took between my publishing job in Manhattan and my Latina neighborhood in Jersey, between my Chicana mixed-race girlfriend in the Bronx and my Colombian mother in Jersey. My experience with sexual abuse, racism, and classism was part of a larger narrative, but so, too, was my desire for a more expansive understanding of feminism. Again, I was not la única. My own writing and thinking belonged to a feminist of color tradition that exists in politics, scholarship, and the arts.

When Bushra and I began working on the first edition of this book, mainstream media outlets were not using the word "intersectionality"—a term and theory Dr. Kimberlé Crenshaw created in the

1980s to identify how black women face institutional practices that recognize gender or race bias but not where those two meet. Today, the word "intersectionality" is all over social media and in national newspapers.

The contributors from the first edition of *Colonize This!* have been a part of this change. Since the publication of that edition, they have gone on to lead community organizations and create new scholarship about and by women of color. They have taken their feminism into their work inside and outside of government. They have served as doctors, penned their own books, and made films. They have led the way, in other words, by doing.

History, however, does repeat itself. We produced the first edition of this book in the wake of the terrorist attacks of September 11, 2001, when police, government officials, and the entire country, it seemed, were racially profiling brown, Arab, and Muslim men and women. More than fifteen years later, we worked on the second edition in the wake of the 2016 presidential election, and the ban on people traveling to the United States from five Muslim countries. My father yelled at me over the phone to not protest against the white man in the White House, even though that man admitted to being a sexual predator and has openly supported white supremacists. "I'm going to the protest!" I told Papi. I bought cardboard and made signs. I called my Republican senator and left messages. I grabbed the bullhorn at the march downtown.

And I worked on this book.

This second edition of *Colonize This!* is, for me, a protest to the current political regime in our country. It is a response to the deportations of immigrant families, to the relentless killing of black people by police officers, and to the media outlets that describe the abuse of girls by old white men as "sexual encounters." This book, being as it is a gathering of young women of color sharing their experiences and intellectual insights, stands in defiance of what is happening in the courts, in Washington, and on the streets of our country. That said, this new edition didn't begin as a protest.

Initially, Bushra and I had wanted to see the stories from young women of color who have been at the forefront of key social justice movements for the past decade. From Black Lives Matter and trans visibility to organizing undocumented families and protesting at Standing Rock, young women of color have been working hard for a more socially just world. They have been creating new terminology: #MeToo, Black Lives Matter, UndocuQueer. I was hungry to read the stories of these young women of color. What does feminism look like for young women of color who grew up with the first black president? With a visible transgender movement? With social media platforms?

Bushra and I set out to find nine young women who could answer these questions and join the voices from the first edition. This new edition has essays about working as an abortion doula, handling call-out culture online as a trans Latina, and being catapulted into the spotlight after suing a high-profile university for failing to protect women from sexual assault on campus. The new essays address being undocumented and an artist, coming of age with Michelle Obama and Disney movies, and what happens when gun violence takes your big sister, and #SayHerName is not only a hashtag and a movement but your day-to-day life.

These young women of color are leveraging social media to their advantage. They are using it to organize and to break silences and also to learn about feminism and to redefine it. They have grown up in a more multiracial United States with faster access to the work of feminists of color, and as a result they are articulating an intersectional feminism that is rooted in the work of the women who have come before us. It is also equally true that institutional barriers—from a lack of daycare when you're a teen mom to the war on black families—persist in the lives of young women of color today.

One new contributor asked, "And you're doing this new edition with your original coeditor?" Yes. In a world where women are so often pitted against each other, and where social media makes bruising each other all too easy, Bushra and I have been blessed. No, that makes it sound like we got lucky. The truth is, we worked hard at staying connected over the years even as we published and promoted our own books, as she became a mother, and as I moved around the country. We also worked hard at intentionally making room for each other's perspectives, trusting that talking it through would create a better book in the end. I believe we have succeeded a second time.

A final thought: Working on this new edition has affirmed for me the importance of focusing on what is happening in our communities of color and on being the ones who tell our stories. As Sonia Guiñansaca writes in her essay about undocumented youth: "We did the work to claim our lives." This, I believe, is the way forward: we have to claim our lives and claim our stories. There is no substitute for the power that comes from doing so. It is energizing and empowering, and ultimately it makes everything else possible.

> **" We have to claim our lives and claim our stories. There is no substitute for the power that comes from doing so. "**

March 28, 2018
Siler City, North Carolina

Introduction to the Second Edition

BUSHRA REHMAN

Daisy and I used to joke, "You're Cherríe and I'm Gloria," when we were editing the first edition of *Colonize This!* There was something about the softness and hardness we wanted to evoke. And yes, who was the soft and who was the hard and what did we really mean? But we were young, and we idolized, tried to imagine our lives by holding them up to the women before us.

So you can imagine our joy when Rebecca Hurdis, one of the writers in *Colonize This!*, invited Daisy and me to the twentieth anniversary celebration of *This Bridge Called My Back* taking place at the University of California, Berkeley. Rebecca had written movingly about her discovery of *This Bridge* (her essay inspiring my own discovery, because yes, I was just as misled by whitewashed history).

It felt like a family reunion. So many radical women had gathered: Cherríe Moraga, Gloria Anzaldúa, Barbara Smith, Angela Davis, and many of the writers from *This Bridge*. I was asked to read poetry; Daisy and I were asked to speak about *Colonize This!*, which had not yet been published.

My strongest impression from the conference, the feeling I left with and still hold with wonder, was the intensity of seeing a generation of women of color before me. It wasn't until then that I truly began to believe I could have a future. My whole life, I was constantly told in direct and indirect ways that when I was old, I would end up lonely, without a family and a home, if I persisted with my resistance to marriage, my desire to write. But here at UC Berkeley, feminist, trans, and women of color writers and activists in their fifties, sixties, and seventies were full of life, friendship, and laughter.

I remember a light heart, but if I take another moment to truly remember, it was a light heart among the darkness, a feeling of emergency. It was February 2002, five months after 9/11. I am a New Yorker and a Muslim. Need I say more about the radical, anti-war, onto-the-bullshit-the-government-was-saying place I was in?

I listened carefully while Angela Davis outlined the deliberateness of the prison-industrial complex as a tool of oppression. I listened carefully while Barbara Smith talked about how the words "identity politics" had been lifted from the Combahee River Collective, and how the original intention of the term and the practice were meant solely for revolutionary purposes.

Gloria's talk was almost wordless. She projected a series of images. Is it too dramatic to say it was a spiritual experience, and like every spiritual experience, felt like an odd dream afterward? She drew ripples, spirals, and stones, let us know it was a spiritual journey we were on, not a clamoring for awards and attention.

I was blown away by it all. And when the scholar-activist Nadine Naber, who had just returned from Palestine, began to cry while reporting on the torture, displacement, and murder of Palestinian children and families under Israeli occupation and colonization, I bent my head and cried too.

It's not that I think feminism happens only at conferences. I was working on *Colonize This!* not because I was an expert on feminism (whatever that means) but because I wanted to understand and explain what it could mean to a woman like me.

Who was I at twenty-seven? Rebellious, self-destructive, malnourished, barely scraping by, a disowned daughter, a vagabond; most called me a freak. The only thread I held onto was the writing. It was something I knew, a secret I understood, this thing called writing. I was driven to it despite every force that tried to stop me.

Now, in Berkeley, I was surrounded by women who were further on the path of writing and creating revolution. It was at this gathering that Cherríe agreed to write the foreword for *Colonize This!* and Gloria agreed to write a blurb. Their generosity and kindness overwhelmed me. We were invited to Gloria's home in Santa Cruz. Daisy, her girlfriend Kristina, and I planned a road trip to visit Gloria on Daisy's birthday, but eight days before we did, Gloria, who had been ill, passed away.

Deeply saddened, we decided to keep our intention; we drove from Oakland and stood outside Gloria's house for a moment. Daisy had visited her once before and remembered the tree that had been one of Gloria's favorites. It grew by the ocean near her home. We knew for sure we had found the right one when we saw someone had put a candle at the foot. We sat beneath the leaves in the beautiful Santa Cruz sun and ate birthday cake Kristina had packed in Tupperware for the trip.

Now, we are a few years away from our own twentieth anniversary. I know the writers in *Colonize This!* have inspired me to have courage in the face of the constant barrage of choking oppressions I live and breathe. I know it has done the same for readers who've reached out to Daisy and me, readers who've told us *Colonize This!* changed their lives, brought them to activism, let them know they were not alone. There was only so long I could listen to the hate spewed by this current administration before realizing it was time to bring the voices of *Colonize This!* into the world again. And yet, I was exhausted.

I thought of Gloria, how well she had put this action in the face of weariness into words. I reread "Speaking in Tongues: A Letter to Third World Women Writers," one of her essays in *This Bridge*. The fog in my head cleared a little bit. Gloria was telling me to write; she was saying yes, she understood, that I was tired, overworked, frustrated, angry, weighed down by decades of sadness and guilt, centuries of brutality, and here I was craving sweets, doing everything but the writing, wanting to crawl up into a ball and sleep.

Gloria wrote, "Be simple, direct, immediate." Gloria, I will try.

As I write this, there are youth-led marches to end gun violence taking place all over the world. My partner is live-streaming the march from DC via *Democracy Now!* I am in tears from the power and eloquence of the speakers. It is the youth, and always has been the youth, who have carried the fire and the light forward.

My heart is with the marchers, but I am inside, trying to finish this book, in hopes it will continue to have revolutionary power. For the first time, I think of how Cherríe and Gloria must have seen us. Was it how I see the youth now, taking on leadership and fighting with love and rage against this sickening, violent, corrupt moment we are living in? I am filled with overwhelming gratitude that these young activists can be more radical than we were and humbled to know *Colonize This!* had some small part in moving the marker just a little bit more toward the light.

> **❝ It is the youth, and always has been the youth, who have carried the fire and the light forward. ❞**

March 24, 2018
Brooklyn, New York

Introduction to the First Edition

BUSHRA REHMAN
DAISY HERNÁNDEZ

December 7, 2001

This morning I woke up to the news radio. Women were throwing off their veils in Afghanistan and I thought about how for years the women I have known have wanted this to happen. But now what a hollow victory it all is. I am disgusted by the us-and-them mentality. "We," the liberated Americans, must save "them," the oppressed women. What kind of feminist victory is it when we liberate women by killing their men and any woman or child who happens to be where a bomb hits? I feel myself as a Muslim-American woman, as a woman of color, fearing walking down the street, feeling the pain that my friends felt as they were beaten down in the weeks after September 11. Solemnly, we counted as the numbers rose: two, five, seven...My friend telling me: They told me I smelled—they touched me everywhere—and when I talked back, they made fun of me, grabbed me, held my arms back, told me to go back to my country, took my money and ran. My other friend telling me: They punched me, kicked me, called me queer—they found the pamphlets in my bag, and I'm here on asylum, for being a queer activist—my papers were just going through—I'm not safe in this country as a gay man. My other friends telling me: We didn't want to report it to the police, why just start another case of racial profiling? They're not going to find the guys who did it. They're just going to use our pain as an excuse for more violence. Use our pain as an excuse for more violence. This is what I hear again and again in a city that is grieving, that is beginning to see what other countries live every day.

But where does women of color feminism fit into all of this? Everywhere. As women of color feminists, this is what we have to think about.

—Bushra Rehman

February 12, 2002

At first I think the teacups have fallen. Broken, they sit on a shelf in the attic apartment Bushra and her sister Sa'dia share. The teacups look antique, etched with thin lines that loop like the penmanship from old textbooks. I imagine they have been in the family for years, but then I find out they were created by Sa'dia for her art exhibit. She made the cups and inscribed each one with the name of a woman from her family. Each cup represents that woman and is broken to the degree of her rebellions. Some are cracked a little, others shattered. They are piled on top of each other, as if someone needs to do the dishes.

The teacups broken and the women broken. That's how it feels sitting on this thin carpet, editing these essays on feminism while Washington wages war against terrorism. Life feels like something broken on purpose. During the Spanish evening news, a man in Afghanistan says, "It was an enemy plane and a woman cried." His words stay with me as if they were a poem. It was an enemy plane and a woman cried. I think of that woman and TV cameras in Colombia, my mother's country. The footage shows bloodied streets and women crying. My mother refuses to look. I can't look away. Her eyes are sad and grateful: my American daughter who can just watch this on TV. My aunt gives us cups of tea and tells me to watch what I say on the phone. Rumors are spreading that the FBI is making people disappear. My aunt with the

wide smile. She tapes an American flag to my window, determined to
keep us safe.

—Daisy Hernández

When we began editing this book, we knew only a little about each other. We were two dark-haired women who moved in overlapping circles of writers, queers, artists, and feminists. We had met in New York City through the collective Women in Literature and Letters (WILL), which organized affordable writing programs that were women of color–centered. It was while editing this book, however, that we realized how much a Pakistani Muslim girl from Queens could have in common with a Catholic Cuban-Colombian girl from New Jersey.

We both grew up bilingual in working-class immigrant neighborhoods. Our childhoods had been steeped in the religions and traditions of our parents' homelands, and at an early age, we were well acquainted with going through customs, both at home and at the airports. We followed our parents' faith like good daughters until we became women: At fifteen, Daisy left obligatory Sunday Mass and Catholicism when a nun said the Bible didn't have to be interpreted literally, and no, Noah's ark had never existed. At sixteen, Bushra discovered her body—and stopped praying five times a day.

Of course, there were also differences. Bushra had been raised knowing that violence was as common as friendship between people of color. Her family had moved from Pakistan to New York City to Saudi Arabia to Pakistan and then back to New York City. Daisy, on the other hand, had grown up with white European immigrants who were becoming white Americans, and her familia had only moved from one side of town to the other. We broke with our families in different ways: Bushra left home without getting married; Daisy stayed home and began dating women.

Our personal rebellions led to a loss of family that took us on another path, where we met other not-so-perfect South Asian and Latina women also working for social change. It felt like it had taken us a lifetime to find these spaces with women who gave us a feeling of familiarity and of belonging, something that had never been a given in our lives. With these women we could talk about our families and find the understanding that would help us go back home. We began to realize, however, that working with our own communities was only the groundwork. To make change happen we needed to partner up with other women of color. To work on this book we had to venture out of our safe zones.

And then 9/11 happened. People from our communities turned on each other in new ways. Girls wearing hijab to elementary school were being slapped by other girls of color. Any mujer dating an Arab man was now suspect in her own community. People we considered friends were now suspicious of Middle Eastern men, Muslims, and Arab immigrants, even if they were immigrants themselves. Living near Ground Zero, we watched people respond to their grief and fear with violence that escalated in both action and conversation, and we felt our own fear close to home: Daisy was afraid that, with the surge of pro-American sentiments, her mother would be mistreated for not speaking English, and Bushra feared for her mother and sisters who veil, and for her father and brothers with beards who fit the look of "terrorists."

In response to the war, we wanted to do "traditional" activist work, to organize rallies and protest on the street, but abandoning this book project didn't feel right. Darice Jones, one of our contributors, reminded us of Angela Davis's words: we are living in a world for which old forms of activism are not enough, and today's activism is about creating coalitions between communities. This is exactly our hope for this book. Despite differences of language, skin color, and class, we have a long, shared history of oppression and resistance. For us, this book is activism, a way to continue the conversations among young women of color found in earlier books like *This Bridge Called My Back* and *Making Face, Making Soul*.

After many late-night talks, we chose the title of Cristina Tzintzún's essay, "Colonize This!," for the book, to acknowledge how the stories of women and colonization are intimately tied. But when we first sat down to write this introduction and looked in the dictionary, we found that "colonize" means "to create a settlement." It sounded so simple and peaceful. We rewrote the definition. To colonize is "to strip a people of their culture, language, land, family structure, who they are as a person and as a people." Ironically, the dictionary helped us better articulate the meaning of this book. It reminded us that it's important for women of color to write. We can't have someone else defining our lives or our feminism.

Like many other women of color, the two of us first learned the language of feminism in college through a white, middle-class perspective, one form of colonization. Feminism should have brought us closer to our mothers and sisters and to our aunties in the Third World. Instead it took us further away. The academic feminism didn't teach us how to talk with the women in our families about why they stayed with alcoholic husbands or chose to veil. In rejecting their life choices as women, we lost a part of ourselves and our own history.

This is difficult to write, because initially, white feminism felt so liberating. It gave us a framework for understanding the silences and tempers of our fathers and the religious piety of our mothers. It gave us Ani DiFranco's music to sing to and professors who told us that, no, patriarchy isn't only in our homes. It is everywhere.

There is actually a system in place that we can analyze and even change.

But our experience with white feminism was bittersweet at best. Daisy felt uncomfortable talking about her parents' factory work in the middle-class living rooms where feminists met to talk about sweatshops. Bushra realized how different she was from her feminist sisters when she critiqued the Israeli occupation or when she was asked to choose between her identity as a Muslim and as an American. There was always a dualism at play between our "enlightened" feminist friends at college and the "unenlightened," nonfeminist women in our families. We wondered how it could be that, according to feminist thought, our mothers were considered passive when they raised six children; when they worked night and day at stores, in factories, and at home; and when they were feared and respected even by the bully on the block.

It was only after college, through word of mouth from other women of color, that we learned about another kind of feminism. These groups practiced women of color feminism, sometimes naming it as such and sometimes not saying it at all. Daisy joined WILL, a collective founded by three Latinas to use writing as a political weapon, and that's how she first read Cherríe Moraga's writings on homosexuality and began publishing her own work. Bushra joined the South Asian Women's Creative Collective (SAWCC), where she found a desi audience and began performing her poetry, first in New York City and eventually around the country. It was among these women that we both began developing a feminist way of looking at la vida that linked the shit we got as women to the color of our skin, the languages we spoke, and the zip codes we knew as home.

Our feminism lies where other people don't expect it to. As we write this introduction, the cop who (allegedly) took part in sodomizing Abner Louima has just been released from jail. We see pictures of the cop kissing his wife splattered across the newspapers. This sanctioning of sexual violence and police brutality against a black Haitian immigrant feels like a slap in the face. For us, as women of color, this is where our feminism lies. When the media vilifies a whole race, when a woman breaks the image of a model minority, when she leaves her entire community behind only to re-create it continually in her art and her writing, or when our neighborhoods are being gentrified—this is also where our feminism lies.

> **As young women of color, we have found that our relationship to feminism is both like and unlike that of the women in our mothers' generation. We've grown up with legalized abortion, and the legacy of the Civil Rights movement and gay liberation, but we still deal with sexual harassment, racist remarks from feminists, and the homophobia within our communities.**

As young women of color, we have found that our relationship to feminism is both like and unlike that of the women in our mothers' generation. We've grown up with legalized abortion, and the legacy of the Civil Rights movement and gay liberation, but we still deal with sexual harassment, racist remarks from feminists, and the homophobia within our communities. The difference is that now we talk about these issues in women's studies classes, in classrooms that are multicultural but xenophobic, and in a society that pretends to be racially integrated but remains racially profiled.

We have also grown up with a body of literature created by women of color in the past thirty years— Alice Walker's words about womanism, Gloria Anzaldúa's theories about living in the borderlands, and Audre Lorde's writings about silences and survival. In reading the submissions for this anthology, we found that it was the books that kept young women of color sane through college, abortions, and first romances with women. Many of us just needed the books: we needed another woman of color writing about her fear of loving a dark woman's body, or about being black and pregnant and feeling the scarcity of her choices.

In working with the writers in this book, we often thought of Audre Lorde's words from her poem "A Litany for Survival": *"We were never meant to survive."*[1] Who would think that we would survive—we, young girls prey to the hands of men, the insults of teachers, the restrictive laws of holy texts, and a world that tells us, "This is not your world." For the young women in this book, creating lives on their own terms is an act of survival and resistance. It's also a part of a larger liberation struggle for women and people of color.

With these ideas and essays in hand, we locked ourselves up for weeks at a time until the book took form. We chose to focus on the four major themes of family and community, mothers, cultural customs, and talking back. Our first section, "Family and Community: A Litany for Survival," describes how we band closer to our birth or chosen families because of the hostility in the world, because of someone calling us "spic," "nigger," "fag," or "terrorist," or because political and economic wars are only a phone call away to aunties living in Nicaragua or the Philippines. But family is only a safe zone until you kiss another woman, question the faith, or go to the movies with a white boy. With our communities we're expected to suppress our individual selves and our dissent in order to look strong in the face of racism. In this section, mixed-race women write to those of us who question their belonging to a women of color community. Women also search for chosen families and live different lives after being diagnosed with HIV. Their feminism and community activism are based on the model of family.

"Our Mothers, Refugees from a World on Fire" is about our inclination as young women of color to see our mothers as the "real" feminists, the ones who practice rather than preach. While college may have given us the theories, many of us return home for a working definition of what it means to be a feminist. The mothers in this section are strong women who told us to get married, go to school, pray, and avoid sex. They depended on each other, on sisters, neighbors, and best friends, to watch over us while they themselves were coping with mental illness, poverty, or raising too many kids. They are the women Cherríe Moraga wrote about twenty years ago when she said our parents were "refugees from a world on fire." We were just kids then, playing on the streets and translating for our mothers in supermarkets and at the doctor's office.

"Going Through Customs," our third section, is about what it's like when every part of us is vulnerable at the checkpoint, when we're asked to check our language, our clothing, our food at the door. Many of us have been negotiating identities from the first time we stepped out of our parents' home. When our parents came here with stars in their eyes and fear in their guts, they didn't realize all they would have to give up. When they hoped for a better future for us, they didn't realize they were giving up a chance to have good Muslim, good Nigerian, good Mexican daughters. "Going Through Customs" is our own way of picking and choosing what we will keep from our traditions and what we will bring into our lives now.

Our last section, "Talking Back, Taking Back," borrows from the title of bell hooks's book and shows women talking back to white feminists, white Americans, men on the streets, their mothers, and liberals. For young women of color, so much of feminism has meant talking back and taking back the world that we live in. It is a taking back of our image and a breaking down of roles imposed on us, whether it's that of the model minority or the affirmative action kid. These women talk back when someone tells us that racism is over because there are a handful of African Americans in the honors class, when we can't walk down the street wearing what we want because we'll be sexually harassed, when they tell us that black women have no problem with body image just because all the women in the magazines are white. Here are women talking back to stereotypes and taking back a history that has been denied to us.

We hope that this book will introduce some of the ideas of women of color feminism to women who have thought that feminism is a philosophy about white men and women and has nothing to do with our communities. We also want this book to deepen conversations between young women of color. We believe that hearing each other out about our differences and similarities is an important step toward figuring out how to work with whatever divides us.

We have learned so much from the process and from each contributor. Our own work as writers has taken on more urgency because of this book, and we hope other young women will also be moved to action. We know that one book can't do it all, and our lack of resources sometimes made it difficult to reach women who also lacked the resources of money and time. But we hope that this anthology will inspire other women to fill in our gaps and move the work forward and deeper. As shani jamila writes at the end of her essay in this book: "The most important thing we can do as a generation is to see our new positions as power and weapons to be used strategically in the struggle rather than as spoils of war. Because this shit is far from finished."

—Bushra Rehman and Daisy Hernández
New York and New Jersey, 2002

FAMILY AND COMMUNITY:
A LITANY FOR SURVIVAL

browngirlworld

queergirlofcolor organizing, sistahood, heartbreak

LEAH LAKSHMI PIEPZNA-SAMARASINHA

These are the histories ever present in every young queer/feminist scene, just undocumented—all the ones that weren't in Michelle Tea's or Sarah Schulman's capturing of white queergirl life. We dark funny girls kick ass, change and make history, but the ass-kicking we do doesn't end up in the official records no matter how crucial we are. We don't kick ass the way the white girls do, whether it's in NOW or riot grrrl. For us, it's all about family. And I want to know: When your politics are all about building family—revolutionary queercoloredgirl fam—what happens?

brotherngirlworld is home and heartbreak, the place where my heart meets my cunt and they cum and rip open at the same moment. I have been an activist, been the one who keeps screaming the chants out in front of the US embassy when everybody else wants to light up, the one cooking chili out of donations for three hundred folks on a broken stove. I did that, but I really went to revolution and feminism cuz I wanted a family that would love me, decolonize me, heal me. The feminism I walked into as a bi-queer brown breed girl was all about the women I wanted to fuck, love, and make home with. More than any meeting, I wanted to make places where my girls, my queer dark sistren, could survive. Do more than: Stop self-destructing. Save each other. Not

3

have a nervous breakdown or six by twenty-five. Decolonize our minds, our hair, our hearts. Transform into the phoenixes we were all meant to be.

I'm a loser in that department, though, one who came to this world with a lot of hope and walked away four years later with a string of heart and cherry busts behind me. Pathetic. Growing up, I dreamed of that chosen political fam that would last my whole life, with some departures of years or decades. There's this trope that repeats itself in the books you and I read to save our lives: that if where you grew up is killing you, you can leave and make a chosen, identity-based fam that takes up where your bio-fam left off. That's usually the straight-up white lefty/queer thang. The coloredgirl one I read about in Chrystos, Gloria Anzaldúa, and Cherríe Moraga said somethin' more: that if the reason my bio-fam was killing me was because they were trying to destroy the brown, the poor in me, bleach out to American, I could run to the girls who were not trying to forget. I wanted that. I grew up surviving because I believed in that. It's hard to let go.

Makes perfect sense why. I'm a mixed brown girl, Sri Lankan and New England milltown white trash, who grew up alone and starving hungry for a sane home. I grew up with my dad being the only Sri Lankan in Worcester, Massachusetts, only he'd clear his throat uncomfortably and say he was from "The British Commonwealth." I grew up with my white mama, who called him, laughing, her "houseboy," and told me to not repeat her mistake and marry anyone dumber than me, while she ripped my hair straight and bloody scalped. I was a brown kinky-headed full-lipped girl in apartheid Massachusetts, white boys chasing me down the street to try and fuck the hot Latina they saw, with browning colonial family photos locked up in trunks, simmering electric heat lightning silences exploding whenever I asked the obvious questions. I wanted to run away. Revolutionary change happens through laws and guns, tear gas and tablas, but it also comes through the families and communities we build to replace the dead life we want to flee.

I grew up in the Reagan eighties dreaming of apocalypse and revolution, knowing we would fight and win it all or die. I fled to many activist scenes, looking for that place. Anarcho-punk as a kid, riot grrrl, anti-Giuliani, anti-cop, anti–Contract on America, ass-kicking in general. When I moved to Toronto for queer-women-of-color-only community in the mid-nineties, along with many others, I thought, *I don't want to waste any more time on white folks.* Or on white queers, on white girls breaking down weeping in women's studies classes. No more Queer Nation, those whips and chains are a white thing. How could I have wasted all this time on fuckin' Susie Bright when my people are in the real shackles of the International Monetary Fund and the colonial mind, and when the Indian Peace Keeping Force is raping a third of the women in the Northern Provinces of Sri Lanka?

> **" We're sistas. We treat each other like sistas. That's the blessin'. That's the problem. We get close. And then we fall in love with each other 'cause us third-world diva gals are beautiful and blessed like none other. "**

Later on, I said goodbye to the straight-of-color scene when my ex went het, joined the Nation, got addicted to using the back of his hand, when the good sistas and brothers all forgot why he and I couldn't go on the same bus to Philly for Millions for Mumia—'cause all that woman and queer stuff was seen as a personal issue, something embarrassing like menstrual pads. So I went to my girls, the one place I could trust, the place Angela Davis said I should find, where my gifts could make the most difference.

WHIRLWIND GIRLS

The Black, brown, red, and yellow girls I went home with are found on the edges of women's studies classes, silent or keepin' on raising her hand, a financial-aid baby or fresh from dark middle-class private school. Eating a free meal at the women's drop-in; the sista outsidahs sitting on the steps, bitch-bonding after the mandatory antiracism training about which white girl said the most stupid thing, getting scholarships to fly to conferences we live on for years afterward. For all our everyday fucked-up trauma, we need to carry around a video camera to document our lives, cuz things happen so fast and ain't nobody gonna believe it otherwise.

When I moved to Toronto, I threw myself in the middle of prison abolition, antipsychiatry, and anticolonial women's activism. Staying up all night fucking to the changing cayso/jungle/hiphopmetal/dub beats, then throwing my clothes on and rushing to do the radical women's radio show. Marching with thousands of other broke, dark faces, we stormed up Spadina Avenue to the copshop each time another man of color branded as crazy was shot. Me and one brown and Black girl, we went for $5 jerk chicken dinners from the restaurant we all went to next to the radio station before they tore it down to make another glitzy mall. She and I sat on the back porch of that tiny two-bedroom, smoking weed and getting ready for the club, debriefing after every meeting, plotting, trying to fix each other up, watching the call display glow with her girlfriend's name and not picking up, finally walking down the street at 2 a.m. to the Caribbean Kitchen to get yet another $6.99 curry goat with green mango special. Me, her, her white girlfriend, her Trini brown fag roommate, our little sis and coworker at the only all-Black dyke-run women's center on any campus, our half-desi femme queerboyfavorite auntie; we waz girls together. No place was safe for all of us; the South Asian queer art show thought we were too light or too Black, too broke or too crazy. We were too queer for Mumia, too political for the bar.

I said I loved her. That was when all the problems started.

Flowchart: You meet, someplace. Each other seems somethin'. Sanity, similar faces, seeming nice in a sea of inanity/assholishness. You go for coffee. You do email. You see each other on the same fringes of the same meetings. You go drink after. You go out in a big pack. You go to her house. Then there's the first big revelation of something intense, close and personal. Usually with much apology for being that way. You say you love each other. Sometimes you fall on the bed, grab ass on the dance floor. You check in, be each other's therapists about all the bullshit every week. And then the first time she opens her mouth while lying back with a blunt/a drink/a piece of western sponge cake in her hand, she lets out something that stops you cold: *Bring me back some of that weird Asian stuff when you go to Japan, girl. You know, she was one of those fuckin' Latinas who don't speak Spanish. Yeah, I got this BIG BLACK DICK from Good Vibrations! I don't want any Muslims in my house anymore—not after what happened.*

You freeze in that moment. Fucked up: *Not safe no more.* This is what you always feared, what you knew was gonna happen, what you were stupid for thinking you could avoid. Do you say anything? Maybe you can say something and she can hear it. Or do you say something diplomatic and carefully worded, and afterward do you bitch on the phone to other fam all you couldn't say to her? More often though, you go away. I went away. Froze and threw a look to some other place in the room and tried to pretend it didn't happen and sat on my anger. Just like surviving my mama's house: be quiet until you can leave for real.

Then does it all finally come out after months of you telling yourself that you would say something, and she says, *What the fuck, what, how the fuck could you say this? Have you been thinking about this all along?*

Maybe she gets married, maybe she goes out with a white boy, maybe she goes back to grad school, maybe she goes back on rock, maybe she transitions, maybe she gets all the good gigs, maybe she gets evicted, maybe she goes back to the psych ward, maybe she fucks your lover at the play party and she likes her better than you.

You're her sistagal, until the wrong word, the wrong tone, the wrong polyamory meltdown, the fight about classism in your relationships, melts you both down. And then you can't work together anymore. You can't put on gigs with each other anymore. You can't borrow money or knock on her door at 3 a.m., she can't call you when she's freakin'. Your margin of survival is cut down, but you don't know the way back.

And do you eventually have a circle of fractured half-friends and go home alone?

We're sistas. We treat each other like sistas. That's the blessin'. That's the problem. We come together cause we're both bein' fucked over by the same people. We get close. And then we fall in love with each other 'cause us third-world diva gals are beautiful and blessed like none other. We fly with each other, there is nothin' like us staggering home at 2 a.m. down the sidewalk, nothin' like our brilliance, shrieking, lifesaving giggles, orgasms. Oh, how we fly.

Nothing hurts as much as another brown woman saying the words you least want to hear. Nothing has ripped my heart open as much as seeing her turn and think, *I'll use all the holes you showed to me—all the fucked-up shit I learned to survive everywhere from the seventh-grade schoolyard to the white queer dance floor—to burn your ass.*

All those years a blur of meetings and dance nights and collapsed on the couch after. In building this radical fam, we wanted to build a circle that would be safe, would be a place where the pressure of trauma would not be there. In an attempt to protect each other, we compiled lists of who was good and safe and who was fucked up. A glance, a word dropped, a phrase that was just *wrong*. Survivors are trained from birth to be exquisitely sensitive, for our own survival's sake. At the first sign of a thrown water glass, the first whisper of footsteps coming down the hall at 3 a.m. behind a smiling face, we're gone. We do not forget these lessons—we still need them every day. We still go, go, gone. Those girls and me, they left town, they left city, we left, let each other disappear. We were raised colonized and confused, to trust the enemy, not our own hair. But we would make hard choices to live, leave each other by the side of the road, for now we deserved the best, didn't we?

What's with all these half-smiles? What does it mean when I do my own in self-defense so nobody wrong gets under my skin? Is it just here or is it everywhere? Can we not be dykes without drama? Is drama gonna be what stops us from saving the world?

The mid-nineties witnessed many of us, including the queer girls, moving away from coalition work with white folks to working in our own communities. Although my examples are fully personal and local, these patterns of creating chosen fam and queer-gal-of-color organizing have affected every place we have tried to do exclusive organizing, in the particular wave of politicization that has happened since the mid-nineties. The early nineties saw a revitalization of organizing against the Gulf War, Bush, cop brutality, and the prison-industrial complex. There was no *BLU* magazine, few of the kickass-of-color millions organizing we sometimes take for granted now. By 1995 many brown and Black folks had gotten sick of working in coalitions dominated by old- and new-school white leftists who were arrogant about their intellect and profoundly ignorant about the histories, experiences, and politics of POC communities. Many of us felt we were already dying, and doing change like this wasn't helping us die any less.

Coming together under broad identities like "people of color" or "queergirlofcolor" brought together folks who'd been at war with each other for centuries and didn't necessarily want to just stop. We thought everything would be all chill and problem-free, because we'd all been on the edges of the same meetings bitching about the same dumb white folks and SWGs (silly white girls).

But when your strongest point of unity is that you all hate the same people, you've got problems.

In moving to all POC politics, I found strength, power, found and made authenticity purity tests (yeah, my Punjabi sucks, but *you're* a half-breed) and the brutal mix of gossip with politics. Broad assumptions of "safe space" that left communities shattered by confusion when rapists, abusers, and provocateurs make their presence known.

Dynamics of family building, trust, histories of abuse and trauma factor into every political movement's organization. When we do not understand them, we fall apart, never speak to each other again, and are not able to see what is at stake beyond our own personal survival. We are not able to keep surviving with each other, to build institutions that will save each other on a mass scale, and last.

THE DAY AFTER

I wake up in one of my lovers' arms four days after my twenty-sixth birthday, my mouth filled with thick yellow water, and a voicemail picked up at midnight pounding in my head. Another message from another of my queer of color fam, telling me for various reasons s/he is now going to be one more person I will pretend not to see when we pass each other on the sidewalk. Thanking me

for my freaked-out call worried s/he might've been hit in the skull
with a tear gas canister like the many fired point-blank at the anti-
free trade protests in Quebec City, but continuing, "I don't hate
you, but I just think our lives are going on such different paths that
I can't be in contact with you right now." I can picture the futon
s/he sat on, the one we sat on so many times, that s/he probably smoked a big joint before picking up the phone to call me, silent dial, that s/he worked hard to sound as composed as possible,
because the voice started to break only once. My heart closes her
church doors as the message comes on, *Press 7 to erase this message,
press 9 to save.*

I am leaving you, you are leaving me. We fucked each other over.
To give the details would violate confidentiality. Would violate us.
S/he needed to leave friends behind, me included, to be who s/he
needed to be. But we needed each other to survive.

"Good sleep?" my lover asks.

"One nightmare," I say.

One more person who I cannot work with, be in the same room
with, get gigs from each other, borrow cash or bathtubs, go shopping and cook food together, $2 fish in green curry and jasmine
rice for both of us. One more of many people who kept leaving and
leaving my crew that year, who changed cities, changed jobs, politics, genders, lives, but most of all friendship/organizing circles.

Now on the far side of twenty-five, no longer precocious, semi-
established, I hold my lover and think, no, I don't think this all
means that "identity politics are bullshit." I do think of Gloria
Anzaldúa's essay in *Making Face, Making Soul*, where she says of
queer women of color, "We just can't fucking get along." My lover
serves as a kind of Switzerland in the middle of our community,
being Black and queer but male and often not leaving his house.
He listens to my grief-filled ranting, walking up to the Hong Kong

noodle restaurant where her and I ate so many dinners. When I stop, he says, "I find that, in general, alliances that are based on friendship are the only things that last. Not alliances based on words and letters."

Were we, are we utopian? Not in the way it's used to curse our longings, as if food, respect, and justice are luxury, but in thinking that in this concept, *queer women of color*, surely there wouldn't be any problems. That this category formed on the edges of meetings, in dreams of all of us sitting down together, would erase all the blood that is also between us. How do we learn that sistahood does not mean no more struggles between us?

I have let go of that utopian dream. Especially when I finally started asking folks point-blank if they had chosen family, they mostly said no. Now I look at heart at the same time as I look at identity. I don't know any other way to say it, though it sounds cheesy.

We know how scary this world can be. Physical, emotional, spiritual survival: none of them are givens for us. We need each other. But we also change fast. We make the world change, and we change as fast and slow as it does. When I was a child and when I was a raw, ripped-open eighteen-year-old, I needed a perfect chosen political fam with the desperate need for forever of a fucked-open three-year-old girl. Perfectly valid. But healing my childhood means replacing that jump-off-the-cliff desperate need with a different kind of faith.

When I was younger, in early abuse healing, I used to listen to folks talking about having faith in the universe, having "trust in the process," even when shit was crazy and they were losing every friend and bit of security they'd ever known. I'd suck my teeth. *Of course*, if you had money and goodies (like they mostly did, more than me), the universe came through. If you didn't have privilege, shit happened and you had no fucking cushion. Without a hell of a lot of luck, you wound up on lockdown, stuck in prison or poverty or the psych ward. No second chances for us (broke/crazy/nonwhite/nonnormal). And it is true that right now I've rocked all the privileges and dumb luck thrown my way and made it (for now) out of that sea of trapped people who don't matter, and a lot of folks I know didn't. It is also true that there is something that keeps reaching for all of us, no matter how desperate our life is.

If we keep reaching back and fighting like hell to fix what they fucked up in us, the people you desperately need may leave. But they will also keep coming, in new forms. The world is chaotic and uncertain, but not all of it is our parents' house.

Maybe, through the past five years of whirlwind, I have gotten past the initial point of healing and decolonization to be able to get beyond perfection expectations, get beyond exiling the other, get beyond seeing any betrayal or mistake as worse than that of our enemies, and at the same time knowing how to call shit when I see it. I am married to the idea of being awake. Awake like it says in *The Survivor's Guide to Sex*: not being cynical or automatically untrusting, but being awake to the possibilities that are really present in any relationship.[1]

It's been weird and important, this cautious return from separatism. It's more real to say I grew up a punk-rock crazy freak girl, rather than making myself out as a warrior in brown who never listened to anything but Asian Dub Foundation.

Over two crackling fucked-up phones, Brooklyn to Toronto, my friend Yalini Dream says, "It's the places where we hurt each other when we're close, girl, that our most important work lies in. It's where the big changes happen. Where the world blows open or it doesn't." Between us, lying so close, there, as we screw up, make mistakes, as the big doors open or close.

What it comes down to is that there is no fixed safe or sane place for any of us, as much as we desperately need it. The same shit we said to the white girls about how "safe space" didn't mean "never uncomfortable" space applies to us, too. We have to stay in the icky places, master the art of moving one step past what we know, listen to each other instead of shouting, and do that tricky two-step of both trusting we know when we're being fucked over and knowing the difference between the truly evil and abusive and someone who screws up but is not evil. This is the difference between purity and practicality.

Strive to be kind to each other's whirlwind girl. Strive to remember that each one of us is precious and necessary, that drama and wars put out our light. Strive to remember this is our one, short life, and the choices we make will determine what comes of it. To know that when we need to cocoon to be clear about that, but not to insist that everybody make the same choices that we need to. Politics and passion are lovely, but not enough. Damn. Sounds like a perfect prescription for that sane family I never had, the one whose longing has shaped my life. Not perfect. But good enough. Just good enough.

I dream of making a child and making a family to raise her in. It is just a dream, but it's a potent one that symbolizes much. When I picture the family I want for her, it's different than before. It includes folks who aren't there every day, but who are there when they can be, when they are in town—mentally or physically. This fam involves the lovers and friends I had this past year. Despite everything, I imagine my brown daughter growing up with a white mama like I did. But instead of my racist, crazy one, I see my Newfie trannybutchchick sweetheart cracking jokes and being gentle with her. She ran away from her bio-family seven years ago to become the girl she is, doesn't pretend to be what she's not, apologizes, listens with eyes more open than anyone I've ever seen.

I dream of making this child with my other lover, a man who's the son of Maroons from Jamaica and Black folks who ran like hell past the Mason-Dixon to Detroit to Windsor, Ontario, intermarried with Nishnawbe and Cree. I see this queer, mostly dark family that is part of the changing of the world, living in houses with wrist restraints and Saul Williams on the minisystem, organic mangoes in bulk from the co-op, my fam that lets each other disappear down the paths that are what they need, and lets them come back, that flows in and out, not promising perfection, valuing each other enough not to implode. We are all runawayfreakshow children. Who love each other, who fuck up, but who will not abandon this. This, which is still all we have.

For the fam during the whirlwind years: Adrineh, Darcy, Bo-Yih, and Sam, and for David Findley and Ga Ching Kong for helping with the redefinitions.

#SayHerName
The Day Utopia Came Home

JAMILAH KING

Utopia showed up at our door in May.

I was twenty-two years old, one year removed from college, and living with my mom in San Francisco while I interned for free for a local weekly newspaper. It was a weekend and it was sunny in San Francisco, which was rare, and our home felt heavy, which was not rare.

May had always been a month of unofficial mourning for my mother and me. On April 27, 1990, my fifteen-year-old sister, Tenisha, had been shot and killed. On May 5, she was buried; her tombstone, which my family could not afford to buy, was donated by the family-owned company that made it ("No child should be forced into the ground and left unremembered," the owner told my mother). Four days later, on May 9, Tenisha did not get to celebrate what would have been her sixteenth birthday. And four days after that, May 13, was Mother's Day. Her murder was never solved.

I was only four years old when Tenisha was killed, so I don't remember the details of that very bad month. But I have felt it all my life. I feel it still. Nowhere is that feeling more powerful than in the home we shared—the third story of a Victorian-style apartment building in a neighborhood that black people who were born there call Fillmore, but that's since been renamed by newcomers "North of Panhandle" for the park that sits across the street. My mom first rented our two-bedroom apartment with a Section 8 voucher she had when my sister was only seven years old. My mom still lives there. It has spectacular bay windows that offer breathtaking views of the neighborhood, but also very poor ventilation, so we were often cold.

Whenever May rolled around, my mother oscillated between intense grief that would leave her bedridden and fits of rage. Even today, my sister's ghost is present. If you squint, you can still see the thumbtack holes where she once hung LL Cool J posters on the walls. But she is not here. Once, when I was no older than eight, I heard my mom rationalize in the way that only grief allows: she never wanted to move, she said, because she wanted my sister to be able to find us if she ever came home.

But my sister did not come home; Utopia did.

I didn't know who she was at first. When she rang the doorbell that day, I thought it was someone who was selling something we didn't need, or collecting signatures for something we didn't want, someone who clearly did not know what May meant to us. We rarely had unannounced visitors, and certainly not during our very bad month of May. Everyone who knew us knew that. But when I answered the door, I saw a young woman in her thirties on the other side. She had cashew-colored skin and was dressed from head to toe in green: a leather jacket, a skirt, knee-high boots. I could tell that she was dressed for something important, but I didn't know that this was supposed to be that.

I looked at her, confused, because she didn't immediately say who she was or why she was there. But I noticed that she was carrying a large white shopping bag, and that her eyes were red with tears. Sensing my confusion, she made her first offering:

"Hey, Milah. Is your mom home?"

My mom was home, and at that moment she was at the stairs' landing, yelling down to see who was at the door. The woman, hearing her, told me her name. As I relayed the message to my mom, I was still confused; I could feel the ground beneath me shifting, and there was an absurdity to that shift. I am awkward in tense situations, prone to laughing when I don't know what else to do, and I could already hear the bad jokes I would tell my friends when they asked what I'd done that weekend: "Oh, you know, just played host to Utopia."

But this was no time to laugh, or joke, and I could tell that when I looked at my mom. When she heard me say Utopia's name, my mother's entire demeanor changed. In an instant, her grief married her rage and gave birth to a stoicism I had never witnessed. Her eyes narrowed, her voice grew firm, but calm, her back straightened, and she told me to let Utopia in.

As Utopia came up the stairs, my mother eyed her. "It's been eighteen years," my mother said. "I've been waiting for you all this time."

Utopia met her gaze and offered almost an apology. "I know auntie," she said. "I finally came home."

My confusion melted away and became something stronger. It became anger. Who was this woman with this intense name? And whose home was she talking about? Because this was my mom, not her auntie, and this was my home, and I'd never seen her in it.

As Utopia made her way up the hallway and into my mother's embrace, I knew that my anger was something more. There was the world before my sister died, and the world after it. Each world had its own secrets and stories, and I knew better than to ask about them. My mother and I never processed either world, because the work of living in them was hard enough. But I knew that Utopia was from a world in which my sister had lived. I wanted to know that world, too.

Every so often, my sister's world would show up. Often, I sought it out. I was only four years old when my sister died, and I have almost no firsthand recollection of her. I don't remember her voice, and I can barely make out her face without the help of a picture. Once, I was playing in the living room and found a book tucked away on a bookshelf. It was Chinua Achebe's *Things Fall Apart*, and my sister's name was written inside. Right, I thought to myself. This must be the book she was assigned at school before she died. Those discoveries would often gut me, because it showed me firsthand how reckless a black girl's death could be: one minute, you're doing homework; the next minute, you're dead.

But I'd also think about all the questions I had that my sister would never be able to answer. Did she like the book? What book was her favorite? I didn't know, and she could never tell me, and this, I knew, was wrong.

Every few years, I'd see a flier laying on the dining room table that my mother had gotten from the San Francisco District Attorney's office offering a reward for information about my sister's murder. The narrative in the crime bulletin read as follows:

On April 27, 1990, Tenisha Hardy, 15 years old, was shot and killed while walking with a friend south on Webster Street near Fulton. At least two shots were fired from the corner where a group of young men had gathered.

Utopia, it turns out, was that friend. And she had come home to tell us her story.

It's never easy being someone's little sister, but it's impossible to chase a ghost. All my life I had been running after my sister's story, because the ones I'd heard didn't make any sense. I didn't want the story of her death, because the finality of it was something I knew I couldn't change. I wanted to know how she had lived. But everywhere I went, I was the dead girl's baby sister. And the weight of that identity followed me like a shadow.

When I was growing up, people in the neighborhood would stop me on the street, furrow their brows, and say, "You're Tenisha's little sister, right?" They always did this with the best of intentions. They always wanted to know how my mother was doing, or would offer up a story about something I'd done in preschool, when my sister used to pick me up while my mom was at work driving buses for the San Francisco Municipal Railway. But I always felt like a canvas on which they could project whatever they were feeling: their wonder, their grief, the memories of their youth. I felt like both she and I had been disappeared from the retelling of her life's stories; in death, she became a martyr instead of a teenager. Meanwhile, I was just the dead girl's sister. I wanted a place where Tenisha and I could go away for a while and just sit and talk.

Maybe that is why I had steeped myself in black feminism in college. I had read the works of women like Toni Morrison, bell hooks, and Patricia Hill Collins, hoping that their words could help me make sense of this world in which I'd grown up. They did. Black feminism taught me that my sister and my mother and I were part of a long history of struggle and survival. That the attacks against us were often invisible. And that in each generation the women in my family had learned to fight these forces in their own way.

> **I had read the works of women like Toni Morrison, bell hooks, and Patricia Hill Collins, hoping that their words could help me make sense of this world in which I'd grown up.**

I also learned that at its most basic, feminism is a desire for freedom. A freedom that is unbound by expectation, that allows you to fail and flourish on your own terms, to be a whole and complete person instead of a statistic. It's a freedom worth fighting for, and while that fighting can often happen during protests or direct action, it is often an intimate struggle of collective consequence.

Tenisha was born on May 9, 1974. At the time, our mother, Debra, was nineteen years old and living in Westside Courts, a housing projcct that multiple generations of my family had called home. Westside was a tight-knit community of people who cooked, laughed, lived, and fought among and against each other. For the most part, it was peaceful and quiet. My mom was two years removed from high school and had already worked a slew of jobs: hospital candy striper, library assistant, police station secretary. But money was always tight, and to save up for her first child, she had made a routine of visiting the cafeteria at Mt. Zion Hospital, which was just across the street, where the food was good and cheap. That's where she was one morning, standing in line for breakfast, when her water broke. She told a nurse, who escorted her up the elevator to the maternity ward, where, at around 6:30 that evening, my sister was born.

Tenisha was born into a world that was quickly learning how to fail her. Months after her birth, Richard Nixon resigned the presidency. But before then, his administration had begun what came to be known as the "War on Drugs." Nixon couched the War on Drugs in racially coded language aimed at middle-class white conservatives. The goal, as his administration put it, was to aggressively pursue the radicals, hippies, and dope pushers who were tearing apart the fabric of American civility. But, years later, in a story published by *Harper's Magazine*, Nixon's domestic policy chief, John Ehrlichman, plainly laid out the administration's belief that its real enemies were African-American families like my own. "The Nixon campaign in 1968, and the Nixon White House after that, had two enemies: the antiwar left and black people," Ehrlichman said. "We knew we couldn't make it illegal to be...black, but by getting the public to associate...blacks with heroin, and then criminalizing [it] heavily, we could disrupt those communities."

Ehrlichman added: "Did we know we were lying about the drugs? Of course we did."[1]

Two years later, in 1976, Ronald Reagan ran for president for the first time. He would lose, but his campaign did help develop a lasting caricature of black women like my mother who were on government assistance. He called them "welfare queens," after his campaign seized upon the story of a woman named Linda Taylor who had been convicted in a high-profile case of welfare fraud. "In Chicago, they found a woman who holds the record," Reagan said at a campaign rally that year. "She used 80 names, 30 addresses, 15 telephone numbers to collect food stamps, Social Security, veterans' benefits for four nonexistent deceased veteran husbands, as well as welfare. Her tax-free cash income alone has been running $150,000 a year."[2]

There were Linda Taylors, aka "welfare queens," everywhere, Reagan argued, and they were lazy women, promiscuous women, living large on the government's dime. Reagan would eventually win the White House in 1980 and spend the next eight years slowly dismantling the social safety net that families like mine relied on.

While the Reagan administration was doing its best to fail black women for the benefit of elevating the interests of white men, black feminists fought back. By the 1970s, women like Ella Baker and Fannie Lou Hamer, black women who played instrumental roles in the civil rights movement, had laid out a path of resistance that many others would follow. There was Elaine Brown, who would go on to become chairwoman of the Black Panther Party, and who pivoted its grassroots approach to local electoral organizing. There was Angela Davis, who fought against and beat the FBI's attempts to convict her of murder in retaliation for her unabashed communism. And when the black liberation struggle and the women's movement each failed to grapple with the realities of black womanhood, groups like the Combahee River Collective wrote a manifesto articulating why a struggle focused on race, gender, and class was necessary. It was "the political realization that comes from the seemingly personal experiences of individual Black women's lives," they wrote in 1977.[3]

The women in my family embodied this sentiment. They weren't attending marches or burning their bras, but they were surviving, and often, thriving, against all odds. My grandmother moved to a nearby suburb and opened a group home for girls in foster care, much to the chagrin of her white neighbors, who complained regularly. She mothered more than a hundred girls, most of them black—I'd call some of them "auntie" for years without knowing we weren't related by blood. My mother became the first person in our family to enroll in college, attending full time while raising my sister, and finally graduating with a degree in communications in 1984, thanks to a public assistance program that offered tuition stipends to single mothers. My aunt soon followed. As Audre Lorde wrote in 1988, these acts of individual achievement weren't really individual at all: "Caring for myself is not self-indulgence, it is self-preservation, and that is an act of political warfare."[4]

Tenisha was an outgoing and happy child. She'd stop strangers at the bus stop and sing them Stevie Wonder songs. After dinner, she'd sit at the kitchen table and read my mother's college-level textbooks. By age ten, she was helping my mother do her taxes. When Tenisha was eleven, I came into the world three months premature thanks to pregnancy complications that almost took me and my mother's lives. But when Tenisha got the news that I'd arrived, she ran smiling down the hallway of her Catholic school, screaming, "My sister is here!"

She was wildly popular among her friends. She still loved to sing: her favorites were New Edition and Babyface. She even battle-rapped with boys in the neighborhood, including one lanky boy named Joseph, who would grow up to become JT the Bigga Figga, a hometown rap legend. His later hits, such as "Game Recognize Game" and "Playaz Club," would eventually become Bay Area hood classics.

Tenisha was so good at this—not just rapping, but carrying herself with confidence—that she earned the nickname "Thick Game." She had a crew of girls, mostly in middle school, but some older, and they did everything together. They went to parties and flirted with boys. They learned how to braid hair and wore matching outfits. They stood up for one another and, if anyone challenged them, they fought. But mostly they did the things that teenage girls do: they gathered at our house, sometimes with me in tow, and played music and gossiped.

Once, when I was maybe twelve or thirteen, my mother made one of her annual calls to homicide investigators. She wanted to know what, if any, progress had been made in my sister's case. The detective who had originally investigated my sister's murder had been reassigned. My mother wanted to know who she could talk to in order to get answers. "I'm calling," I heard her say over the phone, "because my daughter was *assassinated*."

At the time, I was fixated on learning about the Civil War. I knew what it meant to be assassinated. Abraham Lincoln had been assassinated. John Wilkes Booth had crept up behind him and put a gun to Lincoln's head, then pulled the trigger. What followed was one of the most consequential periods of American history, overshadowed by the death of a figure who had gone to war in order to preserve the Union. I knew then that only important people were assassinated. Their lives were matters of public consequence, and so, too, were their deaths. Black girls like my sister were not important. Her life was not a matter of public consequence, and neither was her death, according to the most common telling of her story and stories like hers. She is not engraved in a statue, complete with gold door-knocker earrings and a side ponytail. There are no national holidays dedicated to her legacy. There was only a block party that her friends organized in the courtyard of a neighborhood housing project, to which they wore matching jackets emblazoned with her nickname and "Rest in Peace." Someone brought a radio, someone else brought a buttercream-frosted cake that spelled out "Thick Game" in icing.

Left to grieve in private, my mother staged daily rebellions. I wasn't allowed to pledge allegiance to the flag of a country that had such little regard for our lives and for our deaths. My mother would see a group of police officers out in the street, laughing, being carefree, and she would grow hot with anger: How dare they laugh when her child was dead and gone and no one had been held to account for it? She held the state responsible for my sister's unsolved homicide, but she held our community responsible for her death. Sure, the community had nurtured my sister's life, but it was also harboring the person who'd killed her. Even worse, black America had turned in on itself and had begun to blame its children for their own demise. Mothers, black mothers especially, were held responsible.

Lines were drawn and enemies were everywhere. One of my mother's best childhood friends, a woman she'd grown up with in Westside, had left the city amid the carnage of the 1980s for the relative safety of the nearby suburbs. The city was dangerous, and so were the people in it. One day, decades later, this old friend made an offhand comment about my sister, lamenting her death. "The streets took her," she told my mother.

These were the lies we were taught to believe about our children by our lawmakers and our police and our movies and even ourselves: that they were in some way responsible for their own murders, that seemingly simple transgressions seen as rites of passage in white communities—cutting school, smoking weed, walking the streets after dark with a friend—had suddenly morphed into crimes for which black children were tried without a judge or jury. Black childhood was itself criminal and punishable by death, and we, black people, were powerless to stop it, the story went.

My mother refused to internalize this narrative, because she knew her daughter, and she knew herself. "The streets didn't take my child," she told her friend. "A man with a gun did."

My mother isn't the only who has engaged in this type of resistance. It has now coalesced in the social media movement #SayHerName, which counters the attention given to the extrajudicial killings of black men and boys with a call to also amplify the stories of black women and girls who are murdered. Kimberlé Crenshaw, the legal scholar who coined the term "intersectionality," would later release a series of reports through her African American Policy Forum unpacking all of the institutional forces that put black women's lives at risk, including outsized punishment in schools and unwarranted government scrutiny in housing and child-rearing. It's these forces that, too often, prove deadly for black women, and the call to say their names is a direct challenge to acknowledge their humanity and the unique dreams and experiences they had.

On the day that Utopia came home, I learned that the man with the gun had not only taken my sister's life—he had taken Utopia's, too. And, in a way, he had taken his own.

Utopia sat on the edge of my mother's bed as the story tumbled out of her.

Utopia and Tenisha were best friends. Utopia was two years younger, but their birthdays were one week apart—Utopia's was May 2—and they joked and said that they were twins. They both had larger-than-life personalities, characterized by bursts of energy and openness. They laughed often, spoke loudly, and made friends quickly. They wanted to throw a joint birthday party.

April 27, 1990, was a Friday, and Utopia had had a bad day. Her parents fought often and sometimes their fights turned violent. That Friday was violent. Utopia and my sister were supposed to go with friends to see a movie that night after school, but Utopia was worried about her parents. So she and my sister ditched the movie. They took a long walk around the neighborhood. They had somehow gotten a tiny thimble of wine and drank it to help get Utopia's mind off of her parents. But my sister couldn't go home smelling of wine. "She wasn't afraid of anything," she told my mother, laughing. "But she was afraid of you."

My mother could not know that my sister had been drinking instead of going to the movies, so they'd decided to walk it off.

The movie was letting out soon, and they had planned to meet the friends who had gone to the movie at a nearby McDonald's. As they were walking, a man ran in between them, heading in the opposite direction. He owed money to the person chasing him, a corner boy who sold crack and had a gun. The man was running fast, and when he knocked into my sister and Utopia, he sent them falling in opposite directions. Utopia fell one way, my sister fell the other. The boy with the gun fired, and the bullet meant for the man instead hit my sister in the chest. She fell to the ground, dying, but not yet dead.

The neighborhood was small, and people had heard the gunfire. One girl who lived nearby looked outside her window and saw my sister lying on the ground, with Utopia screaming next to her. She called the police. Somehow, their friends from the movies came to the scene. The girls formed a circle around my sister and Utopia, telling them it would be all right, talking to my sister, trying to keep her alert and alive.

Minutes passed—what felt like ten, then twenty, then thirty—and an ambulance arrived. Utopia rode with my sister in the ambulance. The other girls took the bus to the hospital. In the ambulance, Utopia watched helplessly as my sister lost consciousness and began to go into shock. This Utopia remembers vividly, because she saw how the body expels its fluids when it violently and suddenly begins to shut down. The ambulance raced to San Francisco General Hospital, where my sister was pronounced dead at 11:24 p.m.

As I listened, our stories converged. I have vague memories of a group of girls crying outside of the hospital as my mother and I arrived to meet other family members. I remember a waiting room. I remember it being very late. And I remember a nurse, white, red-cheeked, coming into the room, giving a somber declaration of some kind—probably, "I'm sorry"—and the room erupting in wails and screams. I don't remember anything after that.

What I couldn't have known, until Utopia told me, was this: she was allowed to see Tenisha's body after that was all that was left of her. She didn't know what to focus on, so she looked at her hair. They had done each other's hair hundreds of times, braiding it, pressing it, styling it. She touched Tenisha's hair, and then uncoiled the blue knocker that held it together. She unwrapped a red ribbon Tenisha had worn and unhooked a gold necklace she was wearing, a simple chain with a hollowed-out pendant shaped like a penny.

She went home that night and tucked the knocker, and the ribbon, and the necklace away in her closet.

The next morning, a group of boys came to Utopia's house. These were the same boys she knew from the neighborhood and included the one she'd seen holding the gun that had killed her best friend the night before. They told her that if she ever told the police what happened, if she ever identified them, they would kill her and her family.

She was thirteen years old.

For years, Utopia was trapped in a personal hell. She had seen her best friend die in front of her. It could've easily been her. She hated her birthday, because it reminded her of the friend and childhood she'd lost. She also felt immense amounts of guilt at not being able to save my sister and not being able to come forward and help identify the boy who'd killed her. So she stayed away from my mom and avoided the buses that my mother drove around the city. Later, she would go and sit at my sister's grave on her birthday and have a private version of the joint party they had once planned together.

The boys did not get off easy. They did not go to prison, at least not then. The police did not know who they were, but the neighborhood did. The boys fought constantly. One would eventually become addicted to heroin and later hang himself in prison. Another would convert to Islam and become fiercely involved in his mosque; he was no doubt looking for salvation.

I am not sure if he's found it.

Tenisha, Utopia, and the boys are not often described as children of war, but that's what they are. Some of them survived, but many of them did not. It is easy now to look back on the War on Drugs and the crack cocaine epidemic as the result of racist public policies. And they absolutely were. But they were also periods in which the wholesale warehousing and murder of black children were legally permitted. Out of those years grew the strategy of demonizing black women who, like my mother, survived on welfare.

This is not the story I wanted, but it is the one I have. After Utopia gave it to me, she walked into the bedroom that had once been my sister's. Away from my mother, she handed me a small box. Inside were the knocker, the ribbon, and the necklace. They are the only things I own, outside of my body, that connect me physically to Tenisha, the only things that are part of the world she lived in and still part of the one that's left.

Utopia then reached into the white shopping bag she had been carrying when she arrived. She pulled out a book she'd gotten on publishing. She had heard that I was trying to make a career as a writer.

"Here, cousin," she said. "I want you to tell this story."

Colonize This!

CRISTINA TZINTZÚN

I worry about dating whites, especially white men. I worry that even though my skin is white like theirs, they will try and colonize me. I see what a white man did to my beautiful, brown, Mexican mother. He colonized her. It is not love that drew my father to my mother, as I used to think; rather, it was the color of her skin, her impoverished background, her lack of education, her nationality, her low self-esteem, her submissiveness. In his mind these qualities reinforced his superiority. Instead of recognizing the differences between him and her as beauty, my father saw them as a means for exploitation.

My father met my mother in Morelos, Mexico. She was working at a store when he came and asked her for change. He told her that he was from the States and that he would be back for her. She just thought he was a crazy

> **" I read all the feminist literature I could get my hands on. They gave me the support I needed. They made me feel less alone. "**

gringo hippie, and she paid no attention to him. Later that day he came back for her. He told my mother that he and his friend Zauza, named after the Tequila brand, were going to take her to their place. My mother naïvely thought they were kidnapping her—she had never seen gringos dressed so oddly. So she went with them fearing for her life, and they took her to their house, where the rest of their roommates were tripping off acid. My mother was doubly frightened by this—not only were they kidnapping her, but they were going to turn her into a drug addict. After a few hours they took my mother home, and after that they came to visit her regularly.

Two years later my parents got married. They raised my older sister in Mexico for her first year. Then they came to the States to "visit" but never returned to Mexico to live. If my mother could have returned to Mexico safely with us, her children, she would have. She feared that my father would kidnap us—not an unrealistic fear, considering my uncle did the same thing to my aunt when she left him for the first time. Also, it would not have been economically possible to raise three children in Mexico as a single parent; she had to be realistic. My mother was no longer in her early twenties, and therefore she would have been considered undesirable for employment in machista Mexican culture. Her only choice was to raise us in the United States.

Both my father and my mother raised us to be proud of who we were. Shame was not part of my vocabulary. As a child I was proud to identify myself with brown, with poor, with Indian, with "other." I specifically remember my father teaching me the avenues to fight my oppressors. He was the one who taught me feminist theory. He taught me about systemic racism. I listened to my father's advice. I was not like most girls. I always spoke my mind. I had no reservations about acting "unfeminine." I was raised with such fire. I was aggressive. I spoke like the boys did and never gave it a second thought. I was not worried about it if they would like it or disagree, or if they would like me.

I worry about dating white men because of my father. He is a "progressive" man, or so people think. Only those close to him realize his hypocrisy. Most consider him to be a liberal, a feminist, an antiracist, an anticlassist, but I know he is not. He is the wolf in sheep's clothing. He disguises himself as a humanitarian, but this deception makes him the worst offender of them all.

I was told never to submit to any man, but I was only demonstrated submission by my mother and domination by my father. I was raised with eyes closed but ears open. I heard my father tell me that as a womon, a Mexican, I should not let anyone degrade me because of my race or gender, yet this is exactly what he did to my mother. When he made fun of her accent, when he forced her to have sex with him, when he beat her, when he cheated on her, when he told her she was stupid, when he told her that without him she was nothing.

I saw the contradictions between my father's actions and words, but I had trouble processing it all. I did not realize what it meant that my father only cheated on my mother with African-American, Asian, and Latina womyn. But the flashing lights became harder to ignore when I would hear my father tell other white American men that they should go to Mexico and marry a nice Mexican girl. So that she could take care of him, that they are such good cooks, and so submissive that they would make anyone the perfect wife. I heard him encourage my brother to date only Mexican girls. They would be so grateful to go out with a gringo. To my father it did not matter whether my brother liked them or not.

When I would hear these comments, I'd tell my father that he was a racist. That just because he was white and American did not mean that every brown womon wanted him. I'd tell him that just because they were poor and Mexican, he thought he was better than they were. That they were people too, people with emotions not to be toyed with, that they were not his brown dolls! My father rolled his eyes. I was too damned PC, he would say.

I remember the first time I saw sex. It wasn't on TV, or catching my parents. It was my father with another womon, and I was three. My parents used to sell jewelry door to door. Sometimes there would be deliveries to be made, and on such an occasion I accompanied my father while my brother, sister, and mother waited in the car. I remember a petite African-American womon answering the apartment door and my father locking me in the bathroom, telling me to stay in there. I was frightened but also curious why I was not supposed to open the door. When I did, I saw the answer: my father naked having sex with another womon. I quickly shut the door, my stomach churning, knowing that something was wrong. When I went back to the car and told my mother what I had seen, my father called me a liar and my mother chose to believe him, too hurt to admit the truth to herself.

My father never did try hard to hide the other womyn. My mother, however, did try hard to deny and forgive. It was difficult for her to accept the truth. In the beginning, she became angry not only with my father but with the other womyn. She blamed them for "making" my father cheat. My mother felt worthless. She, like many other Mexican womyn, fell into the trap of thinking that without her man, she could not do or be anything. Not until my mother was able to see the value in herself was she able to face reality. She finally saw the truth behind the other womyn's situations: that these womyn were the same as her.

When I think of colonization, I think of my father's "conquests." I think back to all the faces he has colonized. I think back to Dow, the womon from Thailand; Denise, the longtime girlfriend;

Guadalupe, his soon-to-be new wife in Mexico. And I think back to all the faces I never saw. The girls in the whorehouses from here to Mexico to Thailand. I see faces as young as mine. I remember the note I left my father with a package of condoms, before his business trip to Thailand, begging him to think of his actions, begging him for once to think of the lives of these girls. I noticed it, he did not; this was rape. Sex with a thirteen-year-old girl. My father is a rapist. She was forced to work in the brothel; she is not a prostitute—she is a slave. And I want to hold her hand and beg a million apologies. I want to cry with her. I want to look into her eyes, for I can only imagine her pain; she is my sister. We are both human, both equal, but my father does not acknowledge this. For my father even has the audacity to claim that he knows what it is to be a womon of color, because he used to have long hair in the sixties.

As long as I can remember, my father has always been fascinated with womyn of color. He likes to flaunt money and power in front of these womyn. He thinks this makes him superior, more powerful, intelligent. So he chooses to date only womyn of color—these are the womyn he feels he can exploit. Black, brown, or yellow, my father loves them all—he is so multicultural.

When I think of all the womyn my father has used, I feel sick. My father exploits their poverty, their desperation, their need to eat. And for me it is not some far-off image of who these womyn are, or of their economic situations. No, these womyn are my close relatives—my mother, my aunts, my grandmother. You see, my father is not the only person I know who "colonizes" womyn of color. No, it runs in the family. My grandfather is also married to a Mexican womon (my father's stepmother). She married my grandfather so that her daughter would have economic stability, so she would have a father, but what kind of father calls his daughter "his little spic"? My uncle has been married to three different Costa Rican womyn. He smugly says to me, "Any womon can be bought." I just smile and nod. While he thinks he is fucking these womyn, they fuck him. Like Raquel, his second wife, who left him black-eyed and bruised when he raised his hand to her, or Guiselle, who stole $10,000 from him. I admire these womyn—they could never be colonized.

I know that my brother is going to help me stop the circle of colonization. He refuses to partake in my father's racist, sexist, exploitative games. And for him, like me, it is an internal struggle. One that requires me to question what I feel, and most of all my memory. I must make sure, again and again, that my father's superiority complex has not seeped into me subconsciously. I have met other mutt/colonized children like myself, but instead of overcoming their colonization, they succumb to it. They become internally conquered. They shame themselves into believing that half of them is inferior. They choose to deny their culture and heritage. They make such claims—that their brown skin originated from their French background. And sometimes they become the worst type of colonized people, those who try to hide their feelings of inferiority by persecuting those who are like them.

It took me till the age of eighteen to connect the dots of why I exist, of why my family was and no longer is. I saw something amiss, something foul in my father's actions and words. I knew there was a lie. I knew the truth was deep and painful. When I found it, I was left confused. I did not know what to do with it. My whole existence is based on things I cannot tolerate. I was raised with eyes closed because I did not see my family for what it was. It was based on the ideals of "isms." It was there to soothe my father's ego. I often wonder if my father even sees anyone as his equal. I wonder if he knows that when he demeans other womyn of color that he demeans me. His actions and words pierce me to the core. This is not just any man who is saying these things, this is my father. This is half of me. This is where I come from.

I am careful to learn from other people's mistakes as well as my own. I know that in the past I have let comments slide. My first boyfriend (white) found it funny to tell me to go get him a Coke so that he could pretend I was his Mexican maid. His friends called me spic and told me I smelled of tacos. Back then I didn't know how to challenge their discrimination. I kicked the boy who called me spic, but I had no words. For the first time I could not speak. My "friends" then thought such words were not racist, that the only hate word that existed was "nigger." Their definition of racism was so rigid, pseudo-liberal, and white. I knew I was faced with racism, yet my peers could not see this through my brown eyes.

It was my mother's mistake not to challenge my father; it was my mistake not to do the same with the people I dated. I know I will not make these same mistakes twice. I know I cannot be colonized. I realize now that I can't be with anyone who wants to pat me on the head and tell me how neat it is that I am Mexican but never actually wants to hear me talk about it. Far too many times I have tried to speak of my struggles or those of my people to be met with bored or un-understanding eyes. It leaves me frustrated and isolated. When one friend learned what I was writing this piece about, she replied, "Blah, blah. Heard it all before. Nothing new." My body goes numb when she says these things. I want to punch her, slap her. Instead I just call her an asshole. When I am done with this essay, I will make her read it. Her lack of emotion and understanding makes it next to impossible to speak to her. She is as sensitive and caring as an electroshock. I see her words as self-absorbed ignorance, resentful and dismissive of a culture she does not even try to understand. I struggle to make my voice heard so that she and people like her will learn that there is more than just a white experience.

In my parents' relationship my mother constantly struggled for equality. She fought to be seen as my father's equal. In many respects she succeeded; in my eyes and my siblings' eyes she was equal to if not *more* than my father. Her unconditional love and support gave us the strength and independence we needed. When my mother became tired of my father controlling the family money, she became self-employed. With the small amount she earned working, selling jewelry at local festivals, she would buy us the fast food my father wouldn't let us eat. She would take us to dollar movies and bus trips downtown to the children's science museum. Around my mother I could always be myself. I never had to live up to false expectations, unlike with my father.

My mother is the strongest woman I know. She stayed with my father so that my siblings and I could have an education, so that my sister and I would have the means to take care of ourselves, so we would not need to depend on any man as she had. She felt she had no escape from my father—she was not from this country, she did not speak the language, and she did not have anyone to turn to. So my mother did the best she could. My mother hid her tears and cried in her pillow, and I slept soundly. This was her sacrifice. She did not want us to feel her inferiority. She put her feelings of inadequacy aside and raised us to be proud. And for this I am absolutely grateful to my mother. In fact, I feel fortunate that I was raised with such true contrasts. It helped me find balance. My mother now tells me that her biggest fear when my sister and I were growing up was that we would be submissive. We laugh about her worries now. My mother says that she could not have hoped for more feisty, self-assured daughters.

I do not hate my father. I love my father. I respect him as a father but not as a person. If it were not for him, I would not be as proud and outspoken as I am today. If it were not for him, I would not be passionate about womyn's issues. I look at my father and I see the best example of what not to be. He preached one thing but did another. This taught me to question not only him but the world around me. This helped me see through the lies society fed me. It also made me take action. My father always spoke of the injustice in the world, the racist war on drugs, factory farms, homophobia, free trade. He taught me so much, but he left so much out. He spoke and spoke but never did a damn thing about these injustices. He saved his activism for reading books and preaching to those he could feel more intelligent than. It is because of my father that I am a vegan, even though he eats meat. It is because of my father that I don't tolerate homophobia, even though he says "dyke." It is because of my father that I teach English classes to undocumented immigrants, even though my father calls them "wetbacks" and tells me I should charge them for my services. If it were not for him, I would not be committed to a life of activism. I see his true colors, and I am glad he is my father. I do not wish to change what I cannot, my father or the past. Yet, I choose not to speak to him. He is too sad and pathetic to know how to love. To him love is something to manipulate. And my love is far too precious to be treated in such a manner. I know that to continue speaking with him only hurts me. So I must keep severed ties with this man that I still call daddy. I have hope for my mother. After twenty-one years she has signed divorce papers. She was ready—her three children out of high school, her sacrifice complete. I, like her, have been waiting for her freedom for some time now. And at last it will soon be here.

It was my father who instilled the basic principles of feminism in me, but it was feminism that taught me who I am as a womon. During my high school years I felt isolated from my peers. They seemed shallow, spoiled, and sheltered. I was uninterested in their idea of weekend fun, football games, and catering to the needs of rich white boys. I found no relief in the alternateen scene; skipping school to do drugs and secretly wishing to be "popular" bored me. Instead, I opted to be the outcast. I wanted to analyze the culture that maintained my middle-class white neighborhood. I wanted to know why their system seemed to be so afraid of me. Of why, when I questioned something, my new name became dyke or bitch. I made the decision to confront every homophobic, racist, or sexist word I heard. Sometimes it seemed like I never got a chance to shut up. When I wasn't challenging my peers and teachers, I spent my time reading. I read all the feminist literature I could get my hands on. They gave me the support I needed. They made me feel less alone. They made me proud to call myself a feminist and queer. Those books taught me more than my school ever could.

I appreciate the outlet those books created for me. Although they gave me something to identify with, they never gave me anything to identify with as a Latina. I remember reading *Listen Up: Voices from the Next Feminist Generation* and being angry that the book contained only one Latina contributor—who I was only able to tell was Latina not by what she had written, but by her Spanish surname. I felt the book had represented many other minority groups well, but I felt invisible. I find it frustrating that when most books mention womyn of color, "color" and "gender" are presented as something separate. I am not just a woman or just a person of color—I am a womon of color.

In the past year a new part of myself has awoken—my history. And I don't know how to say it or what to do with it. I have lived my whole life until now away from reality. I am based on my father's superiority complex. I stand here before you because of racism. I look into the mirror and wonder, Who am I? What does being based on white superiority make me? This is a question I will have to answer, and I know there is no easy answer. I am mixed. I am the colonizer and the colonized, the exploiter and the exploited. I am confused yet sure. I am a contradiction.

Resisting Sterilization & Embracing Trans Motherhood

LUNA MERBRUJA

I was seventeen years old when I was asked to make a lifetime commitment to sterilization. I was sitting on the doctor's examination table, emotionally raw after being interrogated about my gendered experiences as a child. The doctor was wearing a tired smile as she read through the list of questions in a monotone voice. I lied, I exaggerated, I gave my biggest brown puppy eyes to placate her, to play by the residual transsexual governing policies that began in the late 1970s. These policies shaped how transgender people were diagnosed and understood. Essentially, we have to prove that we're "authentically" transgender and not deviant cross-dressers fulfilling a sexual fetish. These are the roots of "transvestism."

These problematic policies are the reason why trans people must have childhood experiences of hating anything associated with their sex assigned at birth, along with needing to be seeing a therapist for a few months for a referral letter stating that our gender identity is stable and real, and having to live "full time" as our gender in order to receive gender-related medical treatment.

Fortunately, the World Professional Association for Transgender Health (WPATH) that created these policies has come a long way from those practices, and certain liberal states no longer require such extensive "proof."

However, that didn't protect me as a young teenager. When my doctor told me to contemplate my fertility I was shocked; none of the trans people I knew had told me that hormone replacement therapy (HRT) would render me permanently infertile after a year of treatment.

I felt anguish well up in my chest. I had always dreamed of making my brown baby, Zaylani, from my genetic material. I didn't imagine the logistics of it, I just knew in my soul that I was to bring a child into this world. I knew that my life's purpose was to break the cycle of violence by filling this sweet miracle with all the love and goodness this world had to offer. I was meant to be a trans mother. There was nothing that could convince me otherwise.

But I had not known that pursuing a gender transition would destroy that dream. I spent hours debating with myself if transitioning was really worth it. I ran in circles in my head, playing out numerous scenarios—adopting a child, fostering children, not having my own children but being tía to my friend's kids, or maybe just giving up motherhood altogether.

Then I had this overwhelming guilt wash over me. I thought, "Am I selfish for transitioning and giving up a child I've always wanted?" Having grown up in a Native Alaskan and Mexican home, I come from a lineage of mothers who sacrificed their homelands, their happiness, their careers, and their dreams to raise children: Shouldn't I also sacrifice this selfish *want* to transition in order to birth my miracle?

Theoretically, I could have banked my sperm and paid a monthly fee to keep my sperm frozen. However, what kind of poor, brown teenager do you know who has enough money for a sperm-bank deposit? And the $50+ fee every month to keep it frozen? I couldn't realistically afford this option, and it tore me up inside that money was the ultimate factor holding me back from transitioning.

And truthfully, there were social pressures for me to transition quickly and young—every doctor I spoke to talked about how transitioning younger would be "best," because I would be more "passable," and therefore a "Successful Transgender." Even if these health-care providers were loose with their HRT prescription pads, they were also perpetuating cis normativity and pressuring me at a susceptible age to believe that my looks were the most important aspect of my life, so important that sacrificing my fertility was no big deal as long as I was passable.

With all these conflicting feelings, I decided to seek answers in online forums where transgender women talked to each other about our trans womanhood. I desperately sought out the conversations that dealt with fertility, but what I found only worsened my confusion. Most trans women felt such intense dysphoria surrounding their genitalia that they wanted nothing to do with it. Some even went so far as to state that anyone who wanted to keep their genitals and fertility intact was not a "true transgender woman." I couldn't find anything about trans women having children *after* transitioning; most trans women had had their children before transitioning.

After several months, I decided to wait until I could afford to bank my sperm. Ultimately that day never came. Going through high school and beginning college as a visible trans person created so many barriers to simply living a normal college life. When I started exploring my femme freedom by wearing long skirts and cosplay wigs, painting my nails, and lining my eyes to perfection, my peers would walk around me as if I were a monster. A literal bubble of space surrounded me at all times, and I was robbed of the fun, carefree college experiences that so many of my cis friends were having.

I felt a horrid hatred brewing in my guts. I grew mean toward myself. When I saw my face in the mirror, I felt a need to change myself to be beautiful, to be lovable. I was exhausted by the loneliness of being trans. I was making a daily decision to live my truth as a hairy femme at the cost of having any close relationships.

It was during this time that I concluded that being trans meant I was unlovable, and I began to shift my dreams around this loneliness. I became short-sighted about my future and started living self-destructively. I drank way too much way too often. I slept with people who wouldn't let me turn the lights on. I kept feeding this void in my heart until it poisoned me completely; I decided to give up my dreams of having a child and pursue transitioning.

> **" I know that motherhood is sacred, and that I am destined to overcome sterilization to bring a child into this world. I know that someday, small brown fingers will find their way home resting in my palms. "**

I dropped out of university and returned to living with my grandparents. I enrolled in community college to occupy my time, though my true intention was to quietly transition in a rural area where no one knew me. I spent a year seeking HRT from various clinics until I found one that was an hour east of my rural town. I had found a trans-specific health-care clinic that was staffed by trans women of color. In this sacred space, all the girls sat next to each other in the waiting room looking each other up and down, judging each other's softening features and budding breasts. Sometimes it was uncomfortable to feel this competition, but ultimately we were looking to each other to see what possibilities could await us on these drugs that no one seemed to fully understand.

I clearly remember the day I was prescribed HRT: it was a few days before Christmas in 2014, and the weather was particularly dreary. I sat in the waiting room fidgeting with my uncertainty. I was called up to meet my clinician, Janet, who had a thick manila envelope filled with forms to sign. I briefly glanced at the consent release forms, waivers of liability, etc., signing my new name on each highlighted area. After that was done, Janet handed me a paper outlining all the possible side effects of HRT. She asked me if I had banked my sperm yet and I said no. She said I should do it soon, because six to twelve months on HRT would render me permanently infertile. I asked her if there would be any way to restore my fertility, and she said she'd never seen a girl get swimmers after treatment, and that most don't even want to bother with their parts in the first place. I nodded and signed the form, feeling like I was signing away my fertility for the magic of transitioning.

When I got home, I started a spreadsheet to meticulously track every change my body went through. My second puberty sped by quickly and under the radar, as I had hoped. My chest hardened into tender buds, eventually blossoming into fatty breast tissue. My body hair thinned, my veins retreated under soft skin. My nails grew too fast and my hips ached as they began to rotate. I was feeling blissful for my shapeshifting body, except for my reproductive abilities.

Over the months, I watched my ejaculatory fluids thin to a watery substance, losing the thick, white consistency that indicated live sperm. There was a sweet point where I was feeling the changes of HRT and still had some ejaculatory fluids, but my doctor pressured me into taking a higher dose of HRT in order to "maximize" the benefits. Once I maxed out, my sperm was gone. I could no longer squirt any fluid, and I knew I had reached the point of infertility.

I spent many nights crying after ejaculation. I regretted starting a treatment that made me so beautiful and infertile. I loathed my decision but kept accountable to staying on these drugs for a year, to say I'd truly given it a shot. The trouble was, I loved the changes in my body so much that I couldn't imagine stopping HRT.

As a mother, I felt I had made the wrong choice, that I'd sacrificed my child for my selfish transitioning desires. I could not bear to engage with myself sexually for a long time, because the guilt was too intense to shoulder alone. I didn't want to face my infertility anymore, and I wanted my boiling mothering need to subside, to alleviate the anguish I harbored.

I began creating art to cope with my feelings. I wrote articles late into the night. I created intricate care packages for friends, I got really good at painting fun designs on my nails, and I bleached my hair to shit. My friends asked me to perform in a few art shows, so I began generating content for the stage. What I didn't know was that someone else's performance on that same stage would change my entire life.

It was the last Mangos With Chili show in San Francisco at the African American Art & Culture Complex. The cabaret-style show had burlesque performers, spoken-word artists, storytellers, and experimental performances. I was in the latter category, performing a vulnerable piece about leaving an abusive ex-boyfriend. After my piece, I joined the audience and watched my fellow contemporaries perform their art.

Then micha cárdenas, a trans Latina academic and multimedia artist, stepped onto the stage and read poetry in front of a projection of a microscopic circle. She performed her project, titled *Pregnancy*, about how she had stopped taking HRT for a few months, bought a $50 child's microscope, and started examining her ejaculatory fluids for viable sperm. Each poem documented a separate part of her pregnancy, with the microscopic images changing from being still, to wiggling, to moving in a straight line, indicating viable sperm.

Truthfully, I was so entranced that I cannot recall the words, only the sensation of the deepest healing I have ever experienced. In that one performance, I felt hope fill my eyes to tears. I gasped and choked aloud, not caring to silence my emotional response. All those nights mourning my children, regretting my transitioning, and hating myself suddenly lifted off my heart. I wasn't carrying the weight of sterilization anymore; I was carrying the ferocity of trans motherhood.

When micha came offstage, I darted backstage to thank her for her art and to share what joy I felt in feeling hopeful again. Her story was one I could resonate with; it was one of trans Latina motherhood, not some mythical white or cis woman's experience. She told me how it was a community effort since it was several trans women who taught her how to restore fertility. She shared that some were even able to take supplemental hormones to naturally lactate for breastfeeding!

After soaking in the bliss of knowing the truth about our bodies, I felt rage. I was furious that so many trans women were being told lies about our fertility. I was angry that the feminist movement was ignoring the ongoing sterilization of trans people. After a few months of this frustration, I wrote an article for the online magazine *Everyday Feminism* discussing the importance of centering trans women in reproductive justice. I received a ton of flak from transphobic feminists who wanted to deny that trans women could ever experience reproductive issues, particularly because so much of cis white feminism is wrapped up around having a vagina and a womb. There was also a general rejection from trans women about wanting to use my own sperm to conceive a child because it implied a desire to use my penis in a way that was seen as male.

I didn't defend my stances, but I stand by the fact that trans women have motherhoods that are different from cis motherhoods. Regardless of whether a trans woman identifies as "pregnant" with sperm, we have reproductive issues. If we're being murdered at alarming rates, how can we live to be mothers? If we're being sterilized by the state, why aren't more people outraged and teaching trans people the truth about their bodies? Why aren't there more organized efforts to make sperm banking and egg freezing accessible for trans people?

It's not simply trans women who can restore their fertility by stopping HRT; the same is true for trans men. As long as someone doesn't have reproductive or genitalia-related surgery, there is a chance for restoring fertility. There is a caveat for trans children and teenagers who take HRT before their gametes fully develop because it's unclear if disrupting someone's first puberty will result in permanent infertility.

I know that motherhood is sacred, and that I am destined to overcome sterilization to bring a child into this world. I know that someday, small brown fingers will find their home resting in my palms. The house shall shake with my child's ferocious wailing, and I will wear dark circles larger than a diaper bag under my eyes like they're the latest trend. I will swear that I won't raise children like my mother, yet Sundays will always be cleaning days blasting oldies and every holiday will call for a Party City explosion of decorations. Sometimes, at the end of these tiring, joy-filled days, I will cry endless streams of gratitude that I finally made it to motherhood.

What Happens When Your Hood Is the Last Stop on the White Flight Express?

TAIGI SMITH

When I think of home, I envision a place where memories and wounds run deep like murky rivers, a place where dreams sing like unfinished songs, the soil where we lay our roots and our heads. San Francisco's Mission District was the place I called home, a close-knit community where poor and working-class folks lived side by side while struggling to obtain a piece of Americana. After two years of living in New York City, I am ready to return home. It is almost Thanksgiving, and between trips on the D train and fifteen-hour workdays, I barely feel the autumn leaves beneath my feet in Brooklyn. My body shivers from the November chill, while my nose, red from windburn, runs uncontrollably. I find myself wishing for the comforts of home and smile: in a few days I will be in San Francisco, sitting at my mother's table, full of sweet potatoes, pasta, and, if I'm lucky, turkey. At forty-five years old, my mother is still unconventional and has yet to cook a traditional Thanksgiving dinner. She faithfully replaces the turkey with a simpler bird: Cornish hen.

Will my mother, who, like me, spent several years in New York, recognize that at twenty-four years old, I have found myself on the brink of insanity, unsure of where the next year, let alone my entire life, will lead me? Will she be able to see that working at a TV station has made me aggressive, competitive, and edgy, or will she be deceived by my nice clothes, make-believe smile, and pleasant demeanor? I am heading home, to the streets of the Mission, in search of my comfort zone, Shotwell Street, where the memories are good and the streets familiar.

In the summer of 1980, I was a tall, skinny eight-year-old, with big feet and wild braids. My friends and I gathered at our usual spot on Twentieth and Shotwell to amuse ourselves. There wasn't much to do during the long days of summer. We were the children of bus drivers, housekeepers, migrant workers, the unemployed, and the mentally ill. Most of our mothers were raising us alone and struggled, like single moms do, to provide us with the basics. The mothers of the Mission worked long days to afford simple things for us, like Top Ramen, notebooks for school, and shoes that fit. They weren't afraid to scream our names from their windows or yell at us in public.

We lived together on this block surrounded by automotive shops and single-family homes in the heart of the Mission, America's Latino pit stop for high hopes and big dreams. Some families had come seeking refuge from the bloody wars that had ravaged El Salvador and Nicaragua during the 1980s, while others had immigrated toward *el Norte* to escape the desperation of Mexico's barrios. My mother, then a twenty-four-year-old single parent, found the Mission through a friend, and although she'd never admit it, Moms was a hippie—seeking solace from the craziness of the Haight-Ashbury, the

> **" We lived together on this block surrounded by automotive shops and single-family homes in the heart of the Mission, America's Latino pit stop for high hopes and big dreams. "**

legendary stomping ground of the Grateful Dead and reefer-toking flower children. She acted like a womanist even then and didn't know it. I consider her a womanist because of her strength. She has run more than twenty-five marathons in her lifetime, and she still logs about fifty miles a week. She raised me with a loud voice and a burning passion, as if her life depended on my failure or success. She raised me on her own, without welfare and with an intensity that I've never been able to replicate. She was gutsy enough to hitch a ride across country to forge a better life for herself and me, and for this, she remains my hero.

Moms convinced the owner of our building to rent her a one-bedroom apartment for less than $200 a month. We were one of a handful of Black families in the Mission then, so it was almost impossible not to notice us. I learned how to make quesadillas on an open flame at my friend Marcy's house, while her mother spoke to me in Spanish. Most mornings, I would wake up to the sounds of Mexican ballads blasting soothingly from the building next door. Even today, I can still hear the sounds of wailing mariachis playing guitar and singing songs *de amor*. I always knew I was different from many of my Mexican friends and neighbors; we spoke different languages and ate different foods. But I never felt out of place in the Mission. As children of the Mission, we were raised to love and accept each other. Even today, as adults, we remain friends.

The Mission of the 1980s was a place filled with music and dance. On the far corner of Twentieth and Shotwell was an old garage that had been transformed into a dance studio. For months you could hear the sounds of Brazilian drums resonating from the walls of a once vacant garage. At night women and men would emerge from the building salty with sweat, glistening and seemingly exhausted. You could hear them chattering incessantly, in Spanish and English, about Carnaval, the Mission's answer to the legendary Rio de Janeiro annual event. For months dancers packed the studios that laced the Mission to practice for the twenty-four-hour festival of samba, salsa, and steel drumming.

During Carnaval, the neighborhood women transformed themselves with fifty-foot feathered headpieces and barely-there thong bikinis to parade down Mission Street twisting, gyrating, shimmying, and singing. A woman could take off her bikini top and flaunt her breasts without embarrassment or inhibition during this raw celebration of femininity and womanhood. It was not until I, at twelve, put on my own bikini and feathers and danced with the Brazilian troupe Batucaje that I truly felt the electricity generated when women of color come together to celebrate themselves as beautiful cultural and creative beings. Here we could dance, sing, sweat, and flaunt ourselves and our bodies like no other time. This was Carnaval.

I also remember the rallies on Twenty-Fourth and Mission during the 1980s and the sounds of political activists demanding freedom, shouting, "No More, No More, US Out of El Salvador!" They were white and Latino, young and old—most of all, they were loud and unrelenting. Many were women, unafraid of engaging in civil disobedience and unfazed by the threat of arrest. Who would have thought that almost twenty years later, these same women would be fighting against land developers to keep the neighborhood they called home?

I finally made it home for Thanksgiving, but something strange had happened to the Mission. I had only been away for two years, but it had been transformed into a place I found hard to navigate or recognize. Many of my childhood friends had already disappeared, and some of the Latino families I grew up with were nowhere to be found. The brown faces had diminished, and I was trapped in an unfamiliar scene filled with Caucasoids and trendy bars. It was gentrification.

Gentrification: The displacement of poor women and people of color. The raising of rents and the eradication of single, poor, and working-class women from neighborhoods once considered unsavory by people who didn't live there. The demolition of housing projects. A money-driven process in which landowners and developers push people (in this case, many of them single mothers) out of their homes without thinking about where they will go. Gentrification is a premeditated process in which an imaginary bleach is poured on a community and the only remaining color left in that community is white... only the strongest coloreds survived. (I know I'm using the word "colored".)

The word on the street was that the neighborhood was being taken over by white people—yuppies and new media professionals who would pay exorbitant rents to reside in what the *Utne Reader* had called "One of the Trendiest Places to Live in America"—and there was nothing people of color could do. Some were going to housing court in hopes of saving lost leases, but most attempts to fight greedy landlords were unsuccessful. The neighborhood folks, many of whom had protested in the 1980s against the contras in Nicaragua, were now feeling helpless. They were tired of fighting or simply unsure of how to protect themselves. They had seen their neighbors wage unsuccessful battles against landlords, and they were just hoping they wouldn't be next. The streets were now lined with Land Rovers and BMWs, and once seedy neighborhood bars now employed bouncers and served overpriced raspberry martinis. Abandoned warehouses had not been converted into affordable housing but instead into fancy lofts going for $300,000 to $1 million. The Army Street projects had been demolished, leaving hundreds of people, many of them women with children, displaced and homeless. The message was clear: it was time for the Blacks and the browns to get out—the whites were moving in and that was it.

For poor single mothers, gentrification is a tactic "the system" uses to keep them down; it falls into the same category as "work-fare" and "minimum wage." Gentrification is a woman's issue, an economic issue, and, most of all, a race issue. At my roots I am a womanist, as I believe in economic and social equality for all women. When I watch what has happened to my old neighbor-hood, I get angry, because gentrification like this is a personal at-tack on any woman of color who is poor, working class, and trying to find an apartment in a real estate market that doesn't give a damn about single mothers, grandmommas raising crack babies, or women who speak English as a second language.

The shameful thing is that the yuppies have changed the fab-ric of a neighborhood that was by all accounts an affordable, great place to live. The Mission wasn't one of those neighborhoods de-stroyed by the 1980s crack epidemic. It wasn't a destitute com-munity with burned-out buildings and shuttered-up storefronts, where gunshots rang out in the night. It was a cultural mecca where working-class people of color took pride in the community. The colorful murals that decorated the walls of local buildings were a testament to the rich culture of local Latino artistry, and the nu-merous thriving *marquetas* and restaurants were living proof of a small yet growing business district. We had nightclubs, supermar-kets, auto-body shops, meat markets, florists, delis, and clothing stores owned and operated by first- and second-generation Mex-ican Americans. For many of the immigrants, the Mission was a break from the poverty that had surrounded them in Mexico and El Salvador. Although the workdays were long and hard, most of my neighbors were grateful for the job opportunities that came their way. At least in the United States, there was a way to support one's family.

Many of us existed in a microcosm where working for white people as cooks, housekeepers, and migrant workers was a way of life. Many years later I realized this type of work was actually part of a larger system in which poor people (many of them women) did the low-level, low-paid work that no one else wanted to do. As a result of this system, most of us remained poor. Today I see that we were probably making the best of a difficult situation. Even now, we (me and the women I grew up with) insist that we would purchase homes and raise our children in the Mission if we had the financial means—our memories of the community are that good.

The infiltration of our neighborhood by the wealthy and the privileged is heartbreaking. To act as if our neighborhood is something they needed to "clean up" or "take back" is insulting. It is as if our new neighbors deny that our businesses, familial relationships, and community ever really existed in the first place. Many of the white people who have moved into the Mission see us in stereotypical terms—as immigrants, as people with thick accents and brown skin, as people who play loud music and collect welfare. In essence, they ignore who we really are. Our new neighbors can't see that our homes are impeccably clean and that many of the Latino families here are headed by both a mother *and* a father. And although we barely scrape by at times, we go to work and pay our bills. They want to believe we are all on welfare, destined to become single mothers and crack addicts. The truth is, however, that most of us have proven them wrong. We learned well on Shotwell Street from our single mothers and other women: Teena is now a sheriff, Maricela a police officer, Sonia a journalist at the *San Francisco*

Chronicle, and I am a writer and a producer. None of us grew up to be statistics.

I started calling myself a womanist while attending Mills College in Oakland, California. Mills, a liberal arts women's college, catered to families who could pay $22,000 a year. I was able to afford it thanks to a tremendous financial aid package. Many of the white women at Mills who called themselves feminists didn't understand my experiences as a Black woman. In women's studies classes, for example, the individual histories and struggles of Black women were often ignored. It was in an African-American women's studies class that I learned the word "womanist." Dr. Dorothy Tsuruta was at the time the most progressive (and only!) full-time African-American professor at Mills. She was regularly criticized because many of the white women who attended her classes felt alienated. They became upset and felt excluded when Dorothy told them that the term "womanism," as defined by Alice Walker, was meant specifically for women of color. Dorothy was eventually fired from Mills for shaking up a system that really wasn't in the business of liberating young black minds.

For the Black girls at Mills, Dorothy was like manna for our culturally starved souls. She spoke to us in ways we understood, and most important, she recognized it was torturous for us to attend a college where we were so widely misunderstood. I remember when a white female English professor who called herself a feminist declared that slaves had a special bond with their masters that many of us couldn't understand. I was the only African American in the class, and I was stunned by this statement. I declared myself a womanist when I realized that white women's feminism really didn't speak to my needs as the daughter of a Black, single domestic worker. I felt that, historically, white women were working hard to liberate themselves from housework and childcare, while women of color got stuck cleaning their kitchens and raising their babies. When I realized that feminism largely liberated white women at the economic and social expense of women of color, I knew I was fundamentally unable to call myself a feminist.

I really don't need another white feminist to tell me that poverty, teen pregnancy, infant mortality, AIDS, unemployment, and gentrification are class issues. I was once on the board of a progressive young women's reproductive rights organization, and the other board members were very wealthy white women who viewed many of the problems of women of color as "class issues." We would spend hours talking about how white and Black women had a hard time getting along because of our class differences. As a Black woman, however, my problems have always been directly connected to race; for me, class is secondary. Most white feminists I've encountered seem to think class is the source of all problems. While the roots of gentrification have as much to do with class as with race, it is hard to ignore that most of the people being driven out of neighborhoods are not poor whites in Appalachia; rather, they are poor Blacks and browns in the inner-city melting pots. Some would argue that gentrification only occurs in major cities, but as a news producer, I've traveled around the country. I can say firsthand that gentrification is kicking people of color out of communities everywhere. From Saint Paul, Minnesota, to the outskirts of Louisiana, the South Side of Chicago, and the flatlands of East Oakland, we're being evicted from our communities.

When I returned home to the Mission, I attended the open house of a new loft building opening up on Shotwell Street. I was the only Black person there. Because I've had access to higher education, I am now able to support myself and live a middle-class lifestyle, but even if I had the money to live in the Mission, I wonder how many landlords wouldn't rent to me as a young single Black woman. The other people who had come to the opening were white, and they looked at me as if I didn't belong there. I felt as if they wouldn't want me as a neighbor even if I had the money to live among them. While I represented everything they wanted to get away from, it was ironic that they were trying to move into a neighborhood that was historically Black and brown.

I've tried hard to intellectualize gentrification, but the harder I try, the more complicated it becomes. When I was looking for an apartment in Park Slope, Brooklyn, I was making enough to rent a studio off Seventh Avenue, yet all of the real estate agents I spoke with blatantly refused to show me apartments in the pristine, lily-white neighborhood. They kept taking me to Prospect Heights and Fort Greene, which at the time were mostly Black neighborhoods. Gentrification is more about the color of my skin than the money in my pocket.

Although my building in San Francisco had been spared from the claws of wealthy land bandits, it was a cultural war zone spurred on by economic and racial disparities. In fact, the entire community had become a war zone where guerrilla tactics were the weapons of choice. Someone had posted signs all over the neighborhood urging people to deface the live/work lofts, scrape up the fancy, high-priced vehicles that now lined the streets, and flatten yuppie tires. This vigilante had become a sort of folk hero, and the signs were part of an underground movement called the Mission Yuppie Eradication Project. The posters urged fellow Missionites to burn down the million-dollar lofts and make life hell for the new pioneers. In their own defense, the yuppies held a rally—ironically, on the corner of Twenty-Fourth and Mission, the home of the infamous political protests of the 1980s. Although the local media came out for the event, only a few yuppies were brave enough to show up.

My mother had formed a sort of guerrilla coalition in her building. Along with other people of color, she had vowed to fill vacant apartments with friends and family when they heard that their new neighbors wanted to rent to filmmakers, writers, and other artist types. The new renters were communicating via email with the building manager to secure any vacancies, and although the plan almost worked, they failed to fully homogenize the building. It was these people who viewed me with suspicion when I returned to Shotwell Street. Their icy glares easily translated into "What are *you* doing here?" They were suspicious of the Black girl "loitering" around the building. It really didn't matter that I had spent almost twenty years of my life there. They didn't care that I was a published writer, a successful TV producer, or a graduate of Mills College. To them I was another Black woman they were trying to get out of the neighborhood. I needed so badly to say, "This is my neighborhood. I grew up here," but my anger silenced me.

More than the air of wealth that now permeates the neighborhood, it is the attitude of superiority that angers me. It is the look of hate that aggravates me, the icy glare that says, "We are willing to take over this neighborhood at all costs." It leaves me wondering about the future of my friends and neighbors. I realize that women of color may never have a place to truly call our own. At times I think about returning home to the old neighborhood to organize my former neighbors, but doing that would mean giving up the life I've worked so hard to create in New York.

As my mother's only child, it is my responsibility to make sure she will always have a place to live, whether that be in San Francisco or elsewhere. It angers me that someone's greed could take away the apartment she has called home for almost thirty years. Countless women are grappling with having their rented apartments put on the auction block without regard for where they will go next. And the chances are that the person who buys that building/apartment/duplex will probably be a white person with more power and a lot more money. What is to become of all the other mothers and grandmothers in the Mission whose children have neither the income nor the knowledge to help?

I pay an exorbitant rent to live in a Brooklyn neighborhood where the amenities include a round-the-clock liquor store, a marijuana delivery service, illegal all-night gambling, and numerous buildings for Section 8 families and people on welfare. My building is earmarked for upwardly mobile professionals and white people. Throughout the neighborhood, signs of "revitalization" are cropping up. White kids walk smugly down the street, sometimes riding rickety bikes or skateboards. Internet businesses are opening up alongside yoga studios, and I have a fully renovated apartment with superfast Internet access. I am on the cusp of the revitalization, and although I have an amazing apartment in the midst of the hood, I am more than conscious of the fact that the low-income women around me may not be here for long.

I am sure they look at me and the other professionals moving in and wonder, "What are they doing here?" Do my low-income neighbors realize that the new buildings being put up like wildfire are not for people like them but for people like me, who can afford to pay inflated rents for renovated apartments in the hood? I am keenly aware of exactly what is happening, and I realize that neighborhoods don't have to be financially rich to be culturally vibrant, and that white people moving into poor neighborhoods do little good for the people who already live there. When white people move into Black neighborhoods, the police presence increases, cafés pop up, and the neighborhood bodegas start ordering the *Wall Street Journal* and the *New York Times*. You rarely see low-income housing built alongside million-dollar lofts, or social service centers opening next to yoga studios. When I think about this, I am caught somewhere in the middle, because although I have the money to live in a neighborhood that is being gentrified, I still hear the words my Black real estate agent whispered to me: "Just think of this as your own little castle in the hood."

I don't want them to take over my San Francisco neighborhood, but five thousand miles away, in another state and another community, I'm "on the front lines of gentrification," as a neighbor so politely put it. When I come home at night and see the crackheads loitering in front of the building next door, I realize I may have switched sides in this fight. When I dodge cracked glass and litter when walking my dog, I realize that this neighborhood really could use a facelift, and that the yoga center that just opened up on the corner is a welcome change from the abandoned building it used to be.

Parts of my Brooklyn neighborhood are symbolic of what the media and sociologists say is wrong with "the inner city." I live on a block where the police don't arrest drug dealers who peddle crack in broad daylight, where young Black men drive around in huge SUVs but barely speak grammatically correct English, where I see the same brothas every day standing on the street corners, doing absolutely nothing. They don't hustle or harass me but instead politely say "hello," as if they've accepted me. I feel strained by my situation. While I am intimately aware of what is happening to my new neighborhood, I feel powerless. I've been in Brooklyn long enough to know that although it is not the most savory neighborhood, it is a community where people feel connected, where the old folks know each other, where neighbors still chat. But sometimes I feel like telling the young men on the corner, "Get the hell off the street! Don't you see that life is passing you by? Don't you see this is what *they* expect *you* to do? Don't you see they're moving *in*, and in a few years, you're gonna have to get *out*?"

In my neighborhood, men shoot each other, the sidewalks are cracked, and many of the buildings are abandoned, and I've witnessed two drug raids from my bedroom window. When I come home at night, I put on my sweatpants and walk my tiny dog on littered sidewalks past tomboys in goose-down coats, doing each other's hair on stoops of aging brownstones. When I see these girls, I remember my own childhood and think that they deserve more than this. They deserve a neighborhood that is clean and safe and that provides some hope, a place where they can learn that some dreams do come true, and that Prince Charming doesn't drive an Expedition and sell weed to his friends.

Walking the streets, I realize my neighbors and I are alike in many ways. We like the same foods and the same music, and, most important, we are a group of African-American people living together in a neighborhood that is on the verge of change. But in the end we are also very different. If the rents go up, I will have options and they may not. They may have to move and I will get to stay. Although we look the same, we are different. We are connected by race but remain separated by a slip of paper called a college degree. Our block, our hood, our neighborhood has become the next stop on the White Flight Express.

Fast forward. It is 1998. I sip chocolate martinis in what was once an immigrants' watering hole. Ironically, the bar is now called Sacrifice. A jukebox replaces the mariachis and top-shelf liquor takes the place of Night Train. An old flame, Ron, is trying to convince me to marry him. I'm thinking, *I haven't seen this guy in years*, but I thank him for his compliment. And then I see a short man, a few inches over five feet, wearing dirty gray pants and a button-down shirt. His eyes are glazed over and he is barely able to stand. He is singing a song and I recognize the accent, from Juárez or Tijuana. He mumbles something profane in Spanish and appears to be confused by the sea of white faces (and me!).

He searches the room for his compadres, and it becomes evident that this place he had once known so well is now as foreign to him as it is to me. He blinks his eyes a few times and tries to shake himself from this drunken haze, but soon realizes that what he is seeing is no illusion. He stares at the blonde woman with the multiple tattoos and pierced lip and wonders where his friends might be. He has never seen white people in this bar, and as he looks at her, I stare at him and relate to his longing for days gone by. And then he turns from her and looks at me as if to say, "What are you, *una negrita*, doing here?"

We lock eyes and I allow him to see my shame while I share his sadness. I too am lost in a place I knew so well. Like the old man looking for a drink, I am saddened, disillusioned, and disgusted by the changes. Like him, I also feel powerless. He glances around a bit more, struggles to his feet, curses a few words in *Español*, throws down his tequila, closes his eyes, and stumbles out of the door.

HIV and Me
The Chicana Version

STELLA LUNA

When I was a little girl, I dreamed of being an actress. I enjoyed making up silly dances and putting on shows for my friends and family. Being the youngest of five children and arriving six years after my sister, I had the privilege of being the center of attention throughout my childhood. Our family lived in a suburb of Los Angeles that was generally classified as Mexican middle class. My father was a second-generation Mexican American who believed in strong family values and a religious foundation. As in many Mexican-American households, our family always came first. My mother wasn't allowed to work because my father believed her place was in the home taking care of our family. I never saw my mom question this arrangement, but I noticed actions that discreetly displayed her desire. For example, my sister and I weren't allowed to do any of the household chores or cooking. She would say, "One day you are going to be forced to do this stuff to keep your husband happy, so I'm not going to force you to do it now." I happily obliged, but in the back of my mind, I began to visualize marriage as the beginning of a lifelong service to others.

As I grew into my teens, it became quite apparent that dating was a privilege and not a right. Under the watchful eyes of my father and my three brothers, I was given strict rules to obey. I didn't mind these rules, but what bothered me was my mother's constant fear of my getting pregnant. I found this confusing, because my parents never had a sex talk with me, and it hurt to think they had such little trust in me. Years later, my mom would brag to her friends how her girls "didn't have to get married because they were pregnant." She considered this a personal achievement.

After high school graduation I began working full time as a secretary, and I loved having my own paycheck. I began dating one of my coworkers, an Anglo man, and my family was furious. Brett wasn't like the *machista* guys I had grown up with. Instead, he encouraged me to explore my own ideas and become more independent. My dad disliked him and didn't appreciate that "this white guy" was placing all kinds of crazy ideas in my head. My dad's anger heightened when I decided to start spending weekends over at Brett's house. My mom accused me of "ruining myself." I grew tired of the bad blood between my boyfriend and my family, so Brett and I decided to get married. Deep down inside, I honestly knew I wasn't ready to get married, but I just didn't want to see my family hurt and upset anymore. My father was happy with our decision, and my mother insisted that I could still be married in a white dress. I angrily thought to myself, "Why wouldn't I be married in white?"

Soon after we were married, Brett was offered an engineering position in Arizona and we moved. I really didn't want to leave my family, but my dad convinced me that I had to support my husband's career. Soon after our arrival in Arizona, I became very homesick and felt like we had made a terrible mistake. I discovered that Brett and I were very different people, and I couldn't imagine spending the rest of my life with him. I also found that I couldn't be an adequate partner to him, because I was still figuring out who I wanted to be. Brett was also unhappy, and he accused me of being a "daddy's girl" who still needed to grow up. Sadly, I had to agree with him.

We got a divorce a year later. My family was devastated and insisted I immediately move back home. But I had just started a job that I really enjoyed, and a friend had asked if I wanted to room with her. I had never lived on my own before, and I was anxious to see if I could succeed without my family's assistance. I still wasn't sure what I wanted to do with my life, but I knew I had to find out on my own. I wanted to prove to my family that I wasn't a helpless little girl.

I loved my newfound freedom. I began dating again and became involved in a short-lived relationship. Even though it didn't last, the relationship would come back to haunt me in years to come. I had saved up enough money to move into my own apartment, where I became acquainted with a sweet guy living across the hall from me. Within six months of dating we were married. Despite the fact that Jay was Anglo, my family absolutely adored him. I think it was because he had a gentle spirit and an enormous respect for our family. My father trusted Jay because he was a hard worker and held strong values. I felt like I had met my soul mate.

Unlike my first marriage, my life with Jay was so easy and non-confrontational. I remember looking forward to coming home each night and just being together. The early years of our marriage were an incredibly happy time in our lives. Two years later, in 1993, I discovered that I was pregnant, and we were overjoyed when the doctor confirmed through an ultrasound that the baby was firmly nestled in my tummy. He informed us that as a routine procedure, he asked his patients to have blood tests performed to check for anemia, hepatitis, diabetes, and HIV. My husband asked why I needed to be tested for HIV, and the doctor told us that it was a test he offered all of his patients. It seemed unnecessary, but I agreed to the blood work. We left the appointment and didn't think any more about it—until two weeks later, when I received a phone call that would change my life forever.

I was one month pregnant when the call came from my doctor. One of my tests had come back with unexpected results. He asked if I had ever been a drug user. Offended, I said no. He asked if I had ever had sex with someone I presumed to be bisexual. Again, I answered no. I began to feel dizzy. The doctor said that although he was confused with the results, I had tested positive for HIV. Just then, Jay walked through the door, and I handed him the phone and burst into tears. Through my crying I could hear Jay shouting to the doctor that there must be some kind of mistake. I glanced up to look at him and he had tears streaming down his face. He was asked to come into the office the next day so they could run an HIV test on him. The doctor was bringing in a specialist to discuss our options.

Jay grabbed my hands and told me that he was the one who was probably infected first. I wasn't sure how to react. I called a couple of our gay friends and told them about the test results. We hoped that maybe they would be able to bring some insight into this whole nightmare. We knew they had lost a number of friends to this disease, and we felt safe sharing our sad news with them. Our friends came over and spent the evening trying to calm us down. They hugged us as we cried and tried to tell us that it was going to be all right. I would have never made it through that night without them. That evening, we all formed a special bond that has lasted more than eight years.

At the doctor's office the next day, the specialist told us that the life span of someone with AIDS was five to ten years. He said if our baby was born infected, his or her chances for survival were close to none. He encouraged us to abort the baby. We went home that night and thought long and hard about our future and our unborn child. We came to the conclusion that even if I died from AIDS, we still had to give the baby a chance at being born HIV negative and living a full life. We believed our baby was created out of love and it wasn't right to destroy it.

A week later, Jay's test results came back from the lab as negative. My mind went into a tailspin. I instantly recalled the person I had briefly dated between my two marriages, and I assumed he had to be the one who had infected me. I called him and told him, but I never heard from him again. Although it narrowed down only to my relationship with him, he never confirmed it. It amazed me how the disease had been spread around.

My pregnancy progressed normally, except for the additional blood tests I was required to take to ensure that my immune system was still strong. The treatment for HIV-positive pregnant women in the early 1990s was not very progressive. Clinical trials were still being conducted on the dosing of azidothymidine (AZT) to pregnant women to lessen the chances of their children being born with the disease. Because this method was still considered experimental, I wasn't offered any type of drug treatment. Instead, I relied only on herbs and vitamins to keep up my immune system and minimize my stress levels.

Jay tried to be supportive, but I noticed that he was slowly distancing himself from the situation. We had decided not to tell anyone else about the HIV. The only people who knew were our gay friends, my sister, and Jay's best friend at work. This lack of disclosure made it very difficult for me to cope with my feelings. It also began to make me feel resentful toward Jay. I began to think he was ashamed of me. I recalled my feelings when my parents got upset that I had decided to sleep with my first husband before marriage. Maybe everyone did have a right to be ashamed of me. I had hurt the people I loved because of my intimate decisions. I wondered, Did I actually have the right to bring another human being into this world when my immoral behavior had brought on such a horrible disease?

On a cold December morning, my son Alex was born. He seemed to be a very healthy baby. When he was three days old, he was given his first HIV test. The doctor had high hopes, and when the results came back negative, we felt like we were finally out of the woods. I returned to work and we sought out a caregiver for our son. When Alex was six months old, he was given another HIV test to confirm his negative status. We anxiously awaited the results. Sitting at my desk at work, I saw Jay walk in with a stricken look on his face. I immediately told my boss that I had to leave and I followed Jay out the door. We walked hand in hand and he began to weep. Alex's pediatrician had called: our son's test had come back positive.

The pediatrician believed that the disease hadn't yet manifested itself in Alex's system back when the first test was taken. He had given Jay the name of a pediatric infectious disease specialist at the children's hospital. The piece of paper with the specialist's phone number was crumpled up in my husband's hand. We held each other and cried and talked about moving to Seattle. We had always dreamed of living in the Northwest, and we agreed that if we lost Alex to this disease, we would just run away to a place where we didn't feel so much pain.

That night we held on to Alex so tightly. I felt like God was yanking him away from us. We couldn't believe that this beautiful baby was going to die. We didn't know how we were going to survive through this nightmare. The following day, we told Alex's caregiver about his condition. We apologized for not telling her before, but we honestly didn't think that it was going to be an issue. We told her we still wanted her to take care of our son, but after careful consideration, she told us it would be impossible for her to subject her other parents to the risk. Our hearts were broken, but we really tried hard to understand.

The next day I went in to work and put in my two weeks' notice. I told my boss the whole story, and although he was shocked, he was very understanding. That night, he called to tell me his wife had offered to take care of Alex, and it didn't bother her that he was HIV infected. I broke down in tears at his kindness. I thanked him but explained that maybe it was time for me to stay home and spend as much time with my baby as possible. In reality, I thought it was time for my son and me to stay home and prepare to die.

We took Alex to his first appointment. We were scared and didn't know what to expect, but the doctors were wonderful. They told us there was a new medication being tested for HIV treatment and that they could possibly get Alex on a clinical trial. A few months later he was given AZT and two other antiviral drugs. I poured the liquid directly in his baby formula and tried to get over the ugly feeling about giving my son an experimental medicine.

Sitting at home with my son and our diagnosis, I spent a lot of time getting upset about our situation. I even ventured out to an HIV support meeting, but I left the meeting feeling isolated because I was the only female there. I was beginning to feel like I was the only woman in the world with HIV. I really began to wonder what God had against me. One day I spotted an article in the newspaper proclaiming that "the new face of HIV" was a woman who had been diagnosed with the disease and had given birth to a baby. The article concluded by giving information about a women's support group held in the Phoenix area. I immediately called the agency to find out the details and then anxiously waited for the day to arrive.

I was so nervous when I walked into that meeting, but the women immediately put me at ease. I listened to the women's stories and was amazed at the courage they had toward combating HIV. I was also surprised at the diversity of the women. This confirmed my understanding that HIV could infect anyone: all you have to be is human. I became friends with these women. Some had overcome obstacles such as IV drug use, but there were also college students and housewives—women who didn't understand how this had ever happened to them. I began to realize that I wasn't alone in combating the disease. It was such a comfort to know that I had people to talk to who would understand my feelings and not judge me. It is incredible to realize women's strength during times of struggle. I experienced this strength firsthand as I watched the group come together as sisters and empower themselves to fight for their lives and their dignity.

Later, we would use this empowerment as the foundation to advocate on our behalf in the HIV/AIDS community. In the midst of this local HIV women's movement, the renowned HIV/AIDS specialist Dr. David Ho announced to the nation that he and his team of researchers had developed a combination therapy that was proving to slow the progression of HIV in clinical trials. My doctor immediately sent me to a clinical trial site and enrolled me in an experimental program. I began taking a combination therapy (aka drug cocktail) that was similar to the drugs my son Alex was also being treated with. Although I was riddled with horrible side effects, I continued my routine and anxiously waited to see if it was going to improve my blood count. In the meantime, Alex's blood work was showing incredible improvements. In fact, his CD4 blood count, which indicates the immunity in his body, was within normal range.

With such great strides in research, some of the women in my HIV community decided we were now ready to stand up and have our voices heard regarding the HIV issues that affected the women and children in our community. We laid down the criteria for our mission and presented it to a leading HIV/AIDS agency in town. We wanted to convince the government and nonprofit contributors that there was a lack of funding for services geared toward women and children, such as childcare, transportation, and effective treatment programs that specifically focused on the medical and psychological welfare of our families.

The agency believed in our mission and agreed to take us under their umbrella. The HIV Women's Task Force was born. Besides providing our group with a place to hold our meetings, the agency also gave us opportunities to go into the community and talk about our experiences living with HIV. I was honored to be elected to serve on the agency's executive board of directors. In that capacity I spoke to forums across our area about the changing face of HIV/AIDS. Public speaking was important to the community, but it also served as a healing method for all my years of silence. It empowered my spirit and helped me overcome my fear of rejection and shame.

While these wonderful things were happening in the community, my home life had turned into a disaster. Jay had always been a private person, and I felt like he resented my public speaking engagements. Despite the distance growing between us, I continued my community service work. A number of my engagements took me to the state university and the local community college. I listened to students and encouraged them to practice safe sex and be tested regularly.

At about this time I also began to have a strong desire to return to school. In one of my engagements I expressed a wish to someday pursue an education. After my speech a man came up to me and handed me his business card. He told me to give him a call and he would help me pursue my dream. I looked at the card and realized that he was a financial aid officer from the state university.

Jay, however, seemed reluctant to support my idea. He felt we were surviving a major event in our lives, and now it was time to sit back and have a normal lifestyle. Life was crazy enough with my community activism. I was determined not to let his position get me down. I made an appointment with the financial aid officer and we began the process of applying for financial aid for college. A few weeks later I received my acceptance letter from the university.

Jay and I went into marriage counseling, but despite our efforts, we decided to separate three months into my first semester of college. I felt like my world had fallen apart, but I also understood that perhaps we had been through too many trials to ever completely heal our relationship. I really wished that we were able to move past the sad times in our lives and just be happy again. It was hard to imagine what life would be like without the man who I still so desperately loved. Jay, Alex, and I were supposed to be a family. This isn't how my life was supposed to turn out, but I couldn't be angry with Jay for blaming me for this whole mess. I made a vow that I wouldn't cause him any more pain. I was determined to keep myself and Alex healthy, and to try to be the best mother I could.

The following month, Alex and I moved into our own apartment and began an adventure that would prove to be an incredible growing experience. I enrolled Alex in preschool and began working part time as a waitress to help make ends meet. Jay and I decided on joint custody, and he agreed to keep Alex on weekends so

I could work and still have time to study (and some spare time to sleep!). I was thankful for this arrangement.

When I began my first year, I had personal reasons for wanting a college degree. I believed that I was given a second chance, and I wanted to make the most of it. I decided on an English major, with the intent of possibly becoming a teacher someday. In my second semester I enrolled in a class on Chicano/a culture to fulfill a university requirement. At the time I didn't realize that this class would change my way of thinking forever. We explored many aspects of Chicano/a culture and analyzed the reasoning behind many of our traditions. I was introduced to authors like Gloria Anzaldúa and Cherríe Moraga, who broke the silence on Chicana feminism and made a statement about female oppression and colonization. It was incredible to read about redefining my cultural understanding regarding my own sexual and personal identity.

Since my diagnosis, I had been dealing with shame and a lack of self-worth that I felt could only be redeemed by sacrificing myself for my family, my community, and even my own child. I thought that if I gave everything I had inside to the people I loved, I would perhaps be able to prove I wasn't a bad person. The truth was that I really wasn't a bad person. And I didn't need to dedicate my life to defining the kind of person I was. I realized that I was imprisoned not only by a disease but also by a culture that had trained me to be as clean and untouched in soul and body as the Virgen

" I was imprisoned not only by a disease but also by a culture that had trained me to be as clean and untouched in soul and body as the Virgen de Guadalupe. Because of my HIV-positive status, I was considered useless in a culture that reduced women to their bodies. "

de Guadalupe. Because of my HIV-positive status, I was considered useless in a culture that reduced women to their bodies. If I chose to live my life according to this structure, maybe I should just give up and die.

Overcoming the guilt of being HIV infected is quite a challenge for Chicanas. If we disclose our status, it very well may destroy the foundation to which we try so hard to adhere. And this would bring shame to our families and communities. We stay silent perhaps because we believe we rightfully deserve to die. I could finally understand why so many *mujeres* just give up. Many HIV-infected Chicanas don't seek medical care because they are too scared and ashamed to come forward. Who was going to tell these women that they didn't have to live this way?

I was.

I guess this is when you could say I became politicized. The following semester, I enrolled in more Chicano/a studies classes, looking at Chicana history and theory and thinking about issues directly related to the HIV/AIDS Mexican-American community. I began to understand the reasons why Mexican Americans weren't participating in the HIV community. My heart broke when I realized that many of my sisters were going to die because they just couldn't relate to services that weren't culturally and linguistically suited to their specific needs. I changed my major to Chicano/a studies and anxiously look forward to graduation day, after which I planned to help my community by truly making a difference. It is strange to think about how much I have changed. Before college I believed I was a strong person. Now, five years later, I have a new definition of myself. My New Mestiza is strong-willed, empowered, inspired, beautiful, and sexy! It is times like this when I don't see this disease as a detriment. Instead, I accept HIV in my life as a special task that was bestowed upon me to help the HIV community, which is closest to my heart.

I think about my beautiful, healthy child and I remember being told he had no chance for survival. I think back to the prognosis that I had only five to ten years to live, and yet today I am healthy, happy, and managing a disease that almost handed me a death sentence. It is difficult sometimes to realize that my life didn't exactly turn out the way it was supposed to. But in the long run I believe that it turned out to be something more than I ever could have imagined. I remember being asked at a conference, "If you could be cured of HIV today, but when the disease left your body, it took with it all the strength, unconditional love, compassion, endurance, and empowerment that you have acquired since being diagnosed, would you still agree to being cured?"

I thought really long and hard about my answer, and with tears in my eyes I proudly held my head up and replied, "No."

Tenderheaded Before, During, and After Obama

AMBER TAYLOR

You are a soft child. You shed tears because you forgot how to throw a football the day after your father taught you. You stand barefoot in your backyard, orange foam football in hand, wailing because every time you release the ball it wobbles lopsided, unsure of itself in the air, never reaching your father who stands a few yards away.

I did it perfect yesterday! you shriek, stomping through the backdoor.

Your face is red and watery like Italian ice when you run past your mother in the kitchen.

You hear Father say, You need to talk some sense into your daughter, Denise. What the hell is wrong with her?

It's probably just her hormones, Alan. You know she's about to reach that age...

That evening you cry about your shoddy throwing until your throat feels like the voice box has been ripped from it; however, you do not cry when the police come to take your father away.

When your mother braids your hair you always sit between her legs. Sometimes she sits on the white plastic-covered couch in the living room. Sometimes she sits at the edge of her bed. But you are always on the floor, skinny legs stiff, splayed in front of you like broken chopsticks. Sometimes you read from your children's bible book. It tells you that god knows all the useless information about you, like how many strands of hair you have on your head.

The beads that sit between your legs look like hard candies in their clear plastic bag. You dig through them with one hand and hold your plastic bead needle in the other. There are barrettes in the bag, too, most of them in the shape of bows; you're not allowed to wear too many because mother says she doesn't want you looking like a pickaninny.

She cornrows your hair tightly and you yelp when she braids close to your "kitchen," the baby hairs at the nape of your neck. You have to hold your braid close to your head until she finishes it because it feels like she's going to rip the hair away if you don't. She tells you to stop being so tenderheaded, and you ask what that means. Someone who is more sensitive than most, she says.

As you stack beads onto your needle you ask more questions, the same ones as always: When can you wear your hair straight? Why can't you get a relaxer like the other girls at school? Is your nose too big? Why isn't there a black princess? Will there ever be one?

I don't know, Amber. Because your hair isn't unruly like your sister's. No. Because white people are racist, Amber. I don't know.

Why are they racist?

I don't know, Amber.

When will they stop being racist?

I don't know, Amber.

Eventually you stop asking when white people will stop being racist because the answer from your mother is always the same. You start to think the racism will never stop, like how you never stop asking to get your hair straightened until you're old enough to do it yourself.

But then, when you are thirteen, you get something better than a black princess. You get a black first family.

The first thing you notice about Michelle Obama and her daughters is that they wear their hair the way you always wanted to—like a white girl's. They dress better than most people you know and are very educated. You don't know what to make of this, because you know their straight hair won't save them from the misogynoir you can't save yourself from, but you adore them still, because their presence is comforting, and you want to believe they can change things.

> **You also know your feminist community did not prepare you for this moment. If anything, it was your blackness that prepared you.**

To look up to the first lady is to know that you deserve to be seen; it is to know that your skin color will not stop you from being whatever it is that you are meant to be in this life; it is to know that you can be in one of the most influential positions in the country and still be called an ape in heels, a poor gorilla, and a feminist nightmare.

You've never heard the word "feminism" before. Your parents never use the word, but your father does snatch your attention one day when he mentions the women's liberation movement. You catch a chill from the way he says "women's lib," like it is a weapon.

He says it was something that white women started for themselves because white men treated them like second-class citizens.

You ask why he doesn't like it so much if it was just about white women and men.

It was also targeted at black women to destroy black families, he says with a hard look on his face. He says that white women wanted black women to join in on their cause even though black women's needs were different from theirs. He says that black women started choosing white women over black men, and that this created a rift in the black community that has been there ever since.

Part of you calls yourself a young woman and another part of you calls yourself black. Being both, you always thought that there was no need for division, but now you're hurt, and you feel there must be a rift somewhere in you, too.

When your mother first hears of the black senator from Illinois who is running for president, she calls everyone. She phones your Mommy T in Philly; she talks on and on with Ms. Debbie, who still lives in your hometown. She talks extra loudly to her Aunt Helen, who is over one hundred years old and never thought she would live to see a black president. They all wonder how white people will react if he wins. Will he be assassinated? Will there be civil unrest? They can only prepare for the worst.

Still on the phone, your mother marvels over how far we have come as a people. She dwells on the sacrifices our ancestors made for this man named Barack to have this chance to be president. The word "sacrifice" feels heavy to you and makes the toes of your shoes seem like they are plated with lead. You hear tears in your mother's eyes.

Your mother calls everyone to talk about the black senator from Illinois except for your father, because he does not use the word "sacrifice" when he talks about black politicians.

Your father is not at all impressed. He believes Barack Obama will not make a difference for us as a people; he thinks the country will continue to treat black people as disposables, just as it always has. It is your father who tells you to never get your hopes up for this country that you live in, or anything that comes of it—even a black president, even a black first lady and a black first family. So you try to hide your excitement.

On the day the police come for your father, your mother takes you and your sister to the basement. She tells you not to leave until she comes back. You stand quiet and tearless while you hear your father yelling at the police above you.

Later you ask Mother why the police were here and not what Father did to deserve jail time. She doesn't answer you.

You decide whatever your father did, it wasn't worth calling the police to your home; he returns by the end of the week.

While the first black family in the White House is under constant scrutiny for existing, you work hard to make yourself vanish in high school. There is nothing you can do to hide your black face in class. You know there's no makeup to make your skin pale enough, no bleach to make you white quick enough. But you are old enough now to learn how to do your own hair; instead of learning how to braid like your mother, you pick up your flat iron every morning and make your curls obey. Your hair becomes so heat damaged that it forgets how to curl up in the shower when you wash it; it breaks off and peppers the ivory-colored bowl of the sink when you brush it, but you don't care. You're just happy to have one less thing about your appearance stand out.

Even though you adore Michelle Obama now, you have to admit that you didn't initially. In the beginning, you'd poke fun at her from time to time over silly things. You and your sister didn't like her eyebrows. You made fun of how thin and sharp they looked on her forehead whenever you saw her on the news or on magazine covers; you thought she was trying to be trendy with her thin, strongly arched brows, but ended up missing the mark and looked ridiculous. Her smile never looked genuine to you. Her teeth always seemed tense, and paired with her brows, her face told you she was trying too hard to be likable. She almost looked angry to you. Perhaps she was angry, because she knew she had to try very hard to be liked when so many white first ladies before her hadn't.

You don't exactly remember when, but at some point you stopped teasing. In your first year of high school, you and your sister realized that Michelle didn't need two girls around her daughters' ages to tease her when she already received enough insults about her looks from white people.

You learned about feminist crap from college. This is what your mother tells you when you ask her whether you were interested in feminism when you were a girl.

And you suppose that's true. Feminism is crap when it only caters to the needs of white women. But at college you learn about womanism, a kind of feminism that centers women of color and their experiences. You don't take any special classes in women's and gender studies, or in social justice or sexuality; you learn about these things from your new friends.

You walk with them to and from class on rainy days and give the bird to the guy who drives up and down Spring Street with his Gadsden flag whipping from the bed of his pickup truck. You keep condoms in your pockets and attend Black Lives Matter protests and candlelight vigils together. Sometimes you host community events at the Women's Center where you are coworkers. You kick over big plastic sandwich boards all over campus that ask, "Can Blue Lives and Black Lives Matter?" Later you go out past midnight to vandalize the signs together in red Sharpie, replying: "Blue lives do not exist!" You hold each other accountable when you need to and encourage each other always. You admit you don't know everything there is to know about womanism or feminism, but you are certain that it is supposed to feel like this—like community.

When white students at your college complain on social media about the Black Lives Matter protest that you and your black peers lead after the non-indictment of Darren Wilson, they refer to you all as someone's escaped slaves that need to be rounded up. Many of your black peers are stunned to learn that their white classmates would go as far as to call them slaves, but your mind is elsewhere. You desperately want to believe that because the nation collectively respected a black man enough to vote him into the Oval Office twice, the nation will also be willing to stop murdering black bodies.

You are wrong. You are wrong, and it doesn't even surprise you.

It is your last year at Miami University—not to be mistaken for the one in Florida. Your school is named after the Miami tribe who lived in southwest Ohio before the land was stolen from them. Miami University's official mascot used to be the "Redskins," but in the late nineties it was changed to the "RedHawks."

You think the sentiment is nice, but the mascot isn't worth much when most students are still perfectly fine with buying redskin drinks from New Bar a few blocks away from campus.

You and your roommate are in a bar, but not at the one selling drinks named after racist slurs. That doesn't matter to you though, because there are still racists among you. They keep their glasses close to their lips and take gulps of beer frequently; they shout and slap each other on the back every time a state on the map turns red.

Maybe, you think, some of them are happier that a woman is losing than they are that a racist is winning. You cannot tell. You are sure the racists in New Bar are just as excited as the racists here.

You and your roommate leave the bar discreetly, walking quickly for two blocks to get back to your apartment. You think that if there were ever a perfect night for two black girls to get jumped in Oxford, Ohio, it would be tonight—when Trump has officially been elected president; when the white men who dominate the campus culture are drunk off their racist beers and their triumph.

Your heart quivers as something inside yourself braces for impact. You feel like crying. You feel like all the moisture in your body is hot and concentrated at your lower lashes. Tears threaten to spring from your eyes, but they won't come—the sensation is familiar. It is the feeling of wanting to surrender when your body won't allow it.

You are immediately thankful for the friends you have made in college. You know their presence will steady you, as always. But you also know your feminist community did not prepare you for this moment. If anything, it was your blackness that prepared you; the constant warning from your father told you that nothing good would ever come from this country—a place that gave you a black first family and more dead black bodies than you can name in the same fraction of your lifetime. It's no surprise that it gave you a complete monster to be your next president.

When you enter your room you don't bother with the light. You flop into the bed without washing off your makeup or brushing your teeth; the taste of vodka and Sprite lingers under your tongue. You call your mother.

Maybe you say you're nervous about going to class tomorrow, and then she quotes 2 Timothy 1:7 to calm you: *For God has not given us the spirit of fear, but of power, and of love, and of a sound mind.* Maybe you say you can't sleep, and she suggests listening to that instrumental music you like so much.

Maybe you say to her, I think I'm going to cry, and she says, Don't cry, Amber. We are a strong people. We have survived much worse.

You are more sensitive than most, so you cry over silly things. You're very young when you see a white Jesus being crucified on the television in your basement and you cry for him because you don't think your soul is worth redeeming if it means wearing a crown of thorns. You're nine when you cry at Michael Jackson's "Thriller" music video; you like to watch it in the daytime with your sister, but when it's time for bed you think zombie Michael Jackson will come for you, so you stay awake all night. You're a little older when you cry when there are bees in the backyard and they chase you into the house. You're in your teens when you cry at a commercial for the first time—an ad for the 2012 Winter Olympics plays on YouTube and you sob alone on your living room couch for five minutes before you can start watching a Michelle Phan video. You're in college when you see a commercial for Trident gum on television and burst into tears in front of your grandma, who asks you what the hell is wrong with you. You lie and say you don't know, even though you thought it was sweet how the father in the commercial saved all the gum-wrapper cranes he made for his daughter till she went to college.

Your problem is that you don't cry when you actually need to. You don't cry when something really awful happens, because the really awful things that keep happening have happened before and they will continue to happen. Your body tires of crying over the same thing; you build a wall for yourself to hide behind, and you don't try to process the pain. You don't think you're meant to cry this much. But if you are, then you wish that god could have at least made you less tenderheaded.

You do not cry when racial violence comes to your dorm room—when you're with your white roommate squinting up at the little television, and the news says Darren Wilson will not be indicted.

Michael Brown's body that lay in the street for four hours after being slaughtered can be your body next, and more easily the body of your partner, or any of your eight male cousins. You do not cry when your roommate looks at you and says that if you ever have a family of your own in the future, you must leave the country with them, so that this place doesn't kill you all. They will kill you, she says, and they will not care.

The morning after the election, you call your father before your first class.

Some people aren't going to their classes today, maybe I shouldn't either, you say.

You're in the bathroom, leaning over the sink, applying lipstick. Brown. A few shades darker than your own skin.

Your phone buzzes frantically on the toilet seat with notifications from the BLACK PPL MEET @ MIAMI group chat. Your father's voice barks through the speaker: That's weak shit, Amber. Don't come to me with that weak shit.

They're scared.

They shouldn't be. And neither should you. Forget these white people. You go to your classes and do what you went there to do. Get your degree and get the hell out.

It is 2015, and you are twenty years old. You are visiting with a high school friend at her house; it's been years since you've been able to be in each other's company like this, since you both started college.

On the carpeted floor of her family room, the television is blaring and surrounded by her younger siblings' toys.

You reminisce together about how much easier life seemed just a few years ago, while her siblings watch the Disney Channel, until you notice a preview of an upcoming episode of *Doc McStuffins* in your peripheral vision. You already love Doc McStuffins as a character, because she is a caring black girl who uses her talents to heal her toy patients; you wish you'd had a show like hers to watch when you were a kid instead of *Bob the Builder*.

You're beaming when you realize that Michelle Obama will be making a special appearance on this upcoming episode, in which Doc McStuffins visits the capital and is named the official toy doctor for the White House. You turn to your friend and ask rhetorically how awesome it will be when black children are able to see this episode.

I really don't see why it matters, she says.

You're startled. You know that it matters for black children to see black characters on television and a black first lady in the White House. It matters to be visible. It matters for children being raised in a country that still tells them their skin and bodies are inferior.

None of this is said. Instead you quietly realize that all of your feminist friends from college would immediately share your excitement. Most of them are white, but they would acknowledge the importance of black children being able to see themselves in a positive light in Doc McStuffins, along with a positive representation of what they could become in the first lady, instead of being depicted negatively, or erased altogether.

You wonder if you've outgrown some of your high school friends.

You are eighteen years old when you go to Disney World with your high school marching band. On the last day of your trip your mother meets you in the Magic Kingdom, and you go meet Princess

Tiana together. In line you notice a little black girl in front of you, who is also Tiana in her green water-lily dress. You smile at her and tell her how lucky she is to have a Disney princess to look up to while she is still young.

All you had in your childhood was Pocahontas, Jasmine, and Mulan—all of whom you clung to for empowerment, but none of them made you feel worth much as a black girl.

Little Tiana smiles at you without understanding and gives you a twirl in her dress.

Princess Tiana does for you what the Obamas did. They help you to see your black self in what you think is a good way, though neither of them do more for you than that. Neither of them make the racism go away.

You go with your mother to a store in the Magic Kingdom that sits next to Cinderella's castle. It is a store that only sells Disney Princess merchandise. You go because you want to buy a Tiana doll. The store is stocked with dresses, tiaras, wands, dolls, and toys for all of the white princesses, plus Tinkerbell, who is not a princess at all. You are told that you must walk to the far end of the park, to Dumbo's Circus, which is where they keep the black doll.

The little white girls and their mothers look at you and your mother like you're deranged; some of them are scared of you and your tears; they move out of your way when you check every shelf of the store for the fifth time. You curse at their confusion: Why the fuck do they have Tinkerbell in a fucking princess store, but they don't even have Tiana?

What you mean to say is, Why the fuck did they erase me?

You are thirteen. You are restless and you feel like crying, but the tears won't come, because you prefer to hold them back until you're certain the pain is over.

You roll over in bed and stare at the ceiling until the darkness starts to make dots of color in your vision; you stare until the colors start to shift and turn like your stomach. You ask yourself, *I'm alive to see the first black president of this country—shouldn't I be more moved than this?* Your heart recoils and your chest feels hollow. You give yourself a headache thinking about your new but unchanged reality—or perhaps the braids in your hair are too tight.

The sun sets on Disney World. You drag your feet back to Cinderella's castle with your mother; you hug your toddler Tiana doll, feeling embarrassed. You apologize for making a scene in the store earlier.

It's okay, Amber.

How was that okay? Didn't I embarrass you?

I felt bad for you, Amber. Because you realized that life just isn't fair.

Love Feminism but Where's My Hip Hop? Shaping a Black Feminist Identity

GWENDOLYN D. POUGH

The very idea that someone can attribute coming into Black feminist consciousness to the masculine spaces of rap music and hip-hop culture must seem outrageous to some people. When you add the abstract concept of love into the mix, it might become a little bit more astonishing. Even though third-wave Black feminists such as Joan Morgan, Eisa Davis, Tara Roberts, dream hampton, and Eisa Nefertari Ulen have begun to make a case for a Black feminist identity and agenda tied to hip-hop culture, the linking of hip hop and feminism is still a bit much for some to bear.[1] And although the Black feminist diva bell hooks has started the much-needed dialogue on love, feminism, and the revolutionary potential such a combination would grant, there are not a whole lot of feminists openly checking for the L-word. Given the history of oppression women have suffered at the hands of patriarchs who no doubt claimed to love them, it is not hard to imagine why love would be thought of as suspect. Nevertheless, I feel the need to explore the connections between love, hip hop, and my coming to voice as a third-wave Black feminist.

My development as a Black woman and a Black feminist is deeply tied to my love of hip hop. LL Cool J's soulful rap ballad "I

Need Love" (1987) was the first rap love song I heard, and it would not be the last. Rap and rap artists' never-ending quest to "keep it real" is not limited to real-life struggles on American streets. Some rappers show an interesting dedication to exploring aspects of love and the struggles of building and maintaining intimate relationships between Black men and women. Although this reeks of heterosexism—as do many rap love songs—it also points to the very real nature of the relationship between Black men and women and most men and women of color. When you call someone your sister or brother, or a comrade in the struggle against racism, a bond is created. In that bond there is love. Rap music therefore offers space for public dialogues about love, romance, and struggle in a variety of combinations.

This kind of public dialogue is found in the answer/dis raps of the 1980s, which gave rise to the women rap stars Roxanne Shanté and Salt-N-Pepa. These women paved the way for other women rappers by recording very successful songs, which were responses to the hit records of the men who were their contemporaries. Shanté gave the woman pursued in UTFO's "Roxanne, Roxanne" a voice and ultimately let it be known that women would no longer suffer insults and degradation in silence. Salt-N-Pepa's "The Show Stoppa (Is Stupid Fresh)" was a direct refutation to Doug E. Fresh and Slick Rick's "The Show"—a song in which women are portrayed as objects of conquest.

As a Black woman coming of age during the hip-hop era, I saw the answers that Shanté and Salt-N-Pepa put to wax as more than just temporary jams to get the body moving. They let me know I could have a voice as well. They offered the strong public presence of Black womanhood that I had seen in my mother and her friends, but had not witnessed in my generation in such a public forum. Before I ever read bell hooks's *Talking Back: Thinking Feminist, Thinking*

Black, I heard Shanté and Salt-N-Pepa rapping and securing a strong public voice for women's issues in general and young Black women's issues specifically. Their talking back and speaking out against unwanted advances that could easily be read as sexual harassment gave me a model for dealing with similar issues as I braved inner-city streets. In addition, their talking back changed the way I looked at romance and courtship as well as the voice I could have in those socially scripted spaces. I no longer thought I had to simply smile and keep walking when brothers made catcalls or lewd comments as I walked down the street. I felt perfectly fine and justified in rolling my eyes and telling them how rude they were, or that they would never "get the digits" behaving in such a manner. I began to make up rhymes about these street encounters that sought to disrupt the men's behavior by offering a woman's response. One rhyme in particular was a direct reflection on a street corner encounter with a rude guy who also claimed to be an MC. I rapped:

> *I was on my way to the jam, you see.*
> *Saw a fly guy, you know he was sweatin' me.*
> *Told him my name was MC Gwenny Dee.*
> *He looked at me, laughed and asked sarcastically,*
> *Gwenny Dee, hmm, can you rhyme?*
> *I said not only can I rhyme, I'm a one of a kind.*
> *He said, How can this be, you're a girl?*
> *And a female can't make it in an MC's world.*
> *I said, please tell me what you're talking about*
> *when you say females can't turn it out,*
> *when you say that the best MCs are the men*
> *and chances for a female are zero to ten.*
> *Well, I'm here to say, whether you like it or you don't.*
> *So, fellas listen up, 'cause I'm sure you won't:*

Females make the best MCs, you know.
So just step on back 'cause we run the show.
Your gear and your gold make you look fly,
but you rap wack enough to make me cry.
And that's true, you know why,
'cause I don't lie, as a matter of fact, I'm really too fly.
Got to the party everyone was chillin'.
Looked on the stand saw dude justa illin'
Trying like a dummy to rock hard, with a rhyme he stole off a Hall-
mark card.

My own clearly old-school flow and rapping skills aside, this is how I began to use rap to talk back in ways very similar to the women rappers I listened to on the radio. I wrote this rhyme when I was a fifteen-year-old aspiring rapper. The rhymes I wrote and the developing prominence of female MCs on the radio prompted me to look for a DJ and a crew so that I could start my rap career. With very few women rappers to serve as role models, the success of these answer/dis songs let me know that women could make it in the rap arena. They also inspired the kinds of raps I wrote—raps that were pro-woman and critiqued the inequities of gender that my young mind saw. I am not arguing that I had a strong and carefully theorized critique of gender as a fifteen-year-old B-girl. However, strong and successful women rappers and the space that hip hop provided gave me a chance to develop a critique that I now know to be the beginnings of my current Black feminist consciousness.

> " I began to use rap to talk back in ways very similar to the women rappers I listened to on the radio. "

Even though I had no idea what feminism was at the time, I had seen strong Black women all my life. My mother was a single parent and she worked hard to make sure that my sisters and I had the things we needed. She did not call herself a feminist. But she left an abusive husband and told any other Black man who could not act right where the door could hit him. Having this strong female presence in my own home notwithstanding, there was something particularly inspiring about seeing that presence personified in my own generation. Hip hop gave me that.

Another way that hip hop helped me to develop a feminist consciousness was the exposure it gave me to sexual harassment and the attitude it gave me to deal with it. The thing that stands out very clearly about that time for me was being the only girl in someone's basement as we took turns on the microphone. At different times I warded off advances from fellow male MCs and even the DJ. It seemed like every one of them wanted to at least try and get me to have sex with him. When none of their advances worked, they eventually stopped. DJ Ronnie Ron, however, took offense to my performance of the rap I've included here. He thought the rhyme was aimed at him, because he, too, had tried to get with me and failed. So he put on an instrumental cut, grabbed the mike, and proceeded to freestyle a dis rap just for me. I stopped working with him, and after a few other failed attempts at finding a DJ, I stopped writing rhymes.

As I reflect back on that time, I realize now that there was something about writing rhymes and saying them on the mike—hearing my voice loud, strong, and clear—that made me feel empowered. Though I gave up the dream of becoming a rapper, the acts of writing and performing still give me a surge of strength. The only difference is that now I'm writing feminist critiques of rap and performing them at academic conferences and other venues. I also use rap to teach other young women of color about feminism.

As a woman born in 1970, who was nine years old when the first rap record hit the airwaves (The Sugarhill Gang's "Rapper's Delight"), I grew up on rap music. Reading Tricia Rose's discussion of the evolution of hip-hop culture through the changes in clothing commodified by rappers and hip-hop audiences reminds me of my own evolution: from a teenage B-girl wearing Lee jeans, Adidas sneakers with fat laces, LeTigre shirts, gold chunk jewelry, and a gold tooth to an "Around the Way Girl" college freshman sporting a leather jacket, baggy jeans, sweat hood, and fake Fendi/Gucci/Louis Vuitton.[2]

Once I was in college, however, my relationship with hip hop changed when I stopped consuming the female identities put forth by male rappers as the girl of their dreams. As I had once been willing to be LL Cool J's "Around the Way Girl" (1989), I began taking issue with the very notion of Apache's "Gangsta Bitch" (1992). While I still consumed the music, I began to question the lyrics and constructed identities. Although both of these songs sought to give "props" to the girls in the hood, I found myself struggling with the image that Apache put forth. It was then that I realized it wasn't the "bitch" that bothered me. It was the things he applauded that did. Things like the gangsta bitch fighting other women and helping him to sell drugs to other people in the hood bothered me. These things did not fit in with the feminist identity I was developing.

Like many of the academics and Black popular critics now writing about rap, I have a love for hip-hop culture and rap music. This love prompts me to critique and explore rap in more meaningful ways. I am no longer the teenaged girl who spent Friday nights listening to Mr. Magic's *Rap Attack* and writing rhymes, Saturdays reading her mama's Harlequin or Silhouette romance novels, and Sundays writing rhymes and short stories. While I have grown up on and consumed hip-hop culture and popular romance, I feel it is important to note I am all grown up.

Although I still listen to rap music and read a romance novel every time I get a chance, Black feminist/womanist theories and politics inform my listening and reading. Whenever I can, I go back to my undergraduate university to work with the youth participating in the summer Pre-College Academy. These high school students are from the North Jersey area, and I see it as a way to give back. I do it to spread feminist consciousness to new up-and-coming feminists. Young women growing up today are not privy to the same kind of pro-woman rap that I listened to via Salt-N-Pepa, Queen Latifah, Yo-Yo, and MC Lyte. Even though I like Lil' Kim and Foxy Brown, I know that younger women of color need the critical tools to unpack some of the messages they get from these artists.

One student during the summer of 2000 was obsessed with fancy cars. She asked me, "Ay, yo, what you pushing, Miss Pough?" After telling the student that I drove a Ford Escort, she kind of frowned, pushed up her nose, and said, "Oh, that's cute." This student's fascination with fancy cars and her desire to one day "push" one was not a problem in and of itself. There is nothing wrong with desiring nice things, especially when those things are out of reach and they give one something to work for. The problem occurs when students like this young lady have these desires absent of a critique of materialism and the harsh realities that go along with it. It is one thing to desire nice things and quite another to put drugs in one's purse because "the police won't check or suspect you," and because a drug-dealer boyfriend can buy you nice things in return for drug smuggling. It is one thing to want a nice car and quite another to think the only way you will get one is to use your body sexually.

Parents and educators alike admonish rap because of lyrics that use profanity and glamorize sex and violence. Parents do not want their children listening to it, and educators do not see the educational value in it. I believe that the value resides in the critique. This means that we need to create spaces—both inside and outside of the classroom—for young women especially, to make the kinds of connections to larger societal issues that they do not make in the clubs on the dance floors. For me, a critical look at hip hop that is based not only on a love for the music and the culture, but also on a love of the people who are influenced by it, is what I want to inform my Black feminist consciousness and ultimately my action.

June Jordan's poignant essay "Where Is the Love?" haunts me. Jordan discusses the need for a self-love and self-respect that would create and foster the ability to love and respect others.[3] As I think about hip hop and the images of niggas and bitches that inhibit this kind of self-love and self-respect, I am faced with a multitude of questions. I am concerned particularly with rap and the love that hate produced—love that is fostered by a racist and sexist society. This is the kind of love that grows *despite* oppression but holds unique characteristics *because of* oppression. In many ways it is a continuation of the way Black men and women were forced to express love during slavery and segregation, when Black people were not allowed to love one another freely. Family members could be taken away at any moment. The legacy of slavery—it has yet to be dealt with properly—is the legacy that haunts Black people specifically and the rest of the country in general.

This legacy stands behind the war zone in which Black men and women today are living and trying to love, as Joan Morgan writes.

This legacy prompts me to value love as the connecting factor between hip hop and my identity as a Black feminist. Love has been and continues to be a struggle for Black people in the United States. Yet Black people have found ways to love each other and to be together anyway, despite separations and sales of partners during slavery. During the days of segregation and Jim Crow, Black people—especially parents—had to practice tough love to ensure that loved ones would live to see another day and not become the victim of Klan violence.

While the hip-hop generation has the legacy of African-American history to build on, and strands of these kinds of love persist, the hip-hop generation also has its own demons. Life for young Black Americans is different, and the very nature of relationships within hip-hop culture is necessarily going to be expressed differently. What continues to fascinate me is that despite all the historical baggage and contemporary struggles, young Black people are still trying to find ways to love, just as their ancestors did. A recognition of the plight that Black men and women are up against, along with a realization that in spite of it all, living and loving go hand in hand, is central to any brand of feminism that is going to work for young Black women.

A new direction for Black feminism would aid in the critique and exploration of the dialogue across the sexes found in rap music and hip-hop culture. Black feminists such as dream hampton, Tara Roberts, Joan Morgan, and Eisa Davis have begun to explore the relationship between love and hip hop. Rap music provides a new direction for Black feminist criticism. It is not just about counting the bitches and hos in each rap song. It is about exploring the nature of Black male and female relationships. These new Black feminists acknowledge that sexism exists in rap music. But they also recognize that sexism exists in America. Rap music and

Black popular culture are not produced in a cultural and political vacuum. The systems of oppression that plague the larger society plague subcultures of society as well. Black feminists are looking for ways to speak out against sexism and racism while starting a dialogue with Black men right on the front lines of the battlefield against oppression.

On these front lines I will be fighting and hollering out, "Love feminism, but where's my hip hop?"

OUR MOTHERS, REFUGEES FROM A WORLD ON FIRE

Black Feminism in Everyday Life
Race, Mental Illness, Poverty, and Motherhood

SIOBHAN BROOKS

In 1948, when my mother was sixteen, she had sex and got pregnant with my sister Connie. She gave birth to her on Valentine's Day. Teenage pregnancy was seen as deviant behavior (the father had left), so she was removed from the tenth grade in San Francisco and sent back to the South to relearn the proper "traditional values." My aunt, who was eighteen at the time and a firm believer in traditional values, thought my mother was too young to have a child and that she wouldn't be able to give my sister a "good" life. My aunt had married a man in the military, so she went to the South where my sister was being raised by relatives and unofficially adopted her. They moved to Seattle to live a middle-class lifestyle.

In the 1950s, my mother—now a single mom—was placed in a mental hospital for the infanticide of her second daughter, Tara. No one in the family knew much about Tara; they had never met her. "During that time it was very hard for single mothers, especially Black women, to make it economically," my aunt told me when I was sixteen and had arrived in Seattle thirsty for family history. My mother had been very poor, and my aunt suspected she had had problems getting food for Tara. My mother had taken Tara to the hospital, claiming that she had fallen, but Tara was already dead when my mother brought her in. The doctors were suspicious of her injuries, suspecting that she had been thrown against the wall. My mother had a nervous breakdown then and was taken to Napa State Hospital. She had schizophrenia.

When I heard this story as an adolescent, I was upset that my family had not told me earlier what was "wrong" with my mother. This was the reason why I had never heard from Tara. All this time I had thought she was alive. My mother had told me I had two sisters, but I had only heard from her first daughter, Connie. I didn't hate my mother because of it, but I was enraged that everyone in the family knew but me. Such stories are not unusual within traditional Black communities, even if they often remain family "secrets." Abortion wasn't an option for many poor and working-class Black women like my mom. When I think of the reproductive movement among many white middle-class feminists of the 1960s and 1970s—the black-and-white television footage of white women holding pro-choice signs, showing hangers with an X through them—I think it was "their" movement. Those feminists seemed to deal with abortion as a choice for middle-class white women. They didn't deal with the issues of poverty and lack of education, the realities of infanticide and racism, or making abortion accessible for all women.

I never discussed abortion with the women in my family, but I knew they were against it, as they were very involved in the church. Abortion and queerness were viewed as sins. My sister Connie had been much more active in the civil rights movement than in the feminist movement, even though she had worked mostly with Black women. She had attended high school in Seattle during the height of 1960s integration and had seen white parents, especially white women, protesting her very presence at a high school their children attended. She did not relate to white feminism, because the poverty of women like our mother was never on the agenda for them. I think the white mainstream feminist movement rarely considered issues of class regarding motherhood. They felt motherhood was imposed on them, and they were fighting to be in the workplace, not recognizing that Black women and other women of color and poor white women were already in the workplace. Some of these women served as nannies for elite white women, allowing them to attend their "feminist" meetings.

Growing up, I knew better than to get pregnant because of my mother's warnings about how I would end up on welfare, like most of our female neighbors who were single mothers. Many hadn't completed their education. My mother did not hold these views because she claimed to be a feminist; she held these views because she knew firsthand the interlocking systems of racism, poverty, and sexism. She wanted me to survive and have the opportunities that were denied to her growing up. In fact, she never used the words "feminism" or "racism." We also never talked about my father, who I have only recently learned was Puerto Rican. Like many kids growing up in the projects to single mothers, I knew that to bring up issues concerning my father might be grounds for punishment.

In 1972, when Angela Davis was acquitted of murder charges in Marin County, California, I was born in the Sunnydale housing projects in San Francisco. We never discussed Angela Davis in our home. In fact, my mother wanted me to stay away from political activism altogether. Although she didn't say it, I think she feared that I would be killed, like our leaders of the day who had been killed and arrested during this time. Growing up in the 1970s, it seemed to me as if neither the civil rights movement nor the feminist movement was happening. Few people around me ever talked about them. I remember watching footage of Malcolm X and

Martin Luther King Jr. giving speeches, Angela with her infamous Afro and her fist in the air, Black people being hosed down by the police, white women burning bras, and scenes of the Vietnam War.

I remember thinking that we were free now. We weren't being hosed down, and we didn't live under the stifling conditions of Southern racial segregation, with signs that read "Black" and "White." It never occurred to me, however, that our lives in poverty in the projects were testimony that we were *not* free, that racial segregation still existed. None of our neighbors talked much about politics; rather, they just lived life day to day. They were the least economically affected by these movements.

My mother used to live in the hippie neighborhood of Haight-Ashbury, but the rents increased and she had to move. She was a Black single woman without a high school diploma, and the projects were waiting for her. She worked as a maid for hotels, but when I was born she applied for disability, because of her disfigured feet from years of wearing high heels. She was thirty-nine years old. When I was young, she would tell me how she had frantically looked for vacancies and there were none. But Sunnydale always had vacancies. These projects were the largest in San Francisco, built in the World War II years, and they looked like red and white row houses. Sunnydale's residents were predominately Black when my mother moved in. Even then, it had a bad reputation for violence and would later be known as Swampy Desert. I could tell that she felt defeated having to move into the projects, and she tried her best to make it our home. She was also dealing with re-entering mainstream society after her stay at Napa.

As a whole, my family never talked about what their lives had been like in the South, before they migrated to the East and West Coasts. There are only a few times that my mother talked about race. In one incident she was thirteen and went on the Ferris wheel at Ocean Beach. It was her first time riding it and she was excited. She hopped in, and the operator, a young white guy a few years older, buckled everyone's seat belt but hers. She told me how frightened she was when it reached the top, and how she held on for her life as it swayed back and forth. She tried not to look down and felt her sweaty hands loosen with each sway. When the ride was finally over, she went up to the operator and told him that he had forgotten to fasten her seat belt. When he looked at her with sheer hatred, she realized it had been deliberate.

I remember another time, when I was little. I was sitting on the bus in the front and an old white woman got on and ordered me to move. I didn't understand why I should get up for her, but my mother instantly swooped me up and placed me in her lap while this white woman sat down. Because we lived in the midst of racial apartheid and gender oppression, we did not need to talk about it—it was our daily reality.

Feminism was not a concept I grew up with. I never thought of myself in a gendered way, even while I was sexually harassed by the neighborhood boys as a teenager and socialized to be a good girl on account of my light skin and hair texture. But I always knew I was Black, largely from the racist media images on television and in the movies—from the maids in Shirley Temple films to the stereotyped characters in *Good Times* to the portrayal of the "apes" in *Planet of the Apes*. We laughed at these shows, knowing the images weren't really us. But this is how I learned to be ashamed of being Black. Even after the Black pride movement, no one wanted to be the maid, mammy, or the apes.

When I was young, my mother and I would get dressed up on the first and fifteenth of the month and go downtown, so she could cash her welfare check. I would be happy because I knew she would buy me something from Woolworths. She wore her favorite black-and-white suit, makeup, a wig, dark penciled-in eyebrows, orange lipstick that she never applied to the top of her lips, and dark, round sunglasses. I didn't understand that we were on welfare and that was why we stood in a long line with some people who looked "professional" in business suits, but most looked homeless and poor, and some smelled of urine. These people in the lines were also predominately Black and Latino/a, mainly women.

My mother lived in fear of the welfare agencies that were always trying to locate my abusive father to reincorporate him into our lives. If there were any political discussions in my neighborhood among the women, it was how the welfare agencies kept us all living in a constant state of fear of being cut off from welfare. The other discussions were about how as Black women we often lived in fear of Black men attacking us, in fear of being homeless and of being "relocated" by the Housing Authority because of white gentrification. Black women often feared that their sons would be killed by the police, the drug trade, or one another; that their daughters would get pregnant, molested in the local preschool, or raped. These were the two gendered realities for poor Blacks. I didn't have a language for what our oppression was, but it seemed never-ending and was often normalized.

Women in Sunnydale looked after each other and each other's children, even if it could be perceived as nosey. They went food shopping for each other, strategized about how to get more money from the welfare system, drove their neighbors' children to school, and looked after the elderly. Such involvement in my well-being helped fill in the gaps due to my mother's schizophrenia, which often made her frightened of the "outside" world. Because of this fear, she wanted to keep me close at all times. (It didn't help that we lived in the projects, where danger was always unpredictable.) When I was eight, for example, an old Black woman with gray hair and glasses saw me playing outside and inquired as to why I wasn't in school. When I said I didn't know, she contacted a social worker, who helped my mother with the process of enrolling me. Because of that neighbor, I started school at the age of eight in the second grade. This is just the way things were in Sunnydale.

The term "mental illness" was not used among people in my community or usually within the Black community at large. Only recently have we begun to look at issues of mental illness, such as depression, among Black people, especially Black women. While growing up, I read little of the "feminist" literature that dealt with women of color and mental illness, outside of perhaps some fiction. In fact, I never saw my mother as having a mental illness at all, because she was functional. I thought all mentally ill people were hospitalized. The books at my high school library that dealt with mental illness usually talked about white women, as in *I Never Promised You a Rose Garden* or *Sybil*. Neither the feminist movement nor the civil rights movement had dealt with mentally ill women of color. In the mental health field, young Black women are often portrayed as pathological for being single mothers, which is pegged as the cause of our poverty.

One of my earliest memories of my mother was of her talking to herself, and this behavior was considered normal in our household. When I was a child, I tried to mimic it and stopped feeling that it was odd behavior. She would often burst into angry, unpredictable spells of screaming and talking to herself. In fact, she spent a majority of her time alone, smoking in the kitchen and watching television. I would wake up to hear her screaming about things I didn't understand. How a "nigger" was keeping her down, how she wasn't going back to Napa, how in the future she would have a better life, that she was really white, how she was supposed to marry a white man and live in a house. Sometimes it sounded like she was making up words or speaking a language I didn't understand. She would look off into space with darting eyes, a dazed look in her eyes, wearing a torn green turtleneck and a gray skirt, even though she could afford better, screaming furiously, sometimes to the point of hoarseness and drooling.

In the presence of other people, she could appear "normal," but sometimes she would talk to herself into a handkerchief. I suspect the neighbors may have occasionally heard her screaming or beating me with a belt. Sometimes she would scream at me in the third person and say things like, "Get out of Siobhan's room, you little nigger!" and throw me out onto the porch. I'm sure there were times when the neighbors heard her or saw this behavior. My mother was one of the oldest tenants in the community, so there was a place for her. Everyone knew her, including our Greek mailman. In our community we did not use the term "child abuse," but we were aware that it existed. My friends' parents sometimes suspected that I wasn't getting enough food, because I was underweight. They would invite me over for meals and have me take food home. They never said I was being abused, and never made me feel as if there was something obviously wrong with the way we lived.

Domestic violence also occurred in Sunnydale, but it was not called by that name. It was discussed and dealt with among the women, however. I remember a big Black woman who once quickly ran in the nude across the lawn from our neighbor's place, where an older Black man lived, to my mother's place. He was beating her and she didn't have time to put on any clothes. Another one of our female neighbors went to jail for stabbing her husband, who used to beat her. When she came out, the women in the community did not judge her. They knew she did what she felt was right. Looking back at these women, I doubt any of them would have used the term "feminism" to describe their actions. I did not link phrases like "child abuse," "domestic violence," "drug addiction," or "mental illness" to my experience.

To my colored eye, when I saw the TV shows and billboards about abuse sponsored by white feminists who were trying to raise consciousness, it looked like these issues only affected white people. It was as if issues of abuse had nothing to do with us, that only white people were worthy of naming abuse. Suffering and systematic abuse in communities of color was so normalized. We often didn't even know we were oppressed. Some of us thought suffering was just a part of being Black. To have access to health care, a good education, healthy food, and safe, affordable housing, to have aspirations and a desire to improve one's mental and physical health, was often seen as "white."

> ❝ They fail to realize that in telling us there is no place for our rage, they are becoming a part of what is colonizing us—the denial of our reality. They have to accept the fact that they don't understand our experiences and have an opportunity to learn something. ❞

Many of us did not have access to such things, and we often died young—Where was a feminist movement to help us? The Black women I grew up with prided themselves on being "strong Black women," not "weak" like white women, or "crazy" like white people who were in therapy. These women were angry, as they felt they'd been forced into being the backbone of the community. To justify their sexism, some Black men also subscribed to this notion. These women prided themselves in raising children, and in supporting the men and their families on low wages—without health care, let alone mental health care. For a Black woman, being depressed was seen as a type of luxury. Despite my mother's mental state, she paid the bills on time, shopped for food, and refused the free bread-and-butter services the government offered us. When she died recently from emphysema, and I told some of my friends about her mental illness, they asked if she had been on medication. I didn't know she was supposed to be.

As a college student at San Francisco State University, I started calling myself a feminist when I came into women's studies. Like many young women of color from poor and working-class backgrounds, I first learned a language for racism, sexism, and classism in college. I was also coming into consciousness around being Black and learning Black history. I shaved my head of my permed hair.

My first women's studies class was about sexuality and the body, and how our vaginas were never seen as part of our whole body. We read *Our Bodies, Ourselves* (edited by the Boston Women's Health Book Collective) and *Powers of Desire: The Politics of Sexuality* (edited by Ann Snitow, Sharon Thompson, and Christine Stansell) and talked about body images of women (mostly white) in magazines and sexuality. I found this class interesting but very Eurocentric, despite the inclusion of some readings by women of color, such as an essay by Cherríe Moraga. I thought of my Mexican childhood friend Lupé, who lived in the projects, smelled of strawberry hair spray, and wrote in lipstick on her bedroom wall the names of the boys she had kissed—where was she in this?

We discussed the pornography debates, and I learned that many women were doing sex work to pay for school. This led me to work at the Lusty Lady, a peepshow in San Francisco known for its "feminist," "sex-positive" politics and commitment to hiring female managers. I later became a union organizer there and fought to get more women of color hired.

Most of my professors were women of color, but most of the students were white and middle class. They often spoke with the universal understanding that "woman" meant white like them. When race was discussed, at least one white woman would start crying out of white guilt. We could all exist as "women" in the classroom but not within our differences based on race, class, and cultural identity. I felt that these crying spells frequently functioned to mask white women's racism about issues affecting women of color. White middle-class women who had been socialized by the dominant culture to be quiet could speak out in their women's studies classes. But time and again, they could not see that while their participation could be personally liberating, it could be silencing for women of color (and the few men of color), who, because of race and gender, often did not feel entitled to speak. I began to understand why most women of color were in ethnic studies, not women's studies. I felt the racial isolation of being one of the few women of color in the department, since many women of color felt that feminism was a white lesbian thing. Some saw the concept as separating them from the men in their communities. The voices of queer women of color who were active in fighting for our civil rights were often silenced within ethnic studies departments and tokenized in women's studies.

In a class called "Women and Violence," taught by a Black woman who was a lesbian mother, the white women felt the class should only focus on them. There were few women of color in the class, so the professor made sure we felt empowered to speak by prioritizing our participation. I loved this class because we talked about real issues that affected the lives of poor women and women of color. My mother and I had never talked about feminism or racism, but this class made me feel that at least the experiences of poor working-class women of color like us were being studied—we weren't invisible.

Reading works by many poor and working-class women of color gave me a blueprint to write about my own experiences with poverty and mental illness. We read *Bastard out of Carolina* by Dorothy Allison and *Beloved* by Toni Morrison. The class loved Allison's novel—many of the women were from middle-class backgrounds, but they could relate to the reality of sexism and violence within the family. But when we read *Beloved*, suddenly some of the women felt that the class was getting "off track," that we were talking about race, not gender. The other Black female student and I loved it. I felt empowered reading about infanticide, since it was close to home for me.

One white woman raised her hand and protested, "Why are we reading about Black people? I thought this was a women's studies class." The professor lost her temper and told her that in case she didn't know, it was a Black woman teaching the class, and that Black people can also be women. The white woman started crying and angrily left the class. I was amazed at this white woman's sense of entitlement and privilege, of being able to protest and cry in the classroom. I can think of only a few times I've ever seen Black women in my community cry, even when tragedy occurs.

In a class called "Feminism and Marxism," taught by the lesbian Asian-American socialist feminist Merle Woo, a similar incident happened. There were three women of color in the class, including myself—all of us Black. We talked about internalized oppression, the body, and race. The subject of nose jobs came up for the Jewish women in the class, along with skin color and slavery regarding Black people. The Jewish women tried to equate the "Jewish nose" to body images for Blacks. The Black women silently listened to what the white Jewish women had to say, giving each other that "Can you believe these white people?" look. After the

Jewish women were finished, a Black woman expressed that she felt the dialogue was racist. Even though Jewish women also feel pressured to conform to European beauty standards, it is nowhere near the extent that Black women and other women of color do, because in this country Jewish women can pass for white, while we cannot. The Jewish women got upset and accused us of not understanding them. They dismissed our feelings but wanted theirs validated.

Their words were a symbolic form of violence. That the experiences of women of color are dismissed in the classroom reflects the physical violence that happens to us on the street. What I experienced in the classroom was not so different from what had happened to my mother years earlier, when the Ferris wheel's white male conductor would not fasten her seat belt. The mentality is the same: our humanity is not valued.

At the next class, a Black woman who had been one of the few to actually major in women's studies besides myself brought in a definition of white privilege, listing all the ways white people are visually, culturally, racially, and economically privileged relative to people of color. This dialogue happened over a period of two days. The second day, the Black woman left the class. Although I respected her choice, I remained because I didn't feel a need to leave. The Jewish women then thanked me for "understanding" where they were coming from. I was the token "good" Black. This put me in an awkward position: even though I didn't leave the class, my staying didn't mean I agreed with them, either. I stayed because I wanted to bear witness to what was going on. So often, women of color leave white environments because of fear. They feel like their presence doesn't matter, that if they speak they will not be listened to. Even though I didn't say anything, I wanted to stay and have my presence as a Black woman known. Just because they were getting upset that the Black women in the classroom were bringing issues of racism to their attention did not mean that we had to leave the situation.

My upbringing in the projects and my mother's mental illness prepared me for hostile environments. I always had to navigate between the "normal" world and my mother's world, often hoping those two worlds would never meet. I feared my survival would be at risk if I was ever taken away from her. As I became older, I learned to survive balancing the Black world of my community with the white middle-class world that in many ways showed me that my world did not matter. Women's studies was no exception. I learned my skills back home from dealing with racist schoolteachers who placed me in English as a second language (ESL) classes in fifth grade, even though I had only spoken English at home. I had to fend for myself because my mother did not understand what was going on. The ESL teacher finally realized that I should not have been in her class, and I was placed in regular classes. I had to go through this experience alone, but I knew my people back home thought I was intelligent and that I mattered. This knowledge got me through fifth grade, and it got me through women's studies.

This kind of navigating between two worlds is not new to women of color, whether to immigrants or to many of us born in the United States. We come from different cultures, speak different languages, and have different worldviews, many of which are not respected in white environments. Many white women are afraid of difference and try to ignore it or silence us when we bring up our race and class differences. They often say they don't see race, only human beings. But this is a lie and we all know it. They do not seem to understand that for women of color, our race is a central part of our humanity, especially in a white-dominated society, such as the United States. It is incidents like these that make women's studies hard for women of color and that keep the classes mostly white, even at a progressive college like San Francisco State, where the ethnic studies program grew directly out of the civil rights movement. In women's studies we read the work of some women of color, but surprisingly, not that of bell hooks or Angela Davis (even though she used to teach at State). But I did read them in my Black studies classes.

The white women in my classes often did not understand their racial and class privilege, and they frequently didn't see themselves as being racist. In my friend's class on women and nature, for example, which was mostly white, there were white women appropriating Native American culture: carrying dream catchers or wearing Native American jewelry. They had a blast hiking off into the wilderness, but my friend had to get over her fear of nature, a fear many urban women of color have, since many of us are taught at an early age not to go into parks alone for fear of being raped.

Once a white woman and I were talking about class and education, and she said that I must have had the same education as she did because we were attending the same college, learning in the same classroom. She was trying to argue that the problem in this country was really one of class, not race. She was shocked when I told her I hadn't started school until I was eight. Another time, a white woman asked me to get her a scone as I was heading toward the cafeteria. I had never heard of a scone. I could only hope that the pastry would be clearly labeled. These women just assumed everyone was coming from a similar environment as theirs.

The everyday feminism that I grew up with was missing from my classes; the women had the theory but not the practice. Even though many of these women were involved in some sort of "progressive" organizing, it seemed we spent hours in classes and consciousness-raising groups trying to convince them that people of color were humans. Then there were the women in Sunnydale who organized against welfare cuts and drugs in their neighborhood, for better housing and daycare, who would never call themselves feminists. They were more "feminist" in their actions than many of the white women in my women's studies classes.

I think about my mother, who took time to read to me every night before going to bed, bought me school clothes from Macy's, struggled to keep food on the table despite her illness, and loved me enough to instill a sense of self-esteem even though we lived in the projects. I honor her strength in raising a Black girl in the midst of oppressive poverty—a challenge for many poor Black mothers. This is the kind of feminism that doesn't make it to the doors of women's studies classes. Despite the racism, majoring in women's studies made me feel empowered as a queer Black woman. I am proud to call myself a feminist. I learned critical thinking skills in women's studies that changed my life forever, and I met great friends. I attended readings of many Black feminists that I admired, such as Alice Walker, who had defined the term "womanist."

But I often think about the harsh life my mother and many Black women like her have lived in this country as a result of slavery, economic exploitation, and systematic violence. Women's studies classes do not have to be a struggle for power between white women and women of color, yet that is often what they are because of white women's racism. White women must understand that the anger women of color express in and outside of the classroom toward them is not an issue of "hurt feelings" or "misunderstandings." To reduce our experience of that racism to "misunderstandings" is both racist and reductionist. It is akin to men telling women that we are overreacting to their sexism. The anger of women of color is a rational response to our invisibility. It is a rational response to a racist, sexist, capitalist structure. It is not constructive for white women to tell us that our anger is making it hard for them to relate to us, that our anger makes them feel uncomfortable, that we are not willing to find common alliances with them. This is a classic example of white women's racism. They fail to realize that in telling us there is no place for our rage, they are becoming a part of what is colonizing us—the denial of our reality. They have to accept the fact that they don't understand our experiences and have an opportunity to learn something, maybe even about themselves, as opposed to wanting to shut us up. Only then can any true understanding result among us.

As I write this essay, I am reminded of feminists of color who have come before me, including Cherríe Moraga, Audre Lorde, and bell hooks. When I read their writings about the racism of the women's movement in the 1970s, I see that much of what they were writing about can be applied to women's studies programs today. This is the sad tragedy of feminism, that despite such writings, today this is still a large part of our interactions with white women. It seems as if many women's studies programs became an institutionalized version of their white privilege. I lament that women like my mother are not usually considered in women's studies. It is for women like my mother and my friends' mothers that I do activist work with women of color: to bring the everyday knowledge of these women back into feminism.

I would like to dedicate this essay to my mother, Aldean Brooks; my deceased sister, Tara; and my friends' parents.

Bring Us Back into the Dance
Women of the Wasase

KAHENTE HORN-MILLER

The singing begins and your attention is on the beat of the drum, the sound of the rattle, and the men's voices captured in song. A great feeling of empowerment overwhelms you as you go round and round. Pure energy is created as your feet glide across the floor. Your heart soars as you dance and dance. You feel as though you could dance forever. It is as though you are in another place, another time. You see others around you with faces uplifted, a look of utter joy and abandonment on them. A young girl goes to the middle of the floor. She picks up a cane and bangs it down on the wooden planks beneath her feet. The music ceases and the dancers stop and stand with heaving chests. You can almost hear their hearts pounding along with yours.

The young girl begins to speak, everyone's faces turn, and all our attention is on her. In a loud voice, she says: "Thank you! Thank you for finally listening to us!" Her fist is clenched to her chest as she speaks, then her arm sweeps the crowd, her palm open. It is as if she wants to include us in this feeling that she is trying to project with her words. Though we already know what she means. She is thanking the older generations for listening to what the young people have been trying to say. She is thanking them for bringing the Wasase back so that she may dance and become strong again.

She pounds the stick on the floor again, even stronger this time, as though her words have given her strength. A great war whoop is called out by all the dancers as they begin to dance again, their energy renewed. I dance too. I feel it too. I look around me and see the walls and windows of the Longhouse crying in happiness, for we are unified, at least for this moment in time. We all know and feel that we are of the same spirit. We are Onkwehonwe—the original people.

As a Kanienkehaka—the English call us Mohawks—I was raised within the Longhouse tradition. I live in the community of Kahnawake and I am now a mother of two girls. As my daughters get older, I see and feel their enthusiasm for life and all that it has to offer them. They do not know yet of the challenges they will experience. I think of all those things I must try to protect them from, or rather, teach them about so they can have the chance to make up their own minds. Little do they know of what the world is like in all its diversity. I struggle with it myself. I am a student—of life in general, and now formally enrolled in the institutions of the culture that colonized my ancestors—working for a master's degree in anthropology. I am training in ethnography, and as I worked on one account of my community, I came to understand the dynamics within and surrounding the social problems young people here face. This is my story.

It began in September 1997, when a local thirteen-year-old girl attempted suicide. This woke up many people in the community. I—along with other mothers and fathers, aunts and uncles, sisters and brothers and grandparents—was compelled to think about the future and what it offers young children such as my daughter (my second daughter had yet to join us). The suicide attempt made people look closely at their children, as they tried to decipher the messages the kids were communicating through their actions. Drugs and alcohol are not new to any indigenous community, including Kahnawake. This young girl's action forced a response, however. The initial question that everyone asked was: "How do we begin to combat this problem?" This appeared daunting, so the question changed to: "How do we get the energy to start?"

One woman in the Longhouse community—the keepers of our traditional ways—looked through the *Warrior's Handbook*, written by Louis Karoniaktajeh Hall. She hoped it might give some direction. Karoniaktajeh, who passed away in 1993, is considered the philosophical father of the Rotiskenrakete, the Warrior Society. He was instrumental in revitalizing Kanienkehaka spirit and identity through his writings and paintings. In his book she found this passage:

> To fight any kind of war one needs courage, gumption, knowledge of the enemy and strategic planning. The biggest single requirement is FIGHTING SPIRIT.
>
> People with fighting spirit shall not become casualties of a psychological warfare....How does one acquire fighting spirit? Our ancestors discovered the secret long ago. All their men were great warriors. One hundred percent. How did they do it?...One method that has come to us is the War Dance. Our ancestors brought up the spirit of the people by the War Dance, even those who did not dance....Since it works, it should be performed at every opportunity.[1]

The idea of having a War Dance (known as the Wasase) seemed like a good way to start. The woman approached others in the Longhouse with this idea. Her suggestion was met with a positive response, and the process of planning the Wasase began. I was part of this planning process. I wanted to be involved in this movement to provide a future for my daughter and the youth of our community. The Wasase was set to take place on the Kahnawake Mohawk Territory in Quebec, Canada, in October 1997, but during the preliminary stages some people began to question the women's participation. As women, we wanted our roles more clearly defined. We could not see ourselves as merely providing support for the men during the ceremony, which meant remaining outside the Longhouse. This was our battle too. The survival of our children, our sisters, our brothers—we were fighting for our community. We wanted to dance.

And so it was decided that this issue needed to be brought before the participants in the Wasase ceremony. We would decide together what the best solution was. On the day of the event, we met. It became obvious that reactions were all over the place. We young women were adamant about our right to dance. We felt justified about what we were doing. A few of the older women supported us. But others insisted that the women's role was to stand on the side and provide moral support for the men. The men listened. It wasn't really about them, and in our tradition men do not impose their ideas on women. They shared what they knew about the history, the meaning, and the past uses of the Wasase ceremony, but none of them got up to pass an opinion one way or the other. This was our issue.

As is the way in our traditional decision-making process, we threw in our opinions and our personal experiences. As people listened to our stories about drugs and alcohol and the other problems that confronted us, we began to convince everybody of our honesty and sincerity. Eventually the other women saw what we saw—that as mothers, sisters, daughters, and community members, we had a legitimate and powerful role to play in this war that we were fighting. We had proven our case. They understood! We did it! We were going to participate!

Suddenly, everyone awoke to the realization that we had come to one mind, we had reached consensus, without anyone formally announcing the decision. Our voices had been acknowledged. The energy in the Longhouse began to increase as the men and women stretched their legs after such a long day. The time for deliberation was over. People talked about dinner, the kids, who needed a ride, and they gathered their stuff to leave the Longhouse and prepare for the dance. As I left, I realized this was the first time I had ever felt the full power of the Kaienerekowa, our Great Law of Peace, in action as my mother had described it to me. Knowing and seeing are two different things, especially where the Kaienerekowa is concerned. Anyone who does a bit of reading or listening can understand it as a governing philosophy, but you cannot fully comprehend its power and the role that our women play until you participate. This was the first time I had ever felt the strength of the Kaienerekowa at work. And I carry this with me now—an image of the sun shining through the Longhouse windows on our people, the memory of our energy on that late afternoon as new life came into our old traditions. The women of my nation stepped onto the warpath of greater empowerment for all Onkwehonwe.

We were going to dance.

I am a strong Kanienkehaka woman, but I do not consider myself a feminist. Even though many of the early American feminists were inspired by my culture, my experience has been very different from that of women in the dominant society, and I don't purport to understand feminist theory. But I do understand the Kaienerekowa. As a young girl, I was taught by my mother to question everything. This feeds the anthropologist in me, but it is also a key to our traditional culture. We are taught to take nothing at face value. We have to listen to what the natural world is telling us and take the time to understand it, including our roles as women in the natural order of things. We know that if we don't do this, our people won't survive. Everything must be considered, everything is linked. We must think for seven generations to come.

I realize now just how much this has become part of my nature. I must understand things at a deeper level, otherwise I don't feel complete. But, because of my unique position, my identity constantly shifts between scholar and participant, between my duties in Kanienkehaka society and the externally defined field of Iroquois studies. Sometimes it is hard to maintain a clear focus on what I am doing as a researcher; however, my experience is the lens through which you are looking now. As I describe the world I see, I become a role model, challenging the abusive image of the squaw, changing attitudes, empowering my people so they can appreciate and be appreciated.

After the Wasase ceremony was over and I sat in front of my computer screen, I thought back to the discussion in the Longhouse. I knew that some of the women felt it was just "not right" to dance with the men. They compared it to letting men join the Women's Dance. But what did this mean? As women, couldn't they see that we, too, have an important role to play in the particular kind of warfare we were engaged in? I thought that perhaps they were not sensitive to our current situation of being surrounded by the colonizers' society. But perhaps I was just being patronizing to think this way, not giving them the full credit they deserved as "survivors" of a sort. Perhaps the women who objected to our participation just did not know how to reconcile dancing in the Wasase with their traditional roles as they understood them.

What is our culture? And what is adaptation? At first I felt frustrated, for what seemed clear to me was in actuality not so neatly defined. As I asked myself these questions, I decided to look back into the history of the War Dance and of my people to figure out what had brought us to the current debate. In doing so, I realized that this aspect of history needed to be understood and rewritten from a Kanienkehaka woman's point of view. Below are some of my reflections.

For us, performing the Wasase was a means of strengthening us to fight a metaphoric war against drugs and alcohol abuse and the increasing number of suicide attempts in our community. The Wasase is a ceremony that we adopted from the Sioux more than two hundred years ago, and Kanienkehaka communities had used it when we needed to feel empowered in modern confrontations: in 1974, when we took back Ganienkeh in upper New York State, and in 1990, during the Oka Crisis in Kahnawake, when the guns of the Canadian Army were pointed at our women, children, and grandparents. Where the term *wasase* comes from is not known, but it means renewal, and its ability to bring new strength to our society was already evident during the discussions before the ceremony. Then we danced, continuously, with the men in an outer ring surrounding the women in a center ring. This still lives in my mind. We dance while rattles are shaken. We respond with whoops and hollers while a wooden cane is passed from hand to hand until a person feels the need to stop the dance and speak their mind. There is a loud thump as the cane is hit onto the floor. Everyone stops and listens. Then we all respond in acknowledgment and the dancing continues. This goes on until the first daylight, allowing everyone's emotions to be displayed in full view, giving all those present a chance to recognize their mutual commitment to the confrontation.

The specific circumstances of the Wasase's origin have been forgotten. It is this spirit—the unity and energy that is created—that survives. This spirit and strength exists in all of us, in our selves, in our relationships to the land and to each other. No one can take that away from us. It exists in all our cultures. It is just a matter of finding the right tools at the right time to allow the release of this power at the moment when we need it most. It is at these times, when we are most challenged, that we can feel most empowered. And at this particular time, our women needed to feel our strength. By incorporating women into the War Dance, we were keeping pace with the changes in our society, just as we have always adapted our ancient traditions to fit the different types of situations we have encountered.

As I considered what the ceremony had accomplished, I became even more acutely aware of the oppression that we Kanienkehaka have suffered. I grew up with a limited understanding of the history of my people and did not begin to take an active interest in learning about our past until I was working on my undergraduate research papers. At that time, I was searching for meaning in my life, and trying to understand the treatment my people received during the Oka Crisis. During this incident we fought the neighboring town's proposed expropriation of our ancient burial grounds for the expansion of a golf course. As the issue escalated, we found ourselves surrounded by Quebec Provincial Police and the Canadian Army. We knew then that sovereignty and our very survival as a people were at issue.

I had spent my childhood away from the Kahnawake community and the issues that involve being Onkwehonwe, the original peoples. My mother had been a prominent participant in the civil and native rights movements of the 1960s, but she took time out to raise her daughters away from the spotlight. I had no idea of who she was as an activist and a Kanienkehaka woman. "I did not want to limit your development by making you feel you had to fit a mold. I wanted you to be free," she said when I asked why she had never told us about any of this. So she lived and raised us as she had been taught in the Longhouse culture, and we observed.

During the summer of 1990, my mother was doing research in the Kanesatake Mohawk Territory in Quebec to complete her master's thesis, and she ended up behind the barricades during the Oka Crisis with my two younger sisters. I was in a state of turmoil. I had no idea of her previous involvement in such things. I could not comprehend why she was staying there or why she would keep my young sisters with her. I felt like shouting to the world to let everyone know how angry I was. I did not understand where my anger came from. But this was different from any other time in my life, and I wanted to tell people I was Mohawk. I felt a sense of real connection, stronger than I had ever felt before. When my mother came back to Ottawa after the crisis was over, I began to see another side of her. She was more vibrant, with a sense of purpose. One of her brothers from behind the barricades offered me healing and showed me a deep spiritual side of indigenous identity that I had never encountered before.

With his gift I began a long journey of self-discovery, though I was still confused about who my mother really was. As she prepared for the many court battles resulting from her political participation, I headed off for university. When I began my first year of studies, I was still angry and burdened with a sense of loneliness. I felt a need to reconnect with my identity. I decided to do this through my schoolwork. I began to orient my courses toward "Iroquois" topics. I often phoned my mother, who began to teach me what she knew. If she couldn't explain something properly, she faxed me pages from books and newsletters circulating in Kahnawake.

As I began to understand more, I felt a different kind of pride in who I was, a pride based on knowledge and understanding. I finally began to see who my mother is as a Kanienkehaka woman. Without us realizing it, she had raised my sisters and me in the traditions of the Haudenosaunee, the precontact confederation of the Kanienkehaka, Oneida, Onondaga, Cayuga, and Seneca nations, which has been widely referred to by the colonial name of the Iroquois. My mother taught me to stop and think about everything before making a decision, as is done in the Longhouse. She taught me to be confident and straightforward, to believe that, "Hey, I'm a Onkwehonwe woman, and I'm equal to anyone. I can look after myself!" She taught me respect for others and their voices, for other cultures and other nations, for elders, and the most fundamental thing: that I must think about how anything I do will affect the seven generations to come. In a sense, my sisters and I had become my mother's ultimate contribution to the movement.

Many remark, upon visiting Kahnawake today, that it does not look like a reserve. Yet we are constrained by the typical limitations that frustrate the existence of every reserve. Our traditional life was governed by two very important principles: sharing and reciprocity. With these tenets severely limited by government interference over the years, we have lost much of our communal way of life. The Longhouse is the center of our traditional ceremonies. Many older people have returned to the Longhouse after experiencing a lifetime cut off from Kanienkehaka ways, for when they were young, it was illegal to continue the traditions of our ancestors. Through education and church indoctrination, through all the negative stereotypes and assumptions evident in Hollywood films and popular music, they were forced into another way of relating to the world. My people were not allowed to speak our Kanienkehaka language, to have Kanienkehaka names, or to practice Kanienkehaka beliefs, including our songs and our ceremonies.

My own mother was not allowed to use her given Kanienkehaka name, Kahn-Tineta. It is a name whose full meaning cannot be translated into English. Does it mean "she stands in tall grasses," or "she makes a fresh path across a green field"? Does it signify her birth in the spring? Or the memory of some member of our clan who had passed away? Her schoolteachers did not consider the value of the culture she inherited. She was forced to use the generic Christian name Mary, given to her by the nuns at school. At seven years old, she came home from school crying because she had been told she belonged to a dying race.

All of this had a detrimental effect on generations of our women. I realize now that in some ways those women who questioned our right to participate in the Wasase were resisting the effects of Western influences on our culture. European understanding, of our society and of their own, is skewed by male-centered cultural biases. It is worth remembering that the role of Haudenosaunee women did not automatically change after contact. Women continued to do the same things. We had a well-defined and important function in our culture. It is becoming more apparent to all of us that the church and the colonial state worked together to weaken indigenous societies. These colonizing institutions realized that our status had to be changed if they were to break our traditional worldview and teach us "civilized" European ways. As the colonizers

66 As the colonizers imposed their legislation on us—deposing our governments, imprisoning our men, and sending our children to residential schools— the bitterness of these lessons was incised into our oral history. 99

imposed their legislation on us—deposing our governments, imprisoning our men, and sending our children to residential schools—the bitterness of these lessons was incised into our oral history.

The mother of the girl whose suicide attempt inspired our dance told me about her family's experience: "My father was always sort of a Longhouse, but we had to hide. 'Cause they'll get you arrested. You get arrested if you are Longhouse. And everybody is so afraid of you, as if you were a criminal. It's still like that. I don't know when it's going to stop. They're still like that. If you're a Longhouse." The church and the state could not change the physical reality of our lives, but in many ways they changed our thinking, which has been more damaging.

With all of this sad history in mind, it is easier to understand why some women felt impelled to question our participation in the Wasase. But the fact that they felt free to speak up and raise their concerns shows that some of our old spirit has survived. Our ancestors kept something alive. Through the Wasase and our use of the Kaienerekowa to solve the questions surrounding it, we were all empowered. Many of our women are single mothers like me, and in our society our connection with our children is most important. We all support each other. As I raise my children in the Longhouse tradition, I have come to see that the aim of our constitution is to ensure a balance of power and peace. I am proud of the strong role we women have to play in such a dynamic system. Our social importance is not dependent on any particular man. Our philosophy places us at the very center of the nation, reflecting our procreative powers, which mirror the life-giving strength of Mother Earth. We are the foundation of everything. We give birth. We raise the children. We carry our clan titles. We are the caretakers of the land. We are the rational mind of our traditional government. We advise the men and appoint them to office. We deliberate about when it is time to go to war, and we provide the calmness and stability that are needed to survive.

Since I took part in the Wasase, I have come full circle. There was a time when I did not understand who I was or where I came from. As I raise my children and move ahead in my academic career, I see now just how much my mother taught me. She showed me by example. Through participating in our old traditions and writing about them, I have had my eyes opened to my history and future. I now see that we already have the tools we need to succeed and to be able to work together. Our power comes from our men and women participating together in the social and spiritual Kanienkehaka traditions. Our ceremonies create a sense of openness and unity, and with unity comes empowerment, which is necessary not only in times of war but also in everyday life. No feminist theory is as powerful as the philosophy entrenched in the Kaienerekowa. The Wasase helped us find the strength and unity needed to provide a future for the seven generations to come. It showed us that we can all be a part of the dance.

Love Clinic

SOYON IM

"Don't have sex," warns my mother. It is Sunday morning and we are on the phone—11 a.m. her time, 8 a.m. mine. If I don't answer her call, she'll imagine a couple of disastrous scenarios, and I'm not sure which is worse for her—the thought of me lying underneath a wrecked car or a man. Once a week we talk, and every week she tells me not to have sex—sometimes at the end of our conversation, in lieu of saying good-bye.

My mother has been trying to keep me from sex since I was in elementary school. In fifth grade my friend Jenny had a slumber party and I wasn't allowed to go. "A girl shouldn't get used to sleeping at other people's houses," my mother said. The first time she suspected I might go astray was when she caught me slow dancing with David Kim. I was fifteen and David was the first Korean-American guy I ever liked. We met at one of those six-week SAT prep courses that cost hundreds of dollars and convenes during the weekends in some glass-and-steel corporate park. My parents made me attend the classes in the hopes that I would get perfect SAT scores and get into an Ivy League college.

David played tennis regularly and he'd often come to class right after practice, his gym shorts hanging easily on his tall, lean frame, the sides of his hair damp with sweat, his face slightly pink. You could tell he was still warm from exercise. During our tedious

133

lessons I'd take furtive glances, relishing his beauty. *David has hirsute, indomitable legs*, I wrote in tiny letters in my notebook, using the new vocabulary we were learning by rote. *My boredom is abated by David's pulchritude. David is sanguine and virile.*

David actually lived only five blocks away from me, but because we were on opposite sides of the neighborhood's school district lines, we went to different high schools, which was a good thing. If we'd gone to the same school, he'd have known that I wasn't one of the cool kids, and he would've probably never spoken to me, except maybe to ask a question about homework or something dweeby like that. He certainly wouldn't have invited me to a party at his house.

The party was small; there were eight or nine teenagers drinking wine coolers in a dimly lit half-basement. Wham! was on the stereo, and at one point David asked me to dance. "Careless Whisper," a slow number, was on. He started by putting his hands behind my shoulders, then eventually dropping them around my waist. We weren't so much dancing as hugging each other. I'd never stood so close to a boy before, and the warmth of his body was exquisite. He didn't kiss me, but every once in a while, he'd nuzzle his chin against my neck and I'd feel a tingle run all the way down my spine. We'd held each other like that for about twenty minutes when all of a sudden, my mother walked in.

What followed was a scene from a bad soap opera. She grabbed me by the arm and marched me up the steps and out of David's house. Outside, she slapped me across the face. "Do you know how girls at parties like that end up?" she asked. Then she shouted, "They get pregnant! They get herpes and they don't know who the father is!"

My mother had a long career as a gynecologist. I marvel at the irony of how she spent each day dealing with other people's sexuality while denying mine. Then again, she did her residency in a Bronx hospital and saw every ugly disease close up. Sitting behind the metal stirrups of her examining table, she discovered the intimate details of thousands of strangers. Patients confessed to her secrets they wouldn't share with their best friends. *My period is late. I have an itch down there. He gave me warts.* At night, in front of the TV, she'd read medical journals filled with photos of infected genitals turned pimply and black.

My mother's clinical exposure and her Korean conservatism made a fearsome combination. Like an evangelist, she tried to instill the fear of sex in me, thunderously lecturing on the calamities that befell sinners. Sex led to disease; sex led to death; and, inescapably, sex led to more wanton sex.

The more she pressed, the more I had to go against her. As a teen, I was determined not to stay a virgin or marry early. I read women's magazines like *Cosmopolitan* and fantasized about an older, grown-up me having lots of sex with lots of different men. A few articles on G-spots, multiple orgasms, and the appeal of blue-collar men convinced me that I wouldn't have to settle for less-than-stellar sex. I was a fuck-me feminist before I'd had my first kiss. In my mind sex wasn't just about love or hormones, it was a key to my own identity. Sex represented a freedom that my mother had never experienced as a Korean woman—and there was no way I was going to become like my mother.

> **" I was a fuck-me feminist before I'd had my first kiss. In my mind sex wasn't just about love or hormones, it was a key to my own identity. "**

Nor was I going to be like so many girls at school, ebullient when they were dating and then sobbing for days and weeks after they'd been dumped. I observed many guys who, in contrast, shortly after breaking up with a girlfriend, took up with another. How was it that they seemed so unfazed? Why did guys seem to have so much more control in relationships? Why did we girls allow them the power? Why did my mother give in to my father?

At the time I wished my mother would file for a divorce. My parents hadn't lived together for more than ten years, and I didn't see the sense in them staying married. When my mother, brother, and I moved to the United States, my father decided to stay with his corporation in Korea. He visited us for just a few weeks each year, and my mother essentially became a single parent. When I was sixteen, my father left his company and finally joined our family for good. It was a bad arrangement. He constantly picked on my mother and dismissed her views on just about everything. "Bird brain," he'd utter in a poisonous tone that sickened us all. The worst was when he demanded money. Not having any work in the United States, he sought out doomed business ventures and expected my mother to provide the capital. She didn't want to give up her savings—the money she'd earned as a doctor since coming to the United States—but he always got his way.

I'm ashamed to say I wasn't supportive. I hated my father for weakening my mother, but I hated my mother more for not leaving him. At eighteen I left for college, thinking I was escaping my parents. Unfortunately, I left something crucial behind. Two weeks into my first semester, my mother came across an old diary in my room. She read it and discovered that I wasn't a virgin. During the ensuing fight, she repeatedly yelled, "You betrayed me!"

I betrayed her? What about my father? Why was I the one being punished? Feeling angry and exposed, I retreated to my studies, devouring books by feminist thinkers. Olga Broumas, Naomi Wolf, and Susan Faludi became my new role models. I befriended other women emerging from repressive pasts. Guilt-free sex was our credo as we hopped into bed with both genders. I dreaded the holidays when I had to go back home.

While feminism gave me a community of other like-minded women, it didn't give me any clues on how to resolve two very different cultures, how to be both Korean and American, how to speak to my own mother. By the middle of my first year of college, my mother had started calling me on Sunday mornings to remind me not to have sex. At first I gave a good fight and tried to explain to her that being sexually active was acceptable behavior for someone my age and that few people of my generation believe in the good girl virgin stuff. After a while, I realized it was easier to lie.

A decade later I continue to live a secret life, as duplicitous and conflicted as a gay person acting straight to coworkers. I answer my mother's phone calls, assure her that I'm not having sex while my boyfriend lies in bed next to me. I might be in love, but I am deathly afraid of sharing that joy with my mother. Of course I want to tell her the truth, but every time I try, we end up yelling at each other.

"Don't have sex," she pleads.

How do you talk about love and sex with someone who thinks nothing positive of dating? My mother never experienced the kind of first date where you eat dinner, watch a movie, and kiss at the front door. When she came of age in Korea, men and women weren't free to date without scandal surrounding them. When she was twenty-five, my mother's dates were arranged by elders and consisted of drinking tea and shaking hands at the end. By the third meeting she would decide whether she wanted to marry her date. I imagine that for a man, the process is not unlike interviewing for a job. Only those who are well-educated, well-connected, and who promise success need apply. There was no opportunity for the couple to spend time and really get to know each other, fall in love, and have sex. There was also no opportunity to discover the flaws of a seemingly perfect spouse, or the many little ways in which they might not be compatible. That is, until after they got married and it was too late.

Yam-ja-ne is a Korean word used to describe women. It means quiet, sweet, compliant. I've heard it applied to me many times by my parents' friends, who don't know shit about me. They meet me at dinner parties or wedding receptions, and because of the way I dress or the way I do my hair, they pronounce me yam-ja-ne and offer to set me up with their sons and nephews. I feel fifteen all over again, except now I have my mother's consent—not to have sex but to meet prospective suitors.

Geography doesn't matter when it comes to Korean matchmaking. My father's golf buddy gives me the phone number of his son in Chicago. (That's only, what, two time zones away from my home in Seattle?) "He graduated from MIT and is working as a software developer," the man pipes. My parents smile, encouraging me to take the number. For them it's the same game played years ago, when they were comparing test scores and college acceptances. Except now my parents are losing face, because I dropped out of pre-med to study writing. "Our daughter—we don't really know what she does. Let her tell you herself," my mother says to the programmer's father, who continues to check me out. I look yam-ja-ne to him, but if the truth came out, I'd be out of the race. Which is fine by me. I mean, I'm not really going to call this geek in Chicago, so what's the difference?

"Thank you," I say to the man as I take his son's number. I act out the role of the good daughter for my parents; it's the least I can do for turning out the way I did.

"Don't tell anyone about that ju-che-gi," my mother tells me. Ju-che-gi, which means fool, is what she calls my ex-boyfriend Ian, whom I dated for two years. Ian is Dutch and for the first year of our relationship we lived together in Holland. He came with me when I returned to the United States, and we lived in a studio in Queens, a mere twenty-minute drive away from my parents. Because of our living situation, there was no hiding him. It was my most significant relationship, not only because of the duration but because of his contact with my mother. For a while she even liked him.

When I ask why I shouldn't tell others about Ian, she answers, "Men won't like it if they find out you've been used." Because I didn't marry him, Ian is shameful, and the two years I spent with him must be rewritten for others who may not approve, the random golfers and doctors we meet at Korean functions. As if I were one of her patients, my mother keeps my history confidential, striking out the love of my life like a disease.

Is it foolish to think that as we both get older, we'll come to accept each other? Despite all the difficulties we've had, I still long to share more of my life with my mother. If we can't agree on things, I want her at least to know why I make the choices I do, including why I fall for the men I do. Lately, I've started telling her a bit about my boyfriend—while letting her entertain the idea that I'm not having sex with him. It's better this way than not communicating at all.

Every once in a while, she surprises me and gives me hope. "I know American people carry on differently, but aren't you tired of all this dating?" she asked me recently. I could argue that it's better in the long run to learn from many different relationships, but as a commitmentphobe who attracts other commitmentphobes, I have to admit that all those dinners, movies, and STD tests have lost their novelty. Yes, Mom, I'm tired of dating. I'm tired of the mini-relationships that expire like milk. I'm tired of the breakups, even when they're "mutual" and "amicable." When my last boyfriend/potential husband/potential father to your grandchildren dumped me, he said, "I like you a lot, but I'm not sure if I can love you." He may as well have sent me a form letter. *We have reviewed your resume and while we are impressed with your experience, we do not have a suitable position that fits your qualifications. Thank you very much.*

Even though I want a long-term, loving relationship, I wonder if I can truly sustain one, given my track record. At the end of our conversation, my mother withholds her usual mantra. Instead, she says, "Just be careful who you get involved with. You've got a lot more to offer than you think."

I could say the same for her.

Echoes of a Mother
Black Women, Foster Care, and Reproductive Rights

SAYEEDA COPELAND

I had many mothers. There were many women who molded themselves into the position—some taught me what was needed in different seasons of my life, while others took on the role as a full-time job.

My biological mother was thirty-one years old when she gave birth to me. I was her fourth child. She struggled with an addiction to crack. At the age of one, I was placed in my mother's only sister's care, in New York, while my siblings were placed in the care of my great grandmother, who lived in South Carolina. Rumor has it that the day the courts decided to separate my siblings and me from my mother, she threw her body on the courtroom floor, pleading to the judge to allow me to stay in the city. I was her youngest child; she couldn't handle having all of her children taken away. The judge agreed.

Regardless of the court's warnings, my aunt allowed my mother to visit me whenever she pleased. My mother was the kind of woman who had no filter on her thoughts and words. She said how she felt with no apologies, and her presence demanded respect. My mother and aunt lived in Harlem, not very far from one another. I remember actually living with my mother for short periods of time. But it was only for a few weeks at a time, and eventually they would end with arguments between my aunt and my mother about my mother not returning me. I remember hiding quietly in bathrooms, doors locked, lights off, to make my aunt believe no one was home. I knew at that young age that I wanted to be with the woman who birthed me, and I didn't understand why I couldn't.

During one of my visits with my mother, my aunt allowed my cousins to come over to play with me. I wanted to buy all of us candy. I thought it was a brilliant idea to find money by searching my mother's coat pockets. I ran to her walk-in closet and moved knitted and cotton sweaters out of my face as I jammed my small hands into each pocket. Fishing for any forgotten quarters, nickels or dimes, I found a handful of change in one coat. Feeling lucky, I reached my hand into the next coat, and something that felt like a pen greeted my fingers. I pulled it out, examined its glass texture, and placed it to my lips. I filled my cheeks with air and blew with all my might into its hole. This strange item didn't make a sound, so I knew it wasn't a whistle. I had never seen anything like it, and felt it was something I should not be playing with, so I returned it to its pocket and closed the closet door.

Later that night while I was still at my mother's apartment, I woke to my mother sitting on the edge of the bed. She had the funny object I'd found earlier in her mouth. I watched as her thumb scratched the lighter until its flame appeared. She coughed hard, and then looked over to me as I began to stir.

"Go to sleep, Mama," she cooed. My mother's voice was low and raspy from the smoke exiting her mouth. I peeled the sheets back and climbed over the mountain of blankets to her. I sat beside her and laid my head on her lap. Her body trembled as she brought the funny object to her lips again. I sat up, waited for her next inhale, and reached up to knock the glass pipe out of her hand.

"Don't you ever do that shit again! Do you hear me?!" she hissed and jumped up to catch the glass pipe before it could hit the floor.

I dozed off that night as the smell of crack, a smell that resembled plastic burning, rocked me back to sleep.

I never tried to stop her again. Her addiction never changed her love for me or my other siblings. I grew to understand that this addiction forced her to make some decisions she would never have made in a sober mindset. It was crack that kept my mother from being the best mother I knew she could be. Eventually the news of my mother's drug use continuing and my aunt allowing me to visit without the permission of Child Protective Services came to light. I was placed in foster care again, this time outside of my family.

My new foster family was a couple who lived in St. Albans, Queens. They were in their early seventies. My foster mother's name was Louise, but I called her Momma and her husband Papa. She woke me up very early one morning. I would have thought it was time for church service by the way she had ironed a new dress for me and laid it out on the guest-room bed. We drove to the courthouse as butterflies beat against my ten-year-old rib cage. I wanted them to ask me for the hundredth time who I wanted to live with, and for the hundredth time I was ready to say my mother.

Due to my age, I was not allowed to go into the courtroom. Momma waited with me on the wooden benches outside. My mother spoke with me briefly before going inside. No more than ten minutes later, she emerged. I searched her face for some kind of emotion—sadness, anger, or happiness—but it was blank. I ran to her, hugging her waist, feeling confident I'd be going home.

"Mommy, what did they say?" I was now holding her hand, looking at the mole that rested in its center.

"Oh, they took my rights away." She said it so nonchalantly, as if discussing the weather. She swatted at the air with her hand and sucked her teeth.

"Does that mean you won't be my mommy anymore?"

"No, it means on paper I can't take care of you. They can never take you away from my heart. On earth, and even when I'm gone, I will always be your mother."

Unlike my mother, I was not able to hold back my tears. I felt defeated. I wondered on the ride back to Queens if she had argued enough for me. Did she fight hard enough for me? Did she really want me?

"Sweety? Sweety?" The nurse's voice sounded like a faint song in my ear. My mind was racing, trying to recall what or who I could go to.

"I'm sorry, what are *prenatal* pills again?" I carefully pronounced the new word.

"Prenatal pills are what you have to start taking. They are for the child's development."

"Child?" My eyes darted across the room, taking in the two signs encouraging mothers to breastfeed.

"Oh, darling. Your test came back positive. You're pregnant!" The nurse's smile was the opposite of the emotions flooding my body. She must have noticed my lack of excitement and instantly offered her services.

"I can call your mother for you if you like. Many girls ask for that so you won't have to tell her the news on your own. I understand how hard it can be." She continued to fill out the prescription paper and placed it in my trembling palm. I gazed out the window at the large lake that hugged my college campus. I began to wonder how long it would take for me to walk directly into the lake and disappear. If I did, I wouldn't have to worry about this budding life inside of me.

"You can't tell her. She's...she's—" The tears were now diving off the cliff of my chin. My mother wouldn't understand...couldn't understand.

"I can place her on speaker phone if you like, to make it easier—"

"My mother is dead." My voice didn't sound like my own. Those words felt like a lie. They were the truth.

"Darling, I am so sorry. Okay, well, let's tell your father and I am here if you need me." She handed me a box of tissues.

"No, he's dead too."

"I'm so sorry. Who do you have as a support system?" Her face filled with pity more than sadness.

I often asked myself the same question. I explained to the nurse that I had been late returning to campus for my sophomore year because my siblings and I had just buried our mother. My mother had fought a good fight against lung cancer. There was no calling her to relay the good news, because despite her death that is what it was, good news. My mother believed that children were blessings from God, and to lose a child, like she did to the system, was shameful.

The only other person I could think of to call, besides my child's father, was my adoptive father. After Momma passed away, Papa had moved down South and I had been adopted by a Jamaican couple who had three biological sons of their own. I struggled with being adopted. I felt displaced, and many times unwanted. It was not easy, but I had formed a strong bond with my adoptive father. So over the phone I told him that I was pregnant. I was too afraid to tell him in person. He asked me if I was joking. After realizing this wasn't one of my pranks, he asked me how far along I was. When I told him, he cleared his throat, told me he had some errands to run, and hung up the phone.

When I told my child's father about my pregnancy, his first words to me were: "You know what to do." He didn't even ask me if I wanted to keep the baby. He couldn't bring himself to say the word *abortion*. After a long pause, he assured me that he would agree with any decision I decided to make. I struggled with the idea of how my life would change either way, whether I decided to keep the child or decided not to.

I sought advice from the campus therapist. I had begun seeing her before I found out I was pregnant, because of my mother's passing.

"You are such a bright girl. You have to do what's right for you," she said.

"I am just torn. I'm getting bigger, I'm more tired these days. I hate going to class because morning sickness is kicking my ass. I don't have the energy."

Her raised pencil eyebrows made her look like she was fighting sleep. "Are you keeping it?"

This question had not been asked out loud, though I had been asking it over and over again in my head.

"I don't know. It doesn't feel real." There were so many factors to consider: my financial stability, support system, shelter, my religious beliefs, my education...

"I live near a Planned Parenthood. I can make an appointment for you. Then after everything is done, you can rest at my house and relax," she said. I imagined waiting at Planned Parenthood nervously wondering if everyone knew I was there to have an abortion. "You can stay in my daughter's room," she offered. "We'll return to campus Sunday. You'll have time to relax and heal.... Just think about it."

The therapist smiled and handed me her card. She told me to email or call her when I made my decision.

The reactions of my adopted father and my boyfriend angered me. These men did not know what it meant to be a woman. They did not understand that there was just not a quick fix. My adopted father was angry that I was pregnant and not married. He was pro-life and expected me to have the child, yet he was upset that it was not the "right" timing, because I still needed to complete college. There is no such thing as the "right" time to have a child. My therapist understood that. Her offering me Planned Parenthood services as an option showed me that I didn't have to keep my child because I had been raised religiously. However, I didn't agree with how she made the procedure sound like a walk in the park.

For women of color, to exercise the right of having an abortion is much more complicated than that. There are factors as to why abortion is not talked about often in the African-American community. Religion plays a role, because some consider it a sin to terminate a pregnancy. In some instances, an additional child can be financially straining, yet black women are expected to be able to handle the burden.

The history of women of color and abortion is also associated with the history of slavery. Black women were forced in many cases to conceive and then watch their children be sold off or killed. Adoption has been viewed in the same light. To willingly give up your child as a woman of color means to be shunned. Journalist P. R. Lockhart discusses the effects of abortion on black women in her article "The Untold Story About Black Women and Abortions," writing, "The human stories behind the debates on abortion and reproductive rights often neglect the unique challenges faced by low-income women, a group that disproportionately includes women of color. Abortion has been an especially controversial issue for black women, who must often

> **" The history of women of color and abortion is also associated with the history of slavery. Black women were forced in many cases to conceive and then watch their children be sold off or killed. "**

navigate political barriers, racism, and cultural expectations of motherhood when seeking to end a pregnancy."[1]

This therapist didn't know what it felt like to be a nineteen-year-old black woman, but she knew that I had choices and that I needed to be aware of them. This journey taught me that it is not about who is judging you. It is about knowing your rights and making your decision and being comfortable with it. I learned that Planned Parenthood offered a variety of services. It also supported me if I didn't want to go through with an abortion.

In the end, my therapist showed me that owning my feminism meant exercising my right to do as I wished with my body with no apologies.

My mother's passing was the hardest thing I have ever experienced. Three months later, my biological grandmother passed away as well. I felt so much grief, yet I only found joy in knowing I had life inside of me. I was not ready to lose another part of my family: my unborn child.

I eventually finished out my semester and moved into a shelter when I was four months pregnant. When I reached seven months, I found my very first apartment, right after my twentieth birthday. The night before I was to give birth, I could not sleep. I paced back and forth in my living room to ease the contractions. It became hard to stand, so I tried crawling, hoping that would help. When all else failed, I found myself bouncing up and down on my pink exercise ball and repenting to God for ever having had sex. I called my aunt, and she told me I should head to the emergency room. I was so nervous, but I knew it was definitely time.

My boyfriend and I checked into the hospital around 2 a.m. I was dilated five centimeters—enough to be admitted. I was wheeled into different rooms and hooked up to machines that monitored my baby's heartbeat. The beeping sounds disturbed me at first because they brought back memories of how my mother's hospital machines used to beep. The bright lights, the huge rooms, the various nurses, and all the introductions frightened me. I felt like a little girl again. I felt scared and wanted my mother. The following afternoon, I felt heavy pressure in my lower abdomen and back. I thought it meant I had to use the bathroom, but nurses quickly filled my room and informed me it was time to push.

The epidural I'd had hours prior was not much relief. I was very emotional, telling my boyfriend that I didn't want to push. I didn't want to have a baby anymore because of the pain. One nurse held my hand and said, "We can be here pushing for the next half hour or the next three hours. The choice is yours."

When I heard those words, I held my breath and pushed with all of my might. My sister, my boyfriend, and the doctor and nurses encouraged me, telling me they could see my baby's head. Later, I learned they hadn't really seen his head—they just didn't want me to give up. I pushed five times, and the fifth time, my son, covered in my blood, entered the world with the softest cry I have ever heard. They placed his warm, slippery body on my chest. I looked down at him through my teary eyes, careful not to let him slip out of my arms as our cries merged into one another's. In that moment I could not imagine ever leaving him, or making him feel what I once felt about my mother. I knew my job was to always let him know I love him and, most importantly, that I want him.

When I was finally moved to the visitor's room with my son, everything felt surreal. I stared at myself in the bathroom mirror, observing my hospital gown, which had fallen off one of my shoulders. My eyes were bloodshot from pushing. I looked as if I had been deprived of sleep for weeks. My sister and boyfriend had left to get food. I changed my son's clothes and held him in my arms.

As I laid him down, I heard a voice that sounded like my mother's. The voice sounded close, as if it were coming from the chair next to the bedside.

"So you had the baby."

The voice was so familiar, like an old song you cannot forget. My eyes searched the room. No one was with me besides my son.

"Yes, Mommy, I did. I had him," I answered back, staring at the empty leather chair.

Just then my boyfriend walked into the room with our dinner. I expressed to him I had just spoken to my mother, that she had come to visit me. He kissed my forehead and said the medicine was probably still making me feel a little out of it. I knew it was not the medicine. I felt closure after that moment, as short and beautiful as it was. I believe that it was a spiritual moment with my mother, her letting me know she was there by my side the whole time.

I made the right decision in having my son. I learned to listen to my own voice, and I learned of the options available to me as a woman in this journey. The birth of my son changed the way I viewed the strength of women. I am grateful for my mother and for the women in my life who took on her role. I learned so much from my mother, both things I want to do as a mother and things I would change. Motherhood is a journey that no one can prepare you for. In the end, I gave birth to a beautiful, healthy baby boy. I know my mother would be proud of him if she were here today.

Dutiful *Hijas*
Dependency, Power, and Guilt

ERICA GONZÁLEZ MARTÍNEZ

It started before I was born, before my mother was born, and before her mother was born. We were groomed to be caretakers, to carry the world on our shoulders without swaying and then humbly accept accolades (*que buena*) for it. We were an impossible fusion of Wonder Woman's strength and La Virgen Maria's sanctity and sacrifice. *Que Dios te ayuda* otherwise. Yes, I am a dutiful daughter, but it stresses me out. There, I've said it, but I don't exactly feel relieved. I feel guilty for thinking it and saying it. I hear those expressions echo in my head—*After all she's done for you... cría cuervo y te sacarán los ojos...la abandonaste.* I feel ungrateful *y como una hija mala* (like a bad daughter).

I was reminded of my place as a dutiful daughter on a recent trip to Puerto Rico. Even though I traveled alone, as usual, I still got the same question from my family. *Why didn't you bring your mother?* I had invited her because I felt guilty about going off to enjoy myself while she hadn't traveled in a few years. But she had declined. In Mami's hometown, as always, I was introduced and identified as *la nena de Norma.* My name, if even mentioned, was secondary. I found this funny—and very telling—to the point that I would outright declare, *Yo soy la nena de Norma.* I had to belong to someone, and that meant Mami, since I wasn't Erica, *fulano-de-tal*'s wife, because I was single.

Aside from the question and introduction—both of which had centered around my mother—there were two other comments that clearly painted the role of daughters as social security. An older woman I met talked about how she was organizing her finances in preparation for her golden years: *Ya que solo tengo dos varones, que puedo hacer?* The mother of two boys, she had savings in lieu of a daughter. On another occasion, an elderly male relative complimented me on my independent spirit. When I thanked him and told him I wasn't in a rush to get married or have kids, he responded with, *Pero quién te va a cuidar cuando te pones vieja?* Giving birth to a daughter was the equivalent of buying life insurance. A daughter would be there to take care of a parent in old age.

I am one of many dutiful daughters. For example, my twenty-four-year-old *amiga* who was raised in South America feels like a return on an investment. When she finished her undergraduate degree, it was demanded that she immediately fly back to the nest to take care of her mother, grandmother, and brother. Initially, this had only meant being physically present. Now there are financial expectations beyond contributing to household expenses. While she would like to have her own home, her sense of obligation—imposed and self-imposed—is a block. Her family's attitude is, If you're not serving a husband, then you're serving us. And hers: I would leave but I would feel so guilty; I wouldn't feel at peace. Interestingly, her brother is exempt from this responsibility.

Another friend, who is twenty-nine, until recently had her life dictated by her predetermined role. "My mother over-depends on me," she said. "It's reversed—I am the parent, she is the child. I see other parents not depending on their kids, and the kids have the opportunity to go out in the world and find themselves. I had to know who I was from early on." When my friend went away to school, her relatives wanted to know why she couldn't attend a local college, but her brother wasn't reproached and guilt-tripped for enrolling in a university hours away. He was free to go; she was free to stay. "He's not a girl, so he's not expected to do the same," she said. Years later, with her decision to relocate, my friend received the same accusations from her family. She told me: "They feel like I'm deserting my mother. They say I am the only thing my mother has. I feel guilty about leaving her, like I'm not being a good daughter."

We love our mothers. We want to be there for them and want them to feel comfortable in knowing and relying on that. What is problematic is the double standard—the patriarchal definition of what it means to be a "good" woman; the reproduction of a superior-inferior power dynamic via culture and religion; the marginalization of women, in particular women of color, in the economy; and the emotional dimension of guilt. These factors are all intertwined to produce a situation that deserves a space for conversation and reflection.

AVE MAREEEAHH!

Marianismo is the crux of our existence.[1] Although the book *The Maria Paradox*, by Rosa Maria Gil and Carmen Inoa Vazquez, simplifies this mother-daughter dynamic as a clash between "old" and "new" worlds, it offers a solid explanation. Using the Virgin Mary as a point of reference, marianismo defines women as obedient servants who "happily" sacrifice themselves for everyone else's good. In marianismo, it is a woman's duty to be subservient and submissive, not to make decisions for herself.

Among the ten commandments of marianismo listed in *The Maria Paradox* are: "Do not forget a woman's place. Do not be single, self-supporting, or independent-minded. Do not put your own needs first. Do not wish for more in life than being a housewife."[2]

I was taught to defy marianismo, however. My friends and I were overencouraged, if not pushed, to pursue university degrees. Our mothers saw education as a vehicle for liberation from economic dependency, typically the factor that kept them in unhappy relationships. My parents spared no expense or effort when it came to education for my sister and me. Getting a college education was mandatory for us, even though it contradicted some tenets of marianismo. In college, I, along with the women I am still close to, began to be exposed to the work and boldness of feminists and womanists. I learned about the concepts of "voice," "the personal being political," and the "masculinization of nationalism." I read enlightening work by Julia de Burgos, bell hooks, Angela Davis, and Assata Shakur.[3] I interacted with amazing professors, including Micere Mugo, Linda Alcoff, Alicia Vadillo, and Terri Northrup; and I was inspired by the mothers who fought against police brutality in New York City, and the accomplishments of the Latin Women's Collective, a now-defunct organization that focused on developing Latinas as leaders.

Even though I grew up knowing that Gloria Steinem was dedicated to women's rights, and recall Equal Rights Amendment posters, my first real understanding of feminism came through the women who looked like me and who spoke to me culturally and politically. They were committed to liberation, of a colony or of one's self. To me, as a Puerto Rican, these questions of race, class, and national liberation were critical. I subscribed to bell hooks's definition of feminism:

Feminism is not simply a struggle to end male chauvinism or a movement to ensure that women will have equal rights with men;

it is a commitment to eradicating the ideology of domination that permeates Western culture on various levels—sex, race and class to name a few—and a commitment to reorganizing society...so that self-development of people can take a precedence over imperialism, economic expansion, and material desire.[4]

I understood that I was a Puerto Rican *woman* and that the woman part of me couldn't be a backburner component. The patriarchy was real and reflected in many of the political campaigns in which I participated. Learning how to identify and address sexism was a process. Attempts to point these things out were on many occasions dismissed, passively agreed with, or responded to defensively with examples of female political martyrdom. I saw how sexism—or rather, not dealing with it proactively—could cripple political work. Instead of feminism being linked to race, class, and national liberation—and made part of our daily work and progress—it was mostly relegated to panel discussions.

Puerto Rican nationalist Lolita Lebrón wore a skirt when she and her armed comrades charged the US Congress in 1954 to defend Puerto Rico's right to be a sovereign nation. In 1915, Luisa Capetillo, a feminist and socialist who organized workers in Puerto Rico, was arrested for wearing pants in public in Cuba. Both Lolita and Luisa inspired me. I was driven to pursue the ultimate freedom of my people and myself. These ideals came into conflict at home, however. It was easier to organize a rally against a tuition hike or get involved in a movement to free political prisoners than to face the painful contradictions of who I was raised to be.

Growing up, my sister and I had *muñecas* and knew to cross our legs when sitting down. We also had an easel, a Starsky and Hutch set, race cars, a toy cash register, and a Fisher-Price doctor's kit. An ex–air force boxer, my father taught us to shoot a BB gun at empty Nestlé Quik cans and how to snap a punch. According to my mother, getting married and having kids was not a priority, and philandering husbands were unacceptable. But the premise of marianismo, women as servants, along with its corollaries of suffering and guilt, were ingrained, both inside and outside of the home.

SUFFERING WILL MAKE A GOOD WOMAN OUT OF YOU

I had a striking introduction to women's suffering in Catholic elementary school. I had picked up a book about Saint Rose of Lima. Even though I was little, I understood she was Latina, because she was from Peru and Peru was in South America. That meant she had some kind of link to me because she spoke Spanish, while all the other saints seemed to be from Europe. As I read the paragraphs at the bottoms of the pages and looked at the pictures on top, I was both horrified and fascinated. Saint Rose had stuck a pin in her head and slept on rocks to prove her commitment to God. She had rejected the advances of Satan—who was drawn both as a hideous giant and a tempting stud figure. I was amazed at the things Saint Rose did to herself. Soon after reading that book, I began petitioning for something or trying to repent for being "bad." I made myself suffer. I wasn't brave enough to resort to rocks, so one night I threw barrettes and bobby pins all over my bed and slept on them. I wanted to serve God, but I didn't want all the pain involved. Yet I understood that the more you suffered, the more saintly you were, which makes you closer to God, and yes, *superbuena*.

In church, women were elements of the equation. The statue of the Virgin Mary watched us or waited to be adored. Her greatness came from bearing a special child and having been chosen to do so by an almighty being, assumed to be male. The nuns, the Sisters of Mercy, sat in the front pews during Mass and ran the elementary school. The women directed the choir, cleaned the rectory, cooked for the priests, and responded to inquiries. But after God, always assumed to be male, the priest was central. He had the power to celebrate the Mass, and, in the name of "Him," absolve us of our sins. The deacons, who were also men, were next in importance. Making a church or school function smoothly, as the nuns did, wasn't enough to merit leading Mass. As classic, dutiful daughters, they had the role of servitude. This male-oriented hierarchy in the church followed the patriarchal organization of society. It also was a reality in my family.

In our house, there was clearly a chain of command. My father, a Vietnam veteran and police lieutenant, was the *jefe*. My mother, a former beautician-salesperson-receptionist-daycare worker, was next in line. My sister and I were the subordinates—though I ruled over her by virtue of being older. My mother was by no means quietly compliant, but my father was frequently the decision maker, an entitlement that came from being the man and the breadwinner as well as having a college degree, compared with my mother's high school education. Mami raised us and maintained our home, while Papi earned the money and paid the bills. When this structure and organization was ruptured, we were faced with redefining our positions.

TRANSFERRING DEPENDENCY

My parents split up after twenty-six years of marriage. I was twenty-two and had just graduated from college. Although the breakup was not a surprise, my mother was unprepared and panic-stricken by the thought of having to survive on her own. She had worked for years before and after marrying my father, but a major stroke at a young age had rendered her physically unable to handle many tasks. She could not contribute an income to the household.

Despite raising us and taking care of the house, her work had not been acknowledged as such because it did not yield money. In the computer age, she wasn't ready to reenter the job market. My mother had been deeply frustrated at her dependency on my father. As a result of her physical limitations and her concerns about raising us properly, her life was in the home. She had been unable to establish herself beyond being a mother or a wife. This is by no means saying that being a mother and a wife aren't wonderful things. But they are aspects of the self in relation to others. My mother was *la mama de... la esposa de...* but maybe she wanted at times to just be herself, in her own right.

Paralyzed by fear, my mother attempted to transfer her dependency on my father to my sister and me at a time when both of us were coming into our own as independent adults. This dependency wasn't necessarily always financial, but instead in the realms of decision making, organization, and action. She had always overly depended on us emotionally. We were her world, and we would get chastised for doing things like staying out late as young adults (translation: staying away from her). Our relationship was already troubled by the power dynamic of the parent as superior and the child—even an adult daughter—as subordinate. Although my mother, in her proud, *jíbara*-never-ask-for-anything way, would not tell me that I had to be the "man" of the house, the pressure was there.

I did not shy away from being there, but I was uncomfortable with her asking me for direction or to make decisions for her. Although she initially, and understandably, felt devastated and confused about the end of her marriage, I wanted my mother to understand that there was the potential of her emerging from this crisis as a new woman. I wanted her to recognize that she could finally take some ownership of her life and make choices based on her own well-being and desires, and that she deserved and had the right to do so.

Throughout the long divorce process, my sister and I responded as we should have—with support, love, assistance, and patience. But there were many occasions when we had to hold our mother by the hand to do something like make a phone call to a bureaucrat. She preferred to have my sister or me deal with any task she found intimidating. When we didn't comply, she acted wounded, not seeing, at least at first, that we were only encouraging her to become self-reliant and establish her own identity, much in the same way she had encouraged us over the years. We had been taught to be the best, and that we were capable of doing anything, by the same woman who was now floundering at what she saw as the frightening prospect of independence, or rather, having to "go it alone," and fearing that she would fail. My mother grew up in poverty in Puerto Rico—a poverty rooted in the United States' domination of the Puerto Rican economy. The possibility of not being able to afford the medical care she needed, or to cover her bills, was scary. She wasn't operating from the perspective that she came from a long line of survivors who had always done what they set out to do—to make life a little better for the next generation.

It was emotionally enervating for all of us. But understanding that this was a space and time for my mother to grow and do things according to her own wants and needs, I gave her tough love. We said no to some requests and yes to others. However we reacted, there was always a level of guilt.

JUDGE, WE FIND *LA HIJA* GUILTY

We have been trained to feel guilty for being less than perfect (even though, as a wise poet once told me, there is no such thing as perfection). Even on occasions when my mother doesn't give me a pitiful look, I project guilt. I can never do enough for her. After all, she carried me for nine months, dedicated herself to my well-being, and has been my biggest cheerleader. How could I ever repay her? But is that even the point? We sustain our guilt by constantly trying to compensate for feelings of inadequacy about being less than "perfect," less than La Virgen, showing our subscription to a *marianista* philosophy. The logic is that I am a *good* person when I *serve* her, and that must be 24/7.

Conveying to my mother that my love for her does not diminish when I don't do what she wants was a challenge—for both of us. Giving myself permission to say no to her—*que Dios me perdone*—and not feeling like a bad person for doing so was a breakthrough. All the sacrifices she made so I could have a better chance would be in vain if I did not bring to the table the knowledge and experiences I have gained. That scenarios of living and power could be different and not necessarily doomsday-negative, even in your fifties, was what I offered. We painfully go back and forth, more often than not trying to exorcise ourselves of some residual issue and climbing to a new plateau.

As a politically conscious, single woman, I have the internal critic as well as the external cultural judge evaluating whether I'm acting like a selfish, individualistic *gringa* or a community-building and respectful Latina. Whenever my twenty-four-year-old friend appears to do something that doesn't have her family at the center, she gets the old *Eso es una cosa Americana.*[5] We both agree that our sense of community and family is a part of who we are, but not breathing and living family as the core of our beings every single minute of the day doesn't make us sellouts or *Americanas.* Claiming our own voices does not mean that we forgo our people's survival strategies and remarkable principles of sharing and looking out for one another.

The issues of class and economics are rarely divorced from any aspect of our lives. Most of my friends struggle to pay their rent, living expenses, and student loans. We're not affluent women who can support another person's entire financial needs or hire attendants and housekeepers. Our mothers, approaching their retirement years, find themselves out of the male-as-principle-breadwinner structure to which they were accustomed. Our mothers also find their role of caretaker disappearing. What do you do when what you have based your identity on—caretaking—is no longer a need? How do you become emotionally and economically independent? How do you carve your own identity? How does a *buena* daughter help out of choice and love, not guilt?

The fears are valid. The fear of being alone, the fear of not having a purpose, the fear of not being able to afford basic necessities. The economy is not striking up the band for women in their fifties with limited skills. If professional Latinas make fifty cents on every dollar an Anglo man makes, imagine how a Latina with limited earning potential survives. An article in the *New York Times* described how older women are finding themselves in the predicament of entering their golden years but having to stay in the workforce as a result of divorce. This is attributed to women who spent years raising children but not having pensions of their own. Even older women who are able to land jobs now have to delay retirement as they play catch-up with someone who worked a lifetime.[6]

> **" Yes, I am a dutiful daughter, but it stresses me out. There, I've said it, but I don't exactly feel relieved. "**

As a dutiful daughter, I felt pressured. I wanted to take care of my mother, to tell her that she could just kick up her feet and relax because I had everything under control. This not being the case, however, I couldn't help but feel inadequate about not meeting my own *supermujer* expectations. I also was afraid of feeling selfish, or of being labeled as such for not putting her happiness before mine. This is why I would agonize over having to inform her or my family that I wanted to go away to school or rent my own apartment. Then I would feel resentful about the comments or looks I would receive.

I didn't want my mother to correlate my not being physically present in her house with not being in her life. And I was afraid of having every aspect of my life revolve around what would make my mother happy. I know my decisions about school and the apartment were the right ones, but that doesn't mean the guilt and anxiety disappear forever. On a few occasions when I haven't been able to reach my mother, I have imagined the worst and chided myself for not living with her, for not protecting her enough. I have felt that if something happened to her, I would be full of regret for not being as dutiful as I could have been, for not preventing something bad from taking place. Yet living together would roll back our relationship.

Although my mother was somewhat better off than some of her pals in similar situations—she co-owns her house and receives financial help from my father—she has to pay for astronomical medical insurance and household expenses by herself. She also doesn't feel comfortable with just relying on payments that help but may not be there one day. This insecurity led her to enroll in a course that provided computer training and job readiness to people in her age group. Not quite a tech nerd, Mami is now more proficient at Microsoft Excel than I am. But trying to find work hasn't been easy. Sometimes she doesn't meet the criteria of the prospective jobs, or feels she is denied certain opportunities because she is older. Other times, the jobs that are available aren't right for her needs. Besides technology skills, the program Mami participated in allowed her to develop a network of friends and her own life. To my delight, she would hang out with "the girls," dictate her own comings and goings, and excitedly recount her day to us. She enjoys volunteer work, where her contributions are valued and appreciated, and she tries to revisit goals she had once set for herself. My mother has created an opening that has allowed for self-development and fulfillment, and she has expanded her experiences beyond the world that was prescribed for her as a dutiful *mujer*.

Our mother-daughter relationship is a work in progress. We—Mami, Sis, and I—struggle through new ways of being in the world that will help redefine what kind of mothers and daughters we will be in the future, and what kind of sons, daughters, and grandchildren we will raise.

I especially thank Mami, Melinda, Blanca, and Women in Literature and Letters (WILL), a nonprofit organization for women of color, for making this essay possible.

Becoming an Abortion Doula

SANDRA KUMWONG

The sun could fall on top of my mother and she would hold it up with her bare palms with no issue. Once a man in a convertible cut her off and she rolled down the window, yelled at him in Thai, and threw her travel mug into his white leather seats. Having a mother who is a million times the person I could ever strive to be means that my existence, my breath, and my work has her voice in it as well.

We kids always laughed in the backseat of our Honda Pilot— a picture of Buddha hanging from the rearview mirror—as our mother drove us back and forth between school, music lessons, and tutoring. What a superwoman, rising to the top of her class in business school at the age of seventeen, working two jobs and learning just how lonely the busiest city in the world can be.

Mom, do you wish there were three kids in the back instead of two?

After I became an intern and then an abortion doula for Planned Parenthood of New York City, my mother revealed to me a secret she'd held dearly for a long time. I never expected her to say the words that one in three women can say: "I've had an abortion."

My mother must have dragged her tired, betraying body to the living room where my father camped out. Her experience was not unheard of. They hadn't slept in the same room more than ten times since I was born. She told him the news only to hear something along the lines of, "We don't want another child, we can't have one. Get rid of it." His words were always final and demanding.

Mom, I wish I had been older. I wish I could have talked you through it like I do with strangers.

My mother is a logical woman. When she found out she was pregnant again, I'm almost positive she thought about all the baby clothes she kept and how she could reuse them. She dressed my brother and me both in pink and blue, because clothes were clothes. Then she must have thought about how I'd nursed Lenny's bruises when Dad hit him too hard, or when I'd let his fists land on me, running in at just the right time. She must have thought about how she'd never bring another child into this broken-glass life: me crying on the bannister, avoiding the blood on the beige carpet, the muffled sound of John Wayne in the eerie silence after a fight, the holes in the cream walls and the ripped curtains.

My mother had her procedure done in an OB/GYN office—much different from the health clinics where I volunteer. She sat alone in a waiting room with pictures of two pairs of hands over a swollen belly on the walls. There are so many traumatizing images that can come up right before a procedure that doulas need to be aware of. A patient can be more upset about the pictures in the waiting room or the picketers outside than the pain from the actual procedure.

I've found that after I've introduced myself and helped to get a patient changed, it's not uncommon for a patient to mention these emotional triggers. As a doula, my job is to listen and hold this space of vulnerability for them.

My mother must have cried so much when she changed into the blue gown and put her feet in the cold stirrups. *Did the nurse hold your hand? Did she tell you that you were brave and strong? I'm sure those words sound better in our mother tongue—did they offer you a translator?*

The nurses at Planned Parenthood can administer medication, set up the monitors, and wipe away tears all at once, but at other clinics or hospitals they can be as pro-life as the people spitting and praying outside. It is delusional to think that all medical providers are pro-choice, much less advocates of reproductive justice.

I would have reminded my mother to tuck her chin to her chest and take slow, deep breaths. To concentrate on relaxing the muscles in her bottom and belly. I would have held her hand in mine and put another hand on her shoulder after asking if it was okay. I would tell her that she was brave, strong, and safe.

Mom, I see you in every patient I meet. I see you in the fifteen-year-olds who have never had a pelvic exam, in the fifty-year-olds with three grandsons, in the thirty-year-old who sometimes forgets to take her pill.

Pro-choice is a language that never sits well with me, because many people don't feel as if it's their choice—*Mom, was it really yours?*

Choice assumes that a person has the autonomy to make a decision. This is not the case for those who have been subjected to systematic dehumanization and oppression. When there are forces that make other choices seem impossible—whole communities of young Black and Brown people being threatened by incarceration, or the mass sterilization of Puerto Rican women, or the generational trauma that is passed down from Japanese families who were once locked in

> **66 Choice assumes that a person has the autonomy to make a decision. This is not the case for those who have been subjected to systematic dehumanization and oppression. 99**

concentration camps, or domestic abuse, which is widespread—choice seems like a fantasy.

If I were the doctor in the emergency room, when my father brought my mother clutching her broken face in her hands, flinching at every loving touch he faked, I'd pull her aside and tell her she was safe with me, that I could get her help. I'd peek my head around the corner to see my father, nervously pacing up and down the hallway wondering if he'd get caught this time. I'd give my mom a sign that someone in this universe cared about her, even if she didn't do anything with that sign.

In many instances like these, the medical system failed to support not only my mother, but also masses of people across the country. I decided to become a doctor, so it would allow me to take my life experiences and become a resource that people can turn to, as the medical field often is a threat or a nuisance for many. Becoming a doctor would be justice for all the times women like my mom were ignored when they were silently asking for help.

I am one of millions of patients who have felt safe and important after receiving care at Planned Parenthood, whether it was a live chat for my questions about healthy relationships or getting my annual exam. I applied as a health center advocacy intern during my sophomore year at Hunter College because Planned Parenthood cared about both my physical health and my emotional health. The health-care professionals I met there had asked me about my relationships and about how I was handling the difficult prerequisites for medical school. Becoming part of an organization that works relentlessly to provide accurate medical care and outreach to its communities has been fulfilling.

As I learned more about how race, class, gender, and sexuality can affect a person's access to reproductive health, I became more involved with "reproductive justice," to use a term coined by the advocacy group SisterSong. Reproductive justice provides a new angle in advocacy recognizing that all facets of a person's identity affect how they make reproductive choices, whether they exercise their right not to have a child or their right to have a child and to parent.

Reproductive justice advocates for the total well-being of women—physical, emotional, spiritual, economic, social, and political. It includes the empowerment of women of color and honors the importance of their voices in feminism. This framework puts into words the exclusion I felt as a daughter of Asian-American immigrants when I was confronted with the word "feminism." When it came to voting rights, health-care access, and immigrant reform, where was my face, my skin color, my language?

I became an abortion doula because I craved so much more than pink pussy hats and quirky feminist T-shirts. I wanted my anger to be something productive and tangible. Working with Planned Parenthood community organizers gave me the spirit I needed to be a doula. When my supervisors at Planned Parenthood told me about abortion doulas who operated in New York City Planned Parenthood health centers, I found myself emailing The Doula Project the same day.

Doulas are traditionally involved with providing emotional, physical, and mental support to women during pregnancy and birth. Training to be a doula can include learning about labor positions, aromatherapy, massage, and breathing techniques. Abortion doulas can be trained in similar support techniques, and they can be the same kind of patient advocate that a birth doula is to a laboring patient. In fact, doulas who support patients through abortion procedures have now become essential to many clinics and hospitals. While birth can be seen as joyous for many, and pregnant women might receive support from loved ones and even strangers, news of an abortion is usually silenced, the story of it stuck in calendars and empty mugs of chamomile tea.

It's extremely humbling being a doula. As a part of medical teams that provide safe abortions, I am well aware that in neighboring states, it's almost impossible to obtain one. In those short fifteen minutes when a patient is in the room for an aspiration abortion—a procedure that typically can be done for pregnancies of up to twelve weeks—I get to be the person I wish I could have been for my mom.

Before I even bought my first pair of scrubs, I attended a three-day abortion doula training run by The Doula Project, and then I shadowed experienced doulas. Since Doula Project interns and volunteers operate in a public hospital and at Planned Parenthood in New York City, the support that we provide to patients is limited to these spaces. Traditionally, a birth doula meets a client a few times before the birth and then makes a postpartum visit. With The Doula Project, I do not see the patients before or after their procedures; therefore, the training focused on how to hold space for them for those few moments we have the chance to provide support.

On the first day of training, the experienced doulas, who have devoted their lives to reproductive health, talked about The Doula Project and the principles of reproductive justice behind doula work. The Doula Project supplies services at low cost or free of charge. Our patients often come from low-income backgrounds and are people of color, so acknowledging that there are systemic barriers to getting a safe abortion makes us better doulas, because our politics need to match our intent. Some of us know about the socioeconomic issues through life experiences, while others must put in effort to understand them. Nevertheless, we cannot provide support for all people if we are the ones helping to perpetuate these barriers. The other days of the training focused on methods of support, self-care, and medical knowledge of abortion procedures, which depend on how far along the patient is.

It was a space of learning and relearning. I was extremely grateful for my experience relating to reproductive justice at Planned Parenthood. I only had to apply my knowledge to my doula practice. The learning part consisted of figuring out what exactly my doula practice would be. How would I convey that I was truly listening to a patient—eyes soft with sincerity as she confided in me? What kind of person did I want to be when confronted with someone else's adversity? The training had grave moments that made us question whether we were each capable of being doulas. I had my doubts when we got into groups and tried to figure out how to respond to real quotes from former patients, such as "God hates me. I'm going to Hell." Or when I thought about how I, as a non-Black person of color, navigate my activism and doula practice. Sometimes only experience can guide a doula through finding their narrative.

However, there were moments of laughter. One of the experienced doulas told us to pay attention to our surroundings, as it is one of our duties to talk over Pandora Radio when it plays questionable songs, like "Baby" by Justin Bieber. We compared our first gynecologist appointments over lunch and gushed over *The Great British Baking Show*. Humor and levity allowed us to cope with the difficulties that surround the subject of abortion, bringing normality to this extremely common procedure.

Although I can talk about abortions at the dinner table now, it was difficult for everyone at that training to ask questions or feel comfortable at certain points. Not everyone came into the training an expert on abortion. My fellow trainee cohort consisted of researchers, graduate students, therapists, alternative healers, and more, but we all had a common goal—to give love and support to our patients during a presidency that will be immortalized for its chaos.

Although we are not usually medically trained staff, it is important for us as doulas to understand the procedures so that we can help with the flow of the room instead of being hindrances and so that we can be informed advocates. I remember feeling nauseous watching a twenty-year-old medical school training video in which they performed an aspiration abortion, but what makes me nauseous now is that the video we watched is one of the only medically accurate videos online.

I guarantee that YouTubing "abortion video" will lead only to traumatizing, fake images that are used as pro-life propaganda. These are the images that are burned into the retinas of the patients who do their own research before they come in. Although the medical team reviews the procedure with each patient multiple times before the doctor even enters the room, having this background knowledge allows me to answer any questions a patient could have: *When will I be able to leave the recovery room? How long will this take?* Sometimes, if I sense that the patient is confused, I ask the doctor to go over the steps again.

The actual abortion only takes about five minutes; the rest is prepping, which is when we break out our doula tool kit: we introduce ourselves, answer questions, offer a hand to hold, offer a shoulder massage, and give advice on how to deal with cramps later on. Every time I do this, I wonder whether my mom was ushered out the door of the OB/GYN office into New York's unforgiving cold without a heat pack.

My experience with The Doula Project was different from that of most other volunteers because I was first an intern for the summer—meaning that I was in the clinic three or four times a week for five-hour shifts, while other doulas usually completed just two shifts a month. Being a doula, whether it is for twenty hours a week or once a month, means constantly checking in with one's own needs and energy levels. The self-care mantra was drilled into us through stories of burn-out by experienced doulas: "You can't take care of somebody else unless you take care of yourself first."

We were told to always take the time to reflect on our clinical experiences. Everyone brings their own traumas and politics into these spaces, and these things can motivate us, but being a doula means putting all of this aside to be present for the patient. The most important thing I learned from the training is that you cannot be a doula without knowing your own body—the body that nourishes you when you're feeding someone else, the body that doesn't falter when you tell it to. You don't think of your emotions as an entity until you lend them to somebody else. You swallow your heartache and lend your strength with a left hand firmly placed on a stranger's shoulder.

I was told at the training that when I was in the moment with a patient, I wouldn't cry.

This has been true for 99 percent of the patients I've been with, but compartmentalization comes with experience and practice. The only time I cried with a patient was when one woman told me she couldn't find the strength to get through another abortion if her partner didn't support her emotionally. She had curly brown hair and was much taller than me. It must have looked comical: a small, peach-skinned Asian girl who couldn't fit into her scrubs, holding her hand. She told me how strong she was the first time, how it almost broke her, but she didn't let it. She was determined to get through this one herself, because if her partner couldn't give it his all, he wouldn't be invited into her grieving in the first place. Many people can't wrap their heads around independent women who can feel vulnerable.

I cried because she reminded me of my mom, and I wanted to tell her so badly to get out of the relationship while she could, because she deserved more than someone who fell through on his promises. But being a doula is not about telling someone else what to do. Sometimes, the hardest part is not figuring out what to say, but having to silently listen.

Abortion stories are not one-size-fits-all. From the curly-haired woman who went home with her less-than-perfect boyfriend to the trans man who just needed me to remind him to breathe slowly, every single patient is so different. Thinking in terms of reproductive justice means respecting the choices that people make, whether they fit into your own paradigm or not, because there is a lifetime of experience that is hidden. Many people walk out of the clinic back into abusive homes, or are returning for their fourth abortion; sometimes the only thing a doula can do is make sure the patient has all the resources she needs, and be the one nonjudgmental person in her life at that moment.

People are resilient and will find a way to keep going until they can't anymore. When people are put into situations that make them cry into a stranger's hand, they will find a way to survive. Being able to access safe abortions is a freedom that brings people from all over the world to the United States. Although stigma and blocking of access is a very real threat to abortions, many people in other countries are not even allowed to demonstrate against archaic anti-abortion laws. Some presidencies are worse than others, but there will always be the voices of those who put their bodies on the line for abortions to combat those who seek to punish pregnant people. Examples of such brave organizations include the Jane Collective, the underground network that trained women to perform safe, cheap abortions even when they were illegal, and Women on Waves, with medical teams that provide contraceptives and information and that perform abortions on international waters outside of countries where abortion is illegal. There are women of every color fighting for the right to terminate a pregnancy, and it's critical to acknowledge the grassroots movements that continue to birth leaders with strong hands and steel voices.

Still, there is work to be done even in the most radical of movements. The world of reproductive health activism is still a field dominated by white women. Teaching white women about reproductive justice is not enough; the change will come when the room is full of people of all backgrounds.

Being a doula is a privilege, and the knowledge and experience that have given me my voice are privileges. I'm dedicating my life to uplifting the next daughter who learned first aid from putting Band-Aids on her mom, so that she does not have to see abortions, health care, or activism as unreachable. Learning about reproductive justice has given me a framework for understanding my work and the change I want to make in a way that doesn't require me to sacrifice my identity.

My presence as an Asian woman has made a difference in the procedure room as well as in the political battlefield. I am from a culture that does not discuss puberty, much less abortion. There is something very powerful about holding space for another woman of color. To have an ideology and be able to contribute to a cause

I believe in is empowering. At a time when all that can go wrong might go wrong, all I can do is hope that the hands I've held will find the strength to continue and fight as well.

To my mother: Thank you for molding me into the warrior I am. Thank you for giving me your hands, soft and calloused. Thank you for your anger and your relentless kindness.

Femme-Inism

Lessons of My Mother

PAULA AUSTIN

My mother taught me everything I know about "feminism," even if she didn't think she was teaching me. She taught me to work hard, to be hard, to fight mean, to fear love (to question love). She taught me the meaning of honor and retribution and fear, and pain that goes way back. She taught me what she knew. She taught me about desire and sex and sensuality. How to flirt, be coy and demure. How to be femme, a high diva, show off my cleavage. How to be looked at, how to be invisible and afraid. How to survive, to stay alive. She taught me what she could. About women's power and authority.

REFLECTIONS

I was four years old when my mother brought me and my three older sisters to the United States from British Guiana, a small Caribbean country on the northern tip of South America. The United States offered a different kind of access to higher education and the ability to change one's economic class, if you could play the game. My mother, Ena, had grown up in colonial British Guiana during the 1930s. She lived in rural Bartica, where people were poor and Black and struggled to feed their children. My grandmother washed the dirty laundry of rich white English people seven days a week.

She stood all day at the washer board and basin and then later at the ironing board. My grandfather had left his family when my mother was ten years old. As a child, my mother scrubbed floors to help her mother. My mother's education ended at the sixth grade. She says she "never had a head for school or book learning." She couldn't keep any job that she got. By the time she was sixteen, she had already had two nervous breakdowns and had been raped by a friend of the family. My mother eventually learned to self-medicate with alcohol. She also learned to do hair and sex work.

Ena's idea of strength lay in the power of her sexuality. Looking good and getting what you needed. On her limited budget she was always clean, well groomed, sexy. Heaving breasts, round, wide hips, hugged in by a long-line brassiere and girdle. Her hair wound up on the top of her head, pressed and shining with hair grease. She knew how to "get" things—money, kerosene to light the lamps, and food for her children. This was her work, to survive and keep her girls alive, while her husband—twenty years her senior—supported his other family across town.

Through her sex work my mother found reason to feel accomplished, adequate, of use to her family, sending her sister, Lucille, to school and feeding Lucille's children as well as her own. Ena found a means by which she could control both her life and her body. Even after my mother married at twenty-one, she continued to have several "boyfriends." There had always been men who coveted her, and she used this to her advantage at a time and in a country where dark-skinned, poor women like her had few opportunities outside of telephone operator, secretary, or teacher to make money. Colonialism, imperialism, and white supremacy created an economic separation between light-skinned Black women and white women, as smart women of leisure, and dark-skinned Black women as thick-headed laborers.

In 1984 I was sixteen. I was a junior in high school, in love with my best friend, Jennifer. This is the same year that Susan Brownmiller published her book *Femininity*. I did not read it until two years later, when I was taking a women's studies course at my liberal arts college in New York City. (It was unheard of that I would go away to college—only white kids did that. So I lived with my mother in Flatbush, Brooklyn, and took the subway to school and work each day.) Brownmiller discussed a femininity rooted in heterosexuality and a female-to-female competition for male attention. She talked about femininity as a type of "feminine armor," not a suit of metal in the traditional sense but rather an overstated and distorted display of weakness that was comforting and safe to men.

As a child, I often watched my mother from the bed. She would take out each clip from her hair, and rings of long, pressed black hair would unravel down her head. She brushed it hard, and back, and pinned it up and to the side. Then she twisted the back in a French roll and brushed a little bang behind her ear and pinned it there. She pulled on her control-fitted panty hose over her shapely thighs and ass. Over her hose she put on her girdle and fastened her long-line brassiere. Sometimes I would have to help pull the hook and eyes together behind her.

I often watched her do her makeup in front of the small mirror that sat on a tiny square table across from the bed I slept on, in the bedroom I shared with my mother and sister. She would dab some foundation from the bottle into her hand and smear it evenly across and around her face. She used concealer around her eyes and covered that with powder. She wore black eyeliner above and below her lid, which she administered with a pencil. She wore eye shadow and mascara. Lastly, she lined her lips, using some shade of burgundy. When she finished dressing, her shoes and pocketbook always matching, the room smelled like her expensive perfume long after she had gone.

This was her ritual each day, the donning of her costume. This was her feminine armor, her feminist attire. This was the very thing that brought her strength and power. I could tell this by the way she stepped out onto the street in her blue polyester floral dress that hugged her hips and thighs, her strong calves shaping down into her white pumps, her ass and pocketbook both swaying. Her sexy gait was evidence of her prowess, and both she and I were proud. She was unknowingly modeling for me.

When I was eleven or twelve, I was punished for wearing makeup. I would wait until my mother was out of the room at bedtime and I would sneak an eyeliner pencil from the makeup drawer, hid it under the bed. In the morning I would pretend I was looking for my shoes and slip the eyeliner into my pants pocket, sneaking it out of the house. Somewhere between the apartment door and the building's front door down five flights of stairs, I would hurriedly apply the makeup, lining my eyes with the blue pencil and combing on the black mascara I had stolen from Woolworths. I was never delicate enough. I was rough, rushed, and heavy-handed. Once applied, as hideous as it may have looked, I stepped out from that apartment building. Out onto Ocean Avenue in Flatbush, where I was a poor Black girl, living in someone else's apartment in an all-white neighborhood, where my family was seen as "the help." And at eight in the morning, on that street with all its white faces staring down at me, or not seeing me at all,

> **"My femme dance is reassuring to men. But there is also power, art, objective, resistance in it."**

I walked with my head high and made it to the bus stop without flinching. It was my armor, too.

MY RADICALISM

My introduction to what "feminism" was and what it could mean for me as a woman of color came when I was twenty. At my private, predominately white college, we read many things, including *This Bridge Called My Back: Radical Writings by Women of Color*. It was the first time I saw in print something I could identify with, the intersection of history, culture, oppression, and identity. It was a rite of passage for me. That year I came out as a lesbian, as visible in terms of my Caribbean culture and heritage, as an abused daughter of a wounded, alcoholic mother. Until this point my existence as a chunky, curly-haired, brown-skinned, large-chested girl had been very much about how to remain unseen. I felt ugly, undesirable, unlovable. During summers as a teenager, in the heat of my Brooklyn neighborhood—which was changing from Jewish affluent to Puerto Rican/West Indian working class—I had felt large and uncomfortable in my T-shirt and shorts as well as in my own skin. Now in college, I began to see myself and the world differently.

There I worked with five white women in a student group. We organized around "diversity" issues on our campus. I learned about leadership, voice, and coalition-building as we worked on racism, sexism, and homophobia at our school. We read and wrote together, staged actions, hung up signs, and held caucuses, panel discussions, and consciousness-raising groups. I learned about internalized oppression, not so much about racism as about sexism, and understood it to be at the heart of my desires for invisibility during those teen summers. Understood it to be at the heart of my sense of myself as ugly and undesirable—and simultaneously sexually perverted. (At this time I was being unhappily sexual with random men at my job.)

This internalization of all the destructive messages I had gotten over the years—which I continued to receive—about brown, round women was at the heart of my short stint of trying to deny my femme self (after I had come out) for a more politically correct (and accepted, by my white lesbian friends) androgynous presentation of myself. Still, in many ways this was an idyllic time: social activism and diversity work in a relatively safe environment. I wouldn't know the real impact of patriarchy and its intersection with racism, sexism, and homophobia until I left school.

After graduation I stayed in New York and found a job working as a secretary. I wanted to teach but wasn't quite sure how to do it, and I needed to support myself. I wanted to move out of my grandmother's apartment, which was downstairs from my mother's employer's apartment. It was this life, after school, where I would face my reality without the built-in support of women from college, with whom I had become accountable for fighting against injustice. There were mornings on the subway being felt up and doing nothing except enduring it. Sexual harassment at the gym and being too ashamed to even feel my indignation until much later. Without the anger and righteousness of my women friends, how could I remember that I had a right to my own body, a right to say no? What a privilege it had been to be able to sit and talk about these things, to scream our rage, to write essays. What would I do with this new sensibility? Out here, alone.

My mother had known racism. She understood its existence as a fact of life, a given. It wasn't something changeable, movable. It was something to be maneuvered around, waded through like muck and mire. It wasn't even something necessarily to be talked about. And she moved through it slowly, her pace crippled by clinical depression, little education, and hard work from an early age. I think she found some strength in doing hair and sex work. She always said to my sister and me, "You have two things against you: you're Black and you're a woman. Nothing is going to be easy." She would urge us to get an education so we would not have to "depend on a man." My sister and I would cringe at hearing ourselves referred to as "Black," certain that it wasn't a good thing. Often, in the same breath, my mother would urge us to marry white men, so that we would have babies with "good hair."

MY ARMOR

I always admired my mother's sense of what was powerful about herself: flirting. I remember hearing my mother on the phone or watching her with company. She flirted with everyone. It seemed a completely natural way of interaction. What I learned, listening to my mother's sultry voice—placating, or asking questions like a little girl, giggling, sighing, her eyes wide and suggestive—was that women who had this skill had power. Did the men, and women, she used this on know what she was doing? Did they allow themselves to be manipulated, or distracted from the task at hand? I don't know—not even now when I use my powers of flirt and distract.

It is moments like being stranded on the highway with a flat tire that what I have learned from my mother becomes necessary. I am on my way back from the beach with a white lover who looks like a boy. I am in a long cotton dress, slits up both sides, high heel sandals, hair in a curly pom-pom on the top of my head. We are somewhere between Durham and Wilmington, North Carolina. I am a northerner with all kinds of frightening stereotypes about the South, all of which come into play when I am stranded on the side of the road at dusk.

We trudge across the highway to what looks like a road toward a town, or a group of houses, at the very least. We end up at a bus repair shop. A man with a deep Southern drawl and greasy overalls emerges from the back of the shop to greet us. My lover is concerned about her baseball cap and butch appearance. I am concerned about being Black. Will I be raped or lynched? Will they realize the person I am with is not a boy? Even with all my fear, there is no question between us that my femme affect is the safest bet here. I ask to use the phone, saying we have broken down. My girlfriend nods, smiles, stands idly by. The man directs me to the phone and I call AAA. I tell them I have a flat tire. "I can't seem to get those screwy things off, you know, they hold the tire in place?" I say. The tone in my voice is of distress and silliness. I shift my weight from hip to hip, smiling at the greasy man as I wait for them to dispatch a truck. My girlfriend does not speak.

There is no real reason for me to maintain my femme performance on the phone with the AAA customer assistant. The garage attendant is not really paying attention to me. Still, I am deeply in character, and it brings me a sense of control in the midst of this danger, as does the two-inch elevation from my shoes, as does my lipstick. The donning of my armor helps to hold the anxiety and panic at bay until I can safely express myself later in the arms of my lover or with my friends.

Off the phone, I talk more with the greasy man about the "screwy things" that we could not seem to remove, and the jack, which we couldn't get to work. When the tow truck arrives, we squeeze into the front seat, with me next to the driver, a white man with a thick drawl, the smell of stale Coke and cigarettes permeating everything in the truck. He has had to move aside several girly magazines to make room for us. We drive ten miles before we can get back to the highway. In an effort to distract him from too much observation about the Black woman and white woman in his truck, one of whom looks suspiciously like a boy, I chatter. More conversation about the "screwy things."

"Lug nuts," he says.

"Oh, is that what they call them?" I giggle. "I just don't know a thing about changing a tire. And what is that?" I point toward the fields of crops as we whiz by.

"T'bacca."

"Ohhh, really, is that what it looks like?" More giggling. My lover's leg is anxiously pressed up against mine.

We finally make it back to my stranded car. The tow-truck guy hoists a large jack from his truck, upon which he begins lifting my car. I flit around him. "Man-size," I say, referring to the jack suggestively. I am aware of my play-acting, feeling powerful in the skill of it. He is responding to it. I think it brings comfort to him. I look the part, like my mama taught me.

The line is thin between the empowerment of "femme" and its potential self-destructiveness. I wonder if it was like this for my mother. She turned to sex work out of necessity. This is not something I have to do. Femme brings with it what we have learned about what it means to be female and woman in this country and culture. As many times as I have felt empowered by it, I have also found the power of my femme affect slipping away, leaving instead the ways I feel defeated, inept, unable to handle difficult situations. Rationally, I know these to be the messages of the oppressors and colonizers. Still, I have competed with other femmes for the attention of butches and transgender men. I have both claimed and loathed the titles of Jezebel and "Hoochie Mama" after having an affair with a woman who already had a wife. And even though this particular relationship was damaging, my femme self finds pride in having been able to steal this woman away from her partner, if only for a moment. Sometimes I hate that part of me.

FEMME-INISM

I have felt left out of feminism, mostly because it leaves out women who looked like my mother—traditionally feminine, of color, poor, powerful despite the impacts of oppression on her psyche. It leaves no room for women who find their power through a perceived powerlessness. Amber Hollibaugh—lesbian sex radical, ex-hooker, gypsy—says that it is no accident that there are so many femmes with a history of sex work. She talks about sex workers moving in the world differently than other women, with their heads held high. Men looked at my mother when she walked down the street, and she never looked down or away. This display of blatant subjectivity flies in the face of what we are taught as little girls, how to be a "good girl."

My femme dance is reassuring to men. But there is also power, art, objective, resistance in it. For my mother and myself, colonization and the battle against it poses a contradiction between appearances and deeper survivals. Joan Nestle, author and founder of the Lesbian Herstory Archives and general femme hero, has said, "There is a need to reflect the colonizer's image back at him yet at the same time to keep alive what is a deep part of one's culture, even if it is misunderstood by the oppressor, who omnipotently thinks he knows what he is seeing."[1]

For me and my mother, our femme existence and our femme performance have been the ways in which we have found pleasure in our bodies, wide-assed, round, and brown. Bodies that society teaches us to scorn. To ignore the way in which femmes reclaim ourselves is to seriously diminish our resistance. It is this resistance that is at the heart of my "femme-inism." My mother's feminism was limited, mixed in with very traditional West Indian and Catholic views of gender and sexuality.

There is no language that can create an understanding of how my femme identity and "feminism" function in me as one, with no space between them. The same way race, gender, sexuality, and class exist simultaneously in me, and how who I am is the filter through which I see everything. The same is true for my femme-inism. Maybe it is how I can reclaim my mother's high-femme practice in a more empowered way. To survive, I had to allow myself to be who I am, constrained for a while by the lesbian feminism of the 1970s, which rejected both butch and femme as a "heterosexist imitation of the oppressive gender roles of patriarchy."[2] Even though I came out as lesbian femme in the 1990s, when folks had begun to write about the separation of sex and gender, making room for the possibilities of gender play as itself a political and erotic option, there was still a very large community of lesbians, young and old, primarily middle class and white, who continued to subscribe to the lesbian feminism of the early women's movement.

I have only to look at my mother to see it is possible for me—and for many poor and working-class women who have struggled to support themselves and their families, who have struggled to be strong through the physical and emotional manifestations of oppression and colonization—to be both femme and feminist. The stories my mother has told me about herself—of an outrageous girl washing her naked self on the back steps in the twilight, of a mother starting a new life for herself and her children in a different country and culture, at the age of forty-two, of a woman whose empowerment knew many bounds, who did what she had to for her children to survive, a woman who somehow, in the midst of her own internalized oppression, transferred racial and gender pride, as well as she could, to her daughters—these stories I keep alive and recount as evidence of the strength of the women in my family.

These stories are the context of my femme-inism. The monster of colonization, acculturation, prejudice, discrimination, poverty, misogyny takes shape in me as I struggle here to bring together, in myself, these two aspects of my mother, which her life only hints at—her true and deep passion and sexuality and her strength to proactively address the limitations of her situation.

Feminist Musings on the No. 3 Train

PHOENIX SOLEIL

I joke that my mom's and my aunt's problems all stem from the Trinity: the omnipotent rules that they accept faithfully without question, the savior man who will marry them and save them, and the Holy Ghosts—the men who are actually in their lives. I came up with that insight on the No. 3 subway train, leaving my mom's home after a visit. In transit between my mom's world and mine, insights like these pour out. If feminism is in the water I drink, my mom's herstory is the dry land that pushes me to swallow.

The actual men in their lives were helpful but more in the background: the Holy Ghosts. My mom grew up in Haiti, where she married my father, and then moved to New York. He left her and returned to Haiti shortly after I was born. He sent me letters and money until he died. My aunt came to live with us a couple of years after my grandmother came. My aunt was "waiting" for a husband. Boyfriends appeared and eventually left. My grandmother came closest to the ideal—she married once, stayed married until her death, had children and grandchildren. She was the matriarch who raised seven children as well as nieces and nephews in Haiti. When my mother was growing up, my grandmother was effectively a single mother, because my grandfather had to live far away from her and the children in the isolated countryside, farming and sending her money. She came to New York to help my mother raise me. She prayed a lot. She rarely talked about herself. She died when I was young.

My uncles would help out doing "manly" things, like driving my mother, grandmother, and aunt places and fixing things that my mom would not even let me near because I was a girl. I noticed men were given more space and authority and took it. My mom said that men drink beer, so we had beer in the fridge just for the suitors and our male relatives. I was told that if I had had a father, I wouldn't have rebelled so much, because he would have beaten it out of me. Some of the men in my extended family were kind and gentle, while others were hard and authoritarian. They were all in the background, peripheral to the women.

My family raised me to wait: for Catholic Armageddon, for a husband, and, once I found the husband, to wait on him. I balked at this. But even as I rebelled, I was afraid I wouldn't escape from the future they projected for me. I lump all of their self-defeating ideas that no amount of discussion and reasoning could change with the first part of the triumvirate—the omnipotent rules, a hodgepodge of beliefs that were often contradictory but sacrosanct. According to these rules, the ideal for a woman was that she stay at home. A woman cooks, cleans, and takes care of the children while her husband works. A woman should be obedient to her husband. They argued women shouldn't be allowed to be priests because they were too frivolous and weak. I wondered who in this network of strong women, extended family included, was frivolous and weak. Yet these women also demonstrated their respect for females with beliefs such as that girls take better care of their elderly parents than boys do.

The strange thing about my family is that most of the time they were feminists in action. The life I have now and the choices I enjoy are due to my mother's sacrifices and her faith. Even as I condemn my female relatives' sexism, I realize they were fighters, surviving and doing things on their own every day. My mom got up and went to work, her example telling me that I could do it as well. She immigrated to America to give me a better life. The women in my life told me I had to do well in school. My mom taught me to read before first grade, which was probably the determining factor in my later academic success. When I graduated from high school, my mom and aunt got uncharacteristically emotional, remarking that it looked like I was going to make it. I have inherited from these women a very pragmatic way of looking at the world, because they did whatever was necessary to get the job done.

> " The strange thing about my family is that most of the time they were feminists in action. "

It is hard going and coming from my mom's and aunt's home. In that journey, I leave the world I've created behind—a world that is flourishing, full of goals, joys, challenges, and possibilities—to enter a very desolate world. They worry about this, they suffer from that, but even when there isn't anything pressing, there is still the dead air. Although they have pushed me to incredible heights, they themselves are stuck. I help but I haven't solved the problem. On the train to and from, I'm looking for understanding.

One of my cousins who grew up in Haiti told me I don't know Haitians. I know my family in New York, and they are a pretty unhappy bunch. She had a point. The calmest and happiest I have ever seen my mother was when we visited Haiti together. There, my extended family seemed to have lighter hearts and more everyday joy. I realized that my mother sacrificed her emotional health coming to the United States. It is hard to be a single mother and an immigrant. It is all speculation how culture, sexism, racism, classism, and personality played a part in my mom's life. What I know is that my mom's sacrosanct belief in the inferiority of women and their role in the world didn't help. It is still not helping. She survived and is surviving. However, I feel she would survive better and, more importantly, be happier without that noose around her neck.

When I visited Haiti as a nine-year-old, I noticed that people spent time in each other's houses. It was very social. One of the games was to tell stories. It is hard to believe my aunt's stories of my mother going out dancing when she was young. Living in the United States made it easy for my mom's life to become small. She never made New York her home. My experiences in France and West Africa have given me a better appreciation of how hard it is to create a new life in a foreign land. People who are able to make a foreign country their home have to be bold and aggressive. My mom was bold and aggressive when she had to be in order to care for her family, but she never put value on *pleasi*, pleasures. Putting effort into making her life in the United States more pleasurable would have seemed extravagant to her. Pleasure is nice if you get it, but you don't fight for it. In Haiti, knowing the language and the culture, she would not have felt isolated. It would have been easier to make connections with new people. Now, all of her friends in New York are people she was friends with in Haiti. She has never had much of a social life in New York. She has spent a lot of her free time praying, watching TV, and sleeping. Religion has been her succor. It has also fed her tendency to keep her life small, with its concentration on passivity and the afterlife.

My mother is living for the afterlife. Once, when she found me crying about something, she said that we're not meant to be happy, that this life is about suffering, and we'll have happiness in heaven.

An important difference between my mom's personality and mine is the value I place on my own wants, needs, and feelings in the here and now. She put an incredible amount of energy into raising me but none into herself. I grew up with greater economic stability, so perhaps that is why I insisted on creating a life that met my emotional and spiritual needs in the here and now. I carry some guilt about this.

My aunt is currently suffering from many maladies, but everyone in my family agrees her trouble stems from depression. She's never been married in a culture that teaches her that it is her job to be a wife. In her world she has had few choices. I wish she'd grown up in a place where she was encouraged to make up her own path and look beyond the choices presented to her by family and culture.

It frustrated me when I was growing up that if something broke in the house they'd lament that if only we had a man in the house, "he could fix things." I did not want them to feel helpless or to feel helpless myself. So I'd go over and fix the TV or VCR or put the fan together. But they'd still go on: "Our lives would be so much better if we had a man in the house." When I'd present the fixed item to them, they'd put on a surprised smile, but I knew I hadn't solved the problem. Years later, I surprised them with a career playing with computer technology and the Internet.

I can understand missing male companionship, but that wasn't the way they talked about it. They talked about the "savior" man specifically within the context of social security and economic survival. I understand that when two people share a life together there are economic benefits, but those benefits were at the forefront of the way the women I grew up with talked about men. This wasn't just limited to discussions about husbands. I noticed that whenever we got into conversations about family, my mom said she wanted children, because she wanted someone to take care of her when she grew older. I was ten when I asked her, "What does a husband do?" In her words: "He would advocate for me. People take advantage of you when you are a woman alone. He would know of opportunities and fight for us in the world."

I understood her answer better after I visited Gambia and Senegal in West Africa. The inability of most women there to achieve financial and social independence underpinned gender inequality in that region. Women were so absent from public culture in Dakar that they were hardly seen walking in the streets. I am sure they had their own culture and life separate from male society, but that male society is the one with access to the public space, the finances, and the political power. A Western-educated Gambian man explained to me that there are some very strong Gambian women who become successful, and they can be very vocal, but there is a line and they will not cross it. I believe my older female relatives grew up in a similar atmosphere. They learned to depend on men to act for them. Even when they take care of themselves, they never stop emotionally or psychologically depending on men...as if they were the Holy Ghost. It seems to be another excuse not to live for themselves, not to create happiness for themselves.

I've had discussions with friends about whether people who grow up under oppression with no access to alternatives know that their situations are wrong. I believe they feel it even if they aren't able to articulate it to themselves. They may not know how to attach this background of oppression to the cause of their current situations, and therefore accept it as normal, but it is there. My mom's and aunt's adherence to the prescribed female role is like an invisible noose around their necks constricting their ability to reach their potential. They live out the effects of it.

The difference between my situation and that of my mom is degree. My mother's access to information, wealth, and power was disadvantaged, and she accepted this as the natural way of the world. Her ideas about family were bound up with the idea of economic and social security. But I live in a society that gives me choices, choices that men in other countries can't exercise. It is easier for me to imagine independence without relating to family and husband. I owe a debt to the feminist movement that I can get a job, live alone, and walk around in jeans and a T-shirt without getting harassed. My mom's concern about economic security adds an urgency to conversations about family that I—with my Western, highly educated background—don't relate to. At the same time, I've grown up with my own issues around gender, race, and class. My access to information, wealth, and power was also at a disadvantage, but I don't accept that as natural.

My impression of life growing up in a working-class Caribbean neighborhood was that you had to be very worried about surviving. Life was hard and difficult, and you had to make as much money as you could to be safe. After moving into the white, liberal arts college world, I was presented with the idea that life is a challenge or an adventure, and you must find the work that will make you happy (notice the word "happy"). I did not want the unpleasant, passionless future of my upbringing; however, the other future of my well-to-do classmates seemed like a fantastic dream. There was a conflict in these two realities, and I did not know how to reconcile them. I took a leap of faith. I ended up living my life searching for and creating my own happiness, despite doubting the workability of this path. It worked for me. Armed with a good education, I had more choices than the people I grew up with. I will probably never have to clean houses like my mom and my aunt. I realize there is not one reality; many realities coexist.

I am conscious of the distance between my family's world and my mostly American life. I look for insight wherever I can find it to help me navigate that space. I hope to understand what happened with my mom and gain some wisdom. I get a lot of the "aha" factor when I think about how gender roles and sexism have framed my life and my mom's. The "aha" factor is when you have always felt something, but couldn't articulate it until someone gives you a naming system that allows you to point at all the pieces. While in Gambia a couple of years after college, I was criticized at a market by a female merchant for being too aggressive when I negotiated for price. She said I was acting like a man and should remember that I am just a girl. I felt horrible and wondered if I had been rude, when I realized her criticism that "I wasn't acting like a girl" came from her acceptance of gender roles and male privilege. By analyzing the incident in this way, I was also creating a mental world where things can be different.

When I was a child, I sensed my family's fear and helplessness even when I didn't understand where it was coming from. This was their reality. My tendency was to think the problem was with me and try to adapt. I thought that if this was my reality, too, maybe I needed to stop fighting it and just deal with it. Wanting something that isn't possible hurts. But my growing feminist thought encouraged me to validate those feelings and find a way to honor them. Now when my aunt says that I dress too masculine and I won't attract a man, I still feel cornered. I also feel grounded, however, because

I understand where she's coming from. I have decided on a way of thinking that puts my honest expression of self above the loss of social standing in my family.

I wasn't just fighting religious doctrine and sexist dogma but a cultural sociohistorical worldview. A teacher once described the Haitians in her class as very obedient and polite. I said that's because their families will beat them if they get in trouble. Sensing my disapproval, she said it is good that they discipline their kids. Yes, but it can be taken too far when they instill fear of authority and beat the spirit out of their children. My mom's concern that I act submissively can be partly attributed to coming from a country where people who stand up get mowed down.

My mom felt that if I loved her, I should obey her in all things and accept everything she said as the truth. When I disobeyed, she'd say, "Even a dog knows his master." As a five-year-old, I had the unarticulated idea that love shouldn't be so limiting. To my Haitian Catholic mom I was a freak. Home was a battleground. My mother would say horrible things to me every day in an effort to make me more docile. I was bad when I laughed too hard. I was bad when I disagreed with my uncle's reasoning. I was bad for running around the house. Their definition of "good" was synonymous with passivity.

One day, on the train after a visit, I realized my mother and my aunt have been too "good" their whole lives. They were the extremes—like my mom not remarrying because, as a devout Catholic, she felt she was still married to my father, even though he was the one who lied to her and left. The rumor about my aunt was that she'd had a great love in Haiti who had wanted to marry her. Her family had been against it, so she'd broken off the relationship. These women followed the rules they were taught too well, and they've paid for it. I watch them still paying for it. When I look at my extended family, I notice that the women who were "bad"—those who did their own thing—are the happiest now. Some of the cousins my age growing up in Haiti are very assertive. On the whole, the female relatives of my mom's generation are more traditional, but even in that group my mother and aunt are extremes.

As a kid I'd watch my mother sit in the living room with a worried frown. I wanted her to stop worrying. I'd ask her what was wrong, and she'd tell me, "Problems. Too many problems." She worried about money, my safety, our health, and more. She was always worried something would knock her off the little bit of peace she had. In one such conversation, my mom mentally handed me a picture of her, my aunt, and my grandmother and me on the streets of New York with no place to go. I fear she carried that picture with her every day of her life. She'd sigh, "If only I had a husband."

My aunt would take me aside periodically and tell me that her most cherished wish was that I get married soon and have a family. Even though I understood her Catholicism and her sexist upbringing, I wanted her to question this belief, so I finally asked, "Why in the face of all the bad marriages do you still think that marriage is some type of guarantee of future happiness?"

"Do you want to become like me, alone, without anyone to take care of you?" she replied.

"Mom married with all her Catholic faithfulness and my father left her, and I'm always overhearing some family gossip about some couple divorcing," I said.

"But you'll have the children. Even if your husband leaves you, you will have the children." Ahhh. The Haitian Catholic version of the sperm donor. My mom's response was less radical: "I'm praying for a good husband for you. He won't leave you."

In my mom's old age, she now imagines there is a man who comes into the house and moves things around. She's sure she left so and so here, and now it is not here. "But Mom, why would he leave the TV, VCR, and jewelry alone?" I ask her.

"It's a very strange world. You don't know all the strange things in it," she says.

And of course he's a man *musha-a*, a mister. I believe he is the devil counterpart, a flip side of the savior, the man who was supposed to save her in the triumvirate. After waiting so long, she made up a demon to take his place.

I'm like my mom in that I want salvation. She tried to escape her existence through prayer. I don't think she believed it was possible to find happiness in this world. I've looked for salvation in love, friends, work, theater, filmmaking, writing, books, and myself. It is a struggle. I've been saved in little and big ways. I wish my mother would find happiness while I'm here to see it.

Waiting is what I fear. That's what I realized on a subway ride from a visit to my mom and aunt. I'm not scared of ending up like my aunt as much as I'm scared of spending my whole life existing in that passive position. Every time they ask me about marriage, I feel my own answer to myself: If I'm not waiting, I have to find the courage to make something happen.

GOING THROUGH CUSTOMS

Chappals and Gym Shorts

An Indian Muslim Woman in the Land of Oz

ALMAS SAYEED

It was finals week during the spring semester of my sophomore year at the University of Kansas, and I was buried under mounds of papers and exams. The stress was exacerbated by long nights, too much coffee, and a chronic, building pain in my permanently splintered shins (left over from an old sports injury). Between attempting to understand the nuances of Kant's *Critique of Pure Reason* and applying the latest game-theory models to the 1979 Iranian Revolution, I was regretting my decision to pursue majors in philosophy, women's studies, *and* international studies.

My schedule was not exactly permitting much downtime. With a full-time school schedule, a part-time job at Lawrence's domestic violence shelter, and preparations to leave the country in three weeks, I was grasping to hold on to what little sanity I had left. Wasn't living in Kansas supposed to be more laid back than this? After all, Kansas was the portal to the magical land of Oz, where wicked people melted when doused with mop water, and bright red, sparkly shoes could substitute for the services of American Airlines, providing a quick getaway. Storybook tales aside, the physical reality of this period was that my deadlines were inescapable. Moreover, the most pressing of these deadlines was completely non-school-related: my dad, on his way home to Wichita, was coming for a brief visit. This would be his first stay by himself, without Mom to accompany him or act as a buffer.

Dad visited me the night before my most difficult exam. Having just returned from spending time with his family—a group of people with whom he historically had an antagonistic relationship—Dad seemed particularly relaxed into his stocky six-foot-four frame. Wearing one of the more subtle of his nineteen cowboy hats, he arrived at my door, hungry, greeting me in Urdu, our mother tongue, and laden with gifts from Estée Lauder for his only daughter. Never mind that I rarely wore makeup and would have preferred to see the money spent on my electric bill or a stack of feminist theory books from my favorite used bookstore. If Dad's visit was going to include a conversation about how little I use beauty products, I was not going to be particularly receptive.

"Almas," began my father from across the dinner table, speaking in his British-Indian accent infused with his love of Midwestern colloquialisms. "You know that you won't be a spring chicken forever. While I was in Philadelphia, I realized how important it is for you to begin thinking about our culture, religion, and your future marriage plans. I think it is time we began a two-year marriage plan so you can find a husband and start a family. I think twenty-two will be a good age for you. You should be married by twenty-two."

I needed to begin thinking about the "importance of tradition" and be married by twenty-two? This, from the only Indian man I knew who had Alabama's first album on vinyl and loved to spend long weekends in his rickety, old camper near Cheney Lake, bass fishing and listening to traditional Islamic Qawwali music? My father, in fact, in his youth had been crowned "Mr. Madras," weight-lifting champion of 1965, and had left India to practice medicine and be an American cowboy in his spare time. But he wanted *me* to aspire to be a "spring chicken," maintaining some unseen hearth and home to reflect my commitment to tradition and culture.

Dad continued: "I have met a boy that I like for you very much. Masoud's son, Mahmood. He is a good Muslim boy, tells great jokes in Urdu, and is a promising engineer. We should be able to arrange something. I think you will be very happy with him!" Dad concluded with a satisfied grin.

Masoud, Dad's cousin? This would make me and Mahmood distant relatives of some sort. And Dad wants to "arrange something"? I had brief visions of being paraded around a room, serving tea to strangers in a sari or a *shalwar kameez* (a traditional South Asian outfit for women) wearing a long braid and *chappals* (flat Indian slippers), while Dad boasted of my domestic capabilities to increase my attractiveness to potential suitors. I quickly flipped through my mental Rolodex of rhetorical devices acquired during years of women's studies classes and found the card blank. No doubt, even feminist scholar Catharine MacKinnon would have been rendered speechless sitting across the table in a Chinese restaurant speaking to my overzealous father.

It is not that I hadn't already dealt with the issue. In fact, we had been here before, ever since the marriage proposals began (the first one came when I was fourteen). Of course, when they first began, it was a family joke, as my parents understood that I was to continue my education. The jokes, however, were always at my expense: "You received a proposal from a nice boy living in our mosque. He is studying medicine," my father would come and tell me with a huge, playful grin. "I told him that you weren't interested because you are too busy with school. And anyway, you can't cook or clean." My father found these jokes particularly funny, given my dislike of household chores. In this way, the eventuality of figuring out how to deal with these difficult issues was postponed with humor.

Dad's marriage propositions also resembled conversations that we had already had about my relationship to Islamic practices specific to women, some negotiated in my favor, and others simply shelved for the time being. Just a year ago, Dad had come to me while I was home for the winter holidays, asking me to begin wearing *hijab*, the traditional headscarf worn by Muslim women. I categorically refused, maintaining respect for those women who chose to do so. I understood that for numerous women, as well as for Dad, hijab symbolized something much more than covering a woman's body or hair; it symbolized a way to adhere to religious and cultural traditions in order to prevent complete Western immersion. But even my sympathy for this concern didn't change my feeling that hijab constructed me as a woman first and a human being second. Veiling seemed to reinforce the fact that inequality between the sexes was a natural, inexplicable phenomenon that is impossible to overcome, and that women should cover themselves, accommodating an unequal hierarchy, for the purposes of modesty and self-protection. I couldn't reconcile these issues and refused my father's request to don the veil. Although there was tension—Dad claimed I had yet to have my religious awakening—he chose to respect my decision.

Negotiating certain issues had always been part of the dynamic between my parents and me. It wasn't that I disagreed with them about everything. In fact, I had internalized much of the Islamic perspective of the female body while simultaneously admitting to its problematic nature. (To this day, I would rather wear a wool sweater than a bathing suit in public, no matter how sweltering the weather.) Moreover, Islam became an important part of differentiating myself from other American kids who did not have to find a balance between two opposing cultures. Perhaps Mom and

Dad recognized the need to concede certain aspects of traditional Islamic norms, because for all intents and purposes, I had been raised in the breadbasket of America.

By the time I hit adolescence, I had already established myself outside of the social norm of the women in my community. I was an athletic teenager, a competitive tennis player, and a budding weightlifter. After a lot of reasoning with my parents, I was permitted to wear shorts to compete in tennis tournaments, but I was not allowed to show my legs or arms (no tank tops) outside of sports. It was a big deal for my parents to have agreed to allow me to wear shorts in the first place. The small community of South Asian Muslim girls my age growing up in Wichita became symbols of the future of our community in the United States. Our bodies became the sites to play out cultural and religious debates. Much in the same way that Lady Liberty had come to symbolize idealized stability in the *terra patria* of America, young South Asian girls in my community were expected to embody the values of a preexisting social structure. We were scrutinized for what we said and for what we wore, for being seen with boys in public, and for lacking grace and piety. Needless to say, because of disproportionate muscle mass, crooked teeth, huge Lucy glasses, and a disposition to walk pigeon-toed, I was not among the favored.

To add insult to injury, Mom nicknamed me "Amazon Woman," lamenting the fact that she—a beautiful, petite lady—had produced

> " South Asian girls in my community were expected to embody the values of a preexisting social structure. We were scrutinized for what we said and for what we wore, for being seen with boys in public, and for lacking grace and piety. "

such a graceless, unfeminine creature. She was horrified by how freely I got into physical fights with my younger brother and arm-wrestled boys at school. She was particularly frustrated by the fact that I could not wear her beautiful Indian jewelry, especially her bangles and bracelets, because my wrists were too big. Special occasions, when I had to slather my wrists with tons of lotion in order to squeeze my hands into her tiny bangles, often bending the soft gold out of shape, caused us both infinite amounts of grief. I was the snot-nosed younger sibling of the Bollywood (India's Hollywood) princess that my mother had in mind as a more appropriate representation of an Indian daughter. Rather, I loved sports, sports figures, and books. I hated painful makeup rituals and tight jewelry.

It wasn't that I had a feminist awakening at an early age. I was just an obnoxious kid who did not understand the politics raging around my body. I did not possess the tools to analyze or understand my reaction to this process of social conditioning and normalization until many years later, well after I had left my parents' house and the Muslim community in Wichita. By positioning me as a subject of both humiliation and negotiation, Mom and Dad had inadvertently laid the foundations for me to understand and scrutinize the process of conditioning women to fulfill particular social obligations.

What was different about my dinner conversation with Dad that night was a sense of immediacy and detail. Somehow discussion about a "two-year marriage plan" seemed to encroach on my personal space much more than had previous jokes about my inability to complete my household chores or pressure to begin wearing hijab. I was meant to understand that when it came to marriage, I was up against an invisible clock (read: social norms) that would dictate how much time I had left: how much time I had left to remain desirable, attractive, and marriageable. Dad was convinced that it was his duty to ensure my long-term security in a manner that reaffirmed traditional Muslim culture in the face of an often hostile foreign community. I recognized that the threat was not as extreme as being shipped off to India in order to marry someone I had never met. The challenge was far more subtle than this. I was being asked to choose my community; capitulation through arranged marriage would show my commitment to being Indian, to being a good Muslim woman, and to my parents by proving that they had raised me with a sense of duty and the willingness to sacrifice for my culture, religion, and family.

There was no way to tell Dad about my complicated reality. Certain characteristics of my current life already indicated failure by such standards. I was involved in a long-term relationship with a white man, whose father was a prison guard on death row, an occupation that would have mortified my upper-middle-class, status-conscious parents. I was also struggling with an insurmountable crush on an *actress* in the Theater and Film Department. I was debating my sexuality in terms of cultural compatibility as well as gender. Moreover, there was no way to tell Dad that my social circle was supportive of these nontraditional romantic explorations. My friends in college had radically altered my perceptions of marriage and family. Many of my closest friends, including my roommates, were coming to terms with their own life choices, having recently come out of the closet but unable to tell their families about their decisions. I felt inextricably linked to this group of women, who, like me, often had to lead double lives. The immediacy of fighting for issues such as queer rights, given the strength and beauty of my friends' romantic relationships, held far more appeal for me than the topics of marriage and security that my father broached over our Chinese dinner. There was no way to explain to my loving, charismatic, steadfastly religious father, who was inclined to the occasional violent outburst, that a traditional arranged marriage not only conflicted with the feminist ideology I had come to embrace, but it seemed almost petty in the face of larger, more pressing issues.

Although I had no tools to answer my father that night at dinner, feminist theory had provided me with the tools to understand *why* my father and I were engaged in the conversation in the first place. I understood that in his mind, Dad was fulfilling his social obligation as father and protector. He worried about my economic stability and, in a roundabout way, my happiness. Feminism and community activism had enabled me to understand these things as part of a prescribed role for women. At the same time, growing up in Kansas and coming to feminism here meant that I had to reconcile a number of different issues. I am a Muslim, first-generation Indian, feminist woman studying in a largely homogeneous white, Christian community in Midwestern America. What sacrifices are necessary for me to retain my familial relationships as well as a sense of personal autonomy informed by Western feminism?

The feminist agenda in my community is centered on ending violence against women, fighting for queer rights, and maintaining women's reproductive choices. As such, the way that I initially became involved with this community was through community projects such as "Womyn Take Back the Night," attending pride rallies, and working at the local domestic violence shelter. I am often the only woman of color in feminist organizations and at feminist events. Despite having grown up in the Bible Belt, it is difficult for me to relate to stories told by my closest friends of being raised on cattle ranches and farms, growing up Christian by default, and experiencing the strict social norms of small, religious communities in rural Kansas. Given the context of this community—a predominantly white, middle-class college town—I have difficulty explaining that my feminism has to address issues like, "I should be able to wear *both* hijab *and* shorts if I choose to." The enormity of our agenda leaves little room to debate issues equally important but applicable only to me, such as the meaning of veiling, arranged marriages versus dating, and how the north-south divide uniquely disadvantages women in the developing world.

It isn't that the women in my community ever turn to me and say, "Hey you, brown girl, stop diluting our priorities." To the contrary, the majority of active feminists in my community are eager to listen and understand my sometimes divergent perspective. We have all learned to share our experiences as women, students, mothers, partners, and feminists. We easily relate to issues of male privilege, violence against women, and figuring out how to better appreciate the sacrifices made by our mothers. From these commonalities we have learned to work together, creating informal social networks to complete community projects.

The difficulty arises when trying to put this theory and discussion into practice. Last year, when our organization, the Womyn's Empowerment Action Coalition, began making plans for the Womyn Take Back the Night march and rally, a number of organizers were eager to include the contribution of a petite white belly dancer in the pre-march festivities. When I voiced my concern that historically belly dancing had been used as a way to objectify women's bodies in the Middle East, one of my fellow organizers (and a very good friend) laughed and called me a prude: "We're in Kansas, Almas," she said. "It doesn't mean the same thing in our culture. It is different here than over *there*." I understood what she meant, but having just returned from seven months in the West Bank, Palestine, two months before, for me over there *was* over here. In the end, the dance was included, but I wondered about our responsibility to women outside of the United States and our obligation to address the larger social and cultural issues of the dance itself.

To reconcile the differences between my own priorities and those of the women I work with, I am learning to bridge the gap between the feminist canon of Western white women (with the occasional African American or Chicana) and my own experience as a first-generation Indian Muslim woman living in the Midwest. I struggle with issues like cultural differences, colonialism, Islam, and feminism and how they relate to one another. The most difficult part has been to get past my myopic vision of simply laying feminist theory written by Indian, Muslim, or postcolonial theorists on top of American Western feminism. With the help of feminist theory and other feminists, I am learning to dissect Western models of feminism, trying to figure out what aspects of these models can be applied to certain contexts. To this end, I have had the privilege of participating in projects abroad in pursuit of understanding feminism in other contexts.

For example, while living with my extended family in India, I worked for a microcredit affiliate that advised women on how to get loans and start their own businesses. During this time I learned about the potential of micro-enterprise as a weapon against the feminization of poverty. Last year, I spent a semester in the West Bank, Palestine, studying the link between women and economics in transitional states, and beginning to understand the importance of women's efforts during revolution. These experiences have been invaluable to me as a student of feminism and women's mobilization efforts. They have also shaped my personal development, helping me understand where the theoretical falls short of solving for the practical. In Lawrence, I maintain my participation in local feminist projects. Working in three different contexts has highlighted the amazing and unique ways in which feminism develops in various cultural settings yet still maintains certain commonalities.

There are few guidebooks for women like me who are trying to negotiate the paradigm of feminism in two different worlds. There is a delicate dance here that I must master—a dance of negotiating identity within interlinking cultural spheres. When I am faced with the movement's expectations of my commitment to local issues, it becomes important for me to emphasize that differences in culture and religion are also "local issues." This has forced me to change my frame of reference, developing from a rebellious tomboy who resisted parental imposition to a budding social critic, learning how to be a committed feminist and still keep my cultural, religious, and community ties. As for family, we still negotiate de spite the fact that Dad's two-year marriage plan has yet to come to fruition in this, my twenty-second year.

Migrant Organizing
A Retelling

SONIA GUIÑANSACA

November 2016. My mother sends me a text, "Ganó el Trump." My throat tightens and my chest collapses into an incredible heartache. I am glad she did not call me, because I have no idea how to answer, what kind of lies to make up, or what kind of miracles to wish for. I don't want to tell my undocumented mother what this means for our migrant communities.

This all feels completely different compared to when Obama won the election in 2008. On the campaign trail, he had promised to help undocumented youth like me. He had promised to help my mother, father, and grandpa. The night he became the first Black president of the United States, I was at a bar on Twenty-Third Street in Manhattan with migrant organizers, and we cheered until our lungs had had enough. Not only was my president Black, but the first lady would be a Black woman who had grown up in Chicago and looked like every teacher and professional I'd looked up to. Two Black girls would be running around the White House. Oh, how we cried that night. For us, young women of color, to watch Michelle, Malia, and Sasha onstage affirmed our right to this country. Laughter filled the streets of the city. A new time for people of color was finally here.

But nothing changed, did it? More deportations took place under Obama. There was a rise of deaths at the border, a rise of privatized detention centers, a rise of unaccompanied minors crossing. There was no comprehensive immigration reform or amnesty, and the Dream Act never passed.

What did change was the rise of undocumented young people organizing.

REWIND

I leave Ecuador in 1995, around the same time Tupac is signing to Death Row Records. I migrate at the age of five to reunite with my parents in New York City. My dad came before I was born, and my mom a year or two after she gave birth to me. But I want it to be known that I existed before "migration." I existed in a magical, multidimensional way with my parents. In those years, before text messages, before Skype and FaceTime, I spoke to my parents on payphones with calling cards.

We survive through phone lines
A cycle of dialing numbers
On the other line waited abuela
On the other line waited memories
On the other line waited birthday wishes
That should have been given in person
While eating guava cake
But we were here
And you were there
On the other line we waited
By payphones we waited
For your voice we waited
That is all we had

When I arrived in New York, my parents came to pick me up from the care of the man who had brought me. I was seated on a plastic-covered couch in a Brooklyn apartment wearing denim overalls and sporting a bad bob haircut. I had a mouthful of cavities. I did not recognize my parents. I'd had no way of knowing what they looked like because we'd been dirt poor in Ecuador, and no one could afford cameras. I had to hear their voices.

My parents, however, did know what I looked like, because distant relatives who would come to Ecuador would visit us and record videos of me dancing and walking around el campo. There is a video of me singing to *Dos Mujeres, Un Camino* in my dad's video collection.

My parents enrolled me in PS 161, where Dominican, Mexican, and Puerto Rican kids were all too familiar with migration. We "assimilated" into the public school system. Our names lost the tildes over the n's. We memorized the Pledge of Allegiance, and we entered linguistic warfare when our Spanish was seen as basic and we were made to learn and speak "proper English."

My undocumented status did not come up so much during this time. At home, it was normal to discuss immigration status; we knew that my parents and my grandpa and I were waiting for "papers." When will our immigration papers come? No one knew. My own immigration status and shaming was not something I had to think about, but I worried for my parents whenever they went to work, or when my dad drove around without a license. This became our prayer: *Avoid. Police. Avoid. Handcuffs. Avoid. Deportation.*

ALGUN DÍA

When I was in middle school and given an opportunity to go out of state for a school trip, my parents told me I could not go. I didn't have the identification to get on a plane. So I stayed put in our neighborhood in Harlem. *Algun día*, they told me. Algun día became two, five, eight, ten, eleven, fifteen years later. In high school, my strict global studies teacher, Mr. Murphy, and English teacher, Mrs. Greene, introduced me to the Young Lords, the Black Panthers, Assata Shakur, Toni Morrison, and many other brilliant Black writers and poets. These readings comforted me as I began to think about college and my future. Here were cultural workers who had chronicled their times by weaving stories and critiques of race and class. I only saw them in these two dimensions.

Feminism did not make its way down Adam Clayton Powell Jr. Boulevard toward my high school, or at least not the academic jargon. I understood feminism informally. It was the absence of Black women heroes in Black History Month, or Latina women heroes in Hispanic Month, or why Mami was paid less than her cis men coworkers, or why many migrant women were doing domestic work.

While I was in high school, my parents took multiple odd jobs to pay rent and bills. Some weekdays, I would accompany them to deliver newspapers. Waking up at 3 a.m., we headed to a warehouse where mostly Black and Brown migrants rolled up newspapers and coupons with those damn rubber bands that snapped on your fingers if you pulled too tight. I pulled them tight so many times, trying to rush so that we could go home early, so that my dad could get some sleep before his other job.

I also interpreted for my parents in situations where they needed someone who could speak English. Gulping down my fears, I stood in between the cable company and my dad. I had to interpret every single word perfectly. This was my service to my parents for their hard work.

As I grew older, I learned how to code-switch and how to fend for my parents. They deserved this and much more. The statement

I will provide for them became almost a song on loop in my mind. Because I wanted to take care of them, it was hard to know that college might not be a reality. "High school will be the highlight of your life," my college adviser told me. Saddened and disappointed, but also determined, I started to research my options, and from another undocumented Black migrant I learned about the City University of New York (CUNY) and applied to Hunter College.

I was not the only one whose school and college adviser failed them. There were a couple of other students in my school, mostly girls from Jamaica and Nigeria who were in a similar situation as me. We exchanged scholarship information, and we cheered each other on. We set our minds on finding ways to continue our education. While the rest of the senior class worried about prom, fellow undocumented classmates and I were figuring out payments and basic enrollment because we were also the first in our families to be applying to college. Fuck a prom dress and limo; we were worried about our college applications being forwarded to immigration, and consequently their coming to deport our families.

> **While the rest of the senior class worried about prom, fellow undocumented classmates and I were worried about our college applications being forwarded to immigration, and consequently their coming to deport our families.**

My friends and I were accepted to CUNY, and at that time, we were able to qualify for in-state tuition. My friend Kayan and I both received scholarships from the Jewish Foundation for Education of Women. That's how we were able to enroll for our first couple of semesters. The whole college process forced me to come out publicly as undocumented to teachers, administrators, and deans. By 2007, more people knew about my undocumented status.

ACADEMIC ROBOTIC TIMELINE (AKA ACHY MEMORIES)

Community leaders tell you that laws will give you meaning
So you begin to recite
Yes, sir. I am a skilled worker
Yes, sir. I can contribute
No, sir. I haven't committed any crimes
Pinned. Against. One. Another
You remember that your mother almost didn't make it through the
*   border*
Or any legislation being drafted on
And this time around
She won't make it into health-care packages
She won't be remembered during press conferences
She will be dissected
Researched, researched, researched
And research about how much she doesn't belong will be published

Thousands of undocumented students across the country were dealing with the same reality I was. In 2008, when I attended a Young People For (YP4) summit in Washington, DC, I met a migrant organizer, Jennifer, who told me of an undocumented-led New York organization that had just been formed to work toward relief for undocumented young people. She was a young woman of color who was telling me there were more folks like me trying to do something about this bullshit immigration system. I joined this immigrant organization, and for the next six years I mobilized and organized undocumented youth in New York City.

We used social media platforms to coordinate, to come out as undocumented to one another, and to build an ecosystem of undocumented organizing and leadership. Imagine our Gchats filled with correspondence about next actions, about where to meet and what supplies to bring. We traded Facebook and Myspace messages about legislation, and which Senate staffers we had to respond to and organize against. Simultaneously, we left each other messages about fears, love, broken marriages, abortions, latest chisme, and depression. We disrupted borders via the Internet. It didn't matter that the mainstream headlines were yet to come. We made digital organizing work for grassroots change. In person, we organized in locations that other established immigrant organizations did not want to associate with, like trailer parks in Alabama.

During this time, it was understood that we had power; we could leverage it, and we could influence legislation. Do you know who was at the forefront of all this? Undocumented Queer women of color, Femmes, and nonbinary and gender-nonconforming folks. We were Black and Brown. We were fat and skinny and in between. We hated caps and gowns, were bilingual, often had strong accents, and worked multiple jobs. We had loud mouths and big personalities. We were introverts, awkward, artists, poets, hijab-wearing, messy daters, and loyal Converse shoe wearers. We had the occasional bad eyebrows.

Contrary to what has been reported, the organizing that has happened among undocumented young people has not been the first movement nor is it isolated. It has been built on a lineage of resistance from those organizing for Queer liberation and Black liberation to the sanctuary movement of the 1980s that protected war refugees from Central America. The 2006 immigrant marches especially gave us direction. So, no, our movement did not come from foundations, nonprofits, or allies. The work came from our casitas in Texas, Illinois, California, Missouri, even Maine. This was before organizations like United We Dream and the National Immigrant Youth Alliance. This was before splits in movements and mainstream tokenization.

Don't believe the hype that the undocumented resistance was built by light-skinned cisgender straight men. Erasure has played a key role in why many of our names go unrecognized: Tania, Lizbeth, Maria, Alaa, Kemi, Daniela, Razeen, Yahaira, Viridiana, Jackie, Tereza, Tam, Cinthya, Reyna, Bamby, _____—insert our mothers' names here, and many other names that have been erased and mispronounced whenever people have written about undocumented, unapologetic leaders and the history of the immigrant rights movement. These were the women and gender-nonconforming organizers responsible for the first online petitions to stop the deportation of undocumented young people. We created the leadership and organizing training toolkits that many folks use today and designed the first National Coming Out poster for undocumented youth. We were the coordinators and participants of the first action that took place in 2010 at the office of Senator John McCain urging him to vote for the Dream Act (#McCain5). We were responsible for taking over the Hart Senate Office Building that same year. Picture twenty-one undocumented youth demanding that senators, both Democrat and Republican, vote on the Dream Act (#Dream21). We were drafters of many local legislative proposals, including the NY Dream Act, and creators of #undocuqueer. We were the ones infiltrating detention centers and leading some of the biggest border-crossing actions. We were the reason why Deferred Action for Childhood Arrivals (DACA) became a reality for thousands of undocumented young people in 2012.

There is a lineage. Let their names be sung and recited over and over again. Let the change they strived for be named. These change-makers were my sisters, my friends, my chosen family, and my support system. We were responsible for changing the nation's sentiments about undocumented migrant young people. We amplified our narratives and forever shifted migration discourse even if we weren't held up publicly. We did the work to claim our lives.

Back then, as we innovated and shifted history, we didn't have the language to contextualize exactly what we were doing. The work was urgent. Feminism was not the word we used. It felt too rigid, like the papers we wanted. First- and second-wave white feminist scholars had never grouped me under their umbrella of feminism, and I had not wanted to be a part of that anyway. White feminism left out women like my mother, women who are poor, migrant, who do not get to graduate from high school, who are domestic workers—women of color who cannot dare to imagine their problems simply being about a right to vote or gender equality just being about ascending to white male roles. I craved equity in my feminism. I craved melanin. I craved a complex understanding of bodies of color living and surviving in a capitalist patriarchy and in a xenophobic, antiqueer, antimigrant, cis-sexist, violent world.

Professor Rupal Oza at the Women and Gender Studies Department at Hunter College had a thick accent that made academic words coming out of her mouth sound just like how I pronounced them. She made me feel like I belonged in her classroom with the white students, and she introduced me to the work of legal scholar Kimberlé Crenshaw, who coined the term "intersectionality" to describe how antidiscrimination laws fail Black women by considering gender and race as separate experiences. I began to realize that the organizing many of us were doing, and even just the way we moved through the world—this is what Dr. Crenshaw was writing about back in 1989. We were Queer, and undocumented, and Brown, and Black, and Latinx, and API, and Femme, and poor, and gender nonconforming, and bilingual, and women, and Muslim, and healers, and nonbinary. When we interacted with institutions and when we pushed for legislation, we brought our full selves to the table.

My understanding of feminism began to grow. Audre Lorde's writing and poetry reminded me that "there is no such thing as a single-issue struggle because we do not live single issue lives."[1] This statement helped me process the way I existed in America, especially as a Queer woman of color *and* migrant (not either/or). And Chandra Mohanty's essay "Under Western Eyes" helped me build my macro-understanding of my positioning in the United States and the Global South.[2]

As I was becoming more unapologetic about my undocumented status then, I was also getting comfortable with calling myself a "feminist." The scholarship and lived experiences of these feminists of color helped me to claim the identity. It felt good to speak an inclusive, intentional, intersectional feminist language and to make it my own. This helped me be in dialogue with June Jordan, bell hooks, Janet Mock, Tracee Ellis Ross, Grace Lee Boggs, Octavia Butler, Sandra Cisneros, Ryka Aoki, Alice Walker, and many others. This feminism was something I could be proud of and claim; my mami querida wouldn't be left behind in this type of feminism.

DEPARTURES AND RECONCILIATION

I am afraid to say that I became resentful of the world around me. I couldn't watch anything without thinking how easy those characters had it or how detention and borders would have impacted the story line. I watched *Walking Dead* and wondered how many mothers and children would have become zombies in detention centers. I watched *How to Make It in America* and wondered about the possibility of Kid Cudi's friend being undocumented.

The organizing work took me away from home. I was not present during my sister's teenage years because I was busy getting arrested for actions or I was at community meetings that ran late into the night. My romantic relationship back then suffered because I had not been honest about my bandwidth and I skipped out on therapy sessions. I took on too many deportation cases and ultimately was alone, haunted by paperwork and the alien numbers of those detained. I, along with everyone else, was doing this work in the name of "migrant rights," but we were also working out of scarcity and trauma.

The identity and empowerment we had built around the words "undocumented" and "dreamer" also began to burn the back of my throat. The mainstream media loved "dreamers," but they did not love "immigrants" or "refugees." I am scared to share this but I admit to being complicit in creating the good vs. bad immigrant narrative. We had debates over caps and gowns, who was more "undocumented," who was good for the camera, whose story was more compelling, who was able to prove they were oppressed, which part of Georgia we could build with, and who we would isolate. Meanwhile, I was beginning to realize that my identity was solely built around the lack of status—which meant it was an identity constructed by the US government.

As I write this, and look back, I think of what Roxane Gay calls a "bad feminist." That was me. I was full of contradictions, but it does not take away from my lived experience or contributions toward migrant rights. If anything, it leaves room for me to be tender to my younger self and understand that I was barely surviving, and that this big amerikkkan machine really had a grip on me and all of us.

But hope began to leave. It left after the Dream Act did not get enough votes in the Senate in 2010, and it left when more of our community members were deported, and when Black migrants were marginalized in our own organizing, and when people did not care about Trans detainees or those with criminal backgrounds.

Those of us who were artists left political legislative organizing for cultural spaces and cultural strategies. No more reactionary work. No more narrative correction of what we were not. We wanted to create narratives that illustrated our experiences with nuance. We were more than just the ways we could be productive for the economic benefit of this country. We were more than labor. We yearned to feel whole. No more "Olympic oppressions." We were done with "good immigrant" storytelling. We did not want storytellers telling our stories. We were going to write our own damn stories.

In 2011, I began to create intentional writing spaces in New York City by and for undocumented writers. These were monthly writing workshops, later accompanied by performance spaces known as "UndocuMics" (safe spaces for undocumented artists to share their work). This, unknowingly, was my attempt to organize cultural space and to innovate intentional pipelines for undocumented artists who were not being given the resources to thrive. It was an attempt to reconcile the need to call something *home*.

I was not alone in this. There were other contemporary undocumented artists, mostly Queer and women of color, also strategizing to create. Informally, we created an artist network, sharing with each other tips, dreams, and applications for residencies and funding. We mentored each other. We cheered for each other. In 2013, Kemi Bello, Marco Antonio Flores, and I started the UndocuWriting retreat—the first-ever writing retreat in the nation for and by undocumented writers. This project was powered by CultureStrike, a national arts organization that I had just started working with during that time. The first UndocuWriting retreat happened in Sausalito, California, by the beach. Twelve undocumented writers from across the country, chosen from a pool of more than a hundred applications, flew for the first time on planes toward the Pacific Ocean to work with faculty writers like Staceyann Chin. Later we partnered with the Voices of Our Nation Arts Foundation (VONA), creating scholarships and additional funding to send undocumented writers to VONA's annual writing program. Kemi and I created Undocumenting.com, the first online platform highlighting undocumented artists. Undocumented artists and cultural workers were building the conditions for culture equity for migrant art ten years ago. Now we want large art institutions, publishing houses, philanthropy hubs, and others to stop perpetuating migrant stories as a form of spectatorship, and instead to invest in the creativity of those who are embodied in undocumented experiences. It is not enough to disrupt borders in the policy field; we must do it in the cultural space. Here is where we do long-lasting disruption and change; here is where we change hearts and minds, where we create a tide of possibility for our communities to imagine what a world without prisons, detention centers, and borders would look like.

My feminism taught me to pay close attention to where the imbalance manifests itself. My involvement in these art and cultural spaces has led me to witness who gets to imagine and create. We already know that our cultural spaces are mostly dominated by white people and white cis hetero men. I am afraid to write that even in our own people-of-color cultural spaces it is mostly cis men who are giving us permission to play and experiment. Their projects are mentored and funded. We perpetuate an absence of visibility of migrant Femme/women of color/gender-nonconforming artists. What this says to me is that even in the imagination, we have a whole battle for gender equity to fight.

PRESENT

As I myself begin to identify as gender nonconforming, life is becoming more complicated. The feminism that I am moving with is one that honors all genders, that honors fluidity, that honors non-Anglo identification, respects all pronouns, and does not center on "pussy" power. The feminism that I am moving with now is one that fights for all people and meets people where they are, and where they are hurting, and allows them to create a language that suits them best.

I am also no longer undocumented. Two years ago I was able to adjust my immigration status through my partner at the time. When the green card arrived in the mail, inside the white envelope was a pamphlet with the words "Welcome to America" written all over it. At this point, I want to say that I took the pamphlet and I tore it into pieces.

I am lying. The pamphlet still sits in a folder in my parents' apartment.

Two years later, I am not sure how to make sense of my shift in immigration status. It often used to feel like I was going to be in this battle for an eternity, like most undocumented people are. What do you do when your whole existence for more than twenty-two years was constructed on the absence of papers? No one prepared me for this moment.

I have certain privileges now, and I have responsibilities. My parents will never be able to retire like most white middle-class families. Papa Jerry, my abuelo, will never get the same health care as I am now able to access. So I am left to imagine alternative ways for him to get medical care that go beyond Vicks and prayers to la Virgen. My mother waitresses for the same universities where I am invited to speak. She stands on the balls of her feet for eight hours straight, and sometimes the money she makes at these jobs does not pay for all her bills. This means I show up for them financially. This sometimes (most times) means I hold emotional space for them. This means that as I think of my own retirement plans or future goals, I carry them with me in every decision. No one is left behind.

Two trips to Ecuador have taught me about the toll that being undocumented has taken. I did not get to be with my grandparents when they died. In Ecuador, I videotaped their tombstones and their old casita, and I traveled back with this footage on my iPhone to show my parents. But I have not healed from all those lost memories. I have not healed from the years taken away from me to move around freely without fear of being deported or separated from my family. I am afraid now to wonder who I am outside of my immigration status. The phrase "I am neither from here nor there" is settling too comfortably in my stomach. The first time I returned to Ecuador, family and friends did not claim me. Instead, they called me "American." Where is home, now?

FAST-FORWARD

On election night in 2016, my mother sends me a text but I do not respond immediately. It's the ending of Obama, the beginning of Trump. Instead I text my Queer, gender-nonconforming, and Trans friends and chosen family. A range of texts fly across the country:

Maybe we have to leave the country
It is not going to be safe

Log off social media
Please be careful
I can't do this anymore
We will organize
I love you

My phone feels heavy from so much sorrow. We know what's coming: We will make it through the Trump years but the "we" will be smaller and wounded. Many people will not make it. In just his first year in office, there will be so much Black death, Queer and Trans death. More people will become incarcerated, deported, and exploited. Temporary Protected Status (TPS) will be taken away from many folks, especially from Black migrants, and courts will uphold the Muslim ban.

In our dark bedroom on election night, I disappear in the bed with my Queer, Trans partner as we hold hands. Whispering as if to avoid speaking into truth, whispering as if to keep this from our gods, we speak about what this will mean for our communities. What will happen to Trans folks? What will happen to our sick and disabled families? What will happen to poor communities? What will happen to undocumented migrant and refugee people? "We will exist as we always do," we say. We will create. We will disrupt, we will heal, we will imagine. We will continue to be here.

Ladies Only

TANMEET SETHI

It is a small photo. You know it is an older print because a white, scalloped border frames the black and white image. My mother and father stand on a hill with a view of the city of Seattle behind them. They are newly married, but they are complete strangers. It is 1963, and my mother wears a sari and large sunglasses, with her hair in a beehive. It was her first time in the United States. Her father wanted a son-in-law who was industrious and able to stand on his own feet. That is how my mother came to this country. It was a short trip back to India for her husband, a three-day engagement and a three-day wedding. And just like that, my mother was transported to a land where she had no friends or family. There were no Indian grocery stores or Indian restaurants. There was no email then. It was an ordeal to even make an international call. My mother says you have to make home wherever you are. This is what she did. And she thrived. I think of this whenever I hear anyone call Indian women "weak."

It is another Sunday morning; I have the routine down now. I am only twelve but I know all the gurus' names in order and can play the harmonium in gurdwara. My religion is Sikhism and this is my place of worship. I feel at home here. At the same time, I never know how to explain my church to my American friends. Women on one side, men on the other. We all sit on the same floor, and my mom tells me that is because, in God's eyes, we are all equal. Why can't we sit together? That is just the way it is, she says. I remember seeing a phrase in one of my schoolbooks—"separate but equal"—and I think I understand.

Her brown baseball cap contains her long, flowing black hair in a bun. She would not be caught dead back home in the pink-and-brown-striped shirt and the brown polyester pants that complete the outfit. It is a Baskin-Robbins, not a fashion runway by any means. Every ten-year-old child's dream, and it is my reality. My parents own this childhood ecstasy and my mother spends her days here, scooping out the thirty-one flavors for the local Louisianans to enjoy. In that outfit I suppose it is hard to recognize my mother. I think most customers are comfortable enough with their assessment of her as a foreigner of some sort. They wince at her Indian accent and dark skin. Most assume she is Latina and start to use their rusty high school Spanish with her. They seem offended when she tells them she does not understand what they are saying. Others just speak very slowly, and for some reason loudly, assuming she will have a hard time understanding them.

I am embarrassed by the way they look at her, like she is an alien of sorts. I wonder why they cannot see what I see. A woman who left all that was familiar to her to come to a foreign land where she is always an outsider. A woman who learned an entirely new way of living at an age when educations were done. A woman who left an upper-class family in India to work for a living with her husband in America. A woman who had to constantly explain her background because no one but her husband understood her memories. For a while I thought she was invisible. But then I realized that these people were blind.

A graceful artist performs the classical dance of Bharatnatyam and we study her, transfixed. Black kohl outlines her eyes in bold, dark borders. Her hair is tied back with garlands of jasmine strung through the curve of her braid. Shining gold necklaces and bracelets outline her form. Heavy bells adorn her ankles and sing her dance with every step. Her outfit is a juxtaposition of fuchsias and bright blues on a silk background that fans out in a peacock splendor when she bends her knees. She bows to Mother Earth first to ask for advance forgiveness for the upcoming steps and leaps. Her hands are poised in distinct positions, changing with every step, for they also tell a story in their own tongue. The orchestra frames the dance with its *raag*, chosen specifically for this storytelling adventure. As she makes defiant moves with her long, elegant fingers and her graceful, bell-covered feet, she transports us along a heavenly story of the gods and goddesses. The spectators, both men and women, are entranced by her gestures and powerful stances. Riveted to their seats, they hang on her every word. She speaks and guides with her steps. As she moves, she acts as our teacher, and we all listen.

My grandmother's key chain is no ordinary key chain. Its chiming sound is subtle but pervasive. Made of sterling silver, it hung ornately on my grandmother's *salwar* and always made an unmistakable sound everywhere she went. The ringing filled my childhood memories of my grandmother's house in India. It hung a few inches long, with three rows of silver bells and a paisley-shaped border. Salwars do not have pockets, and its hook was an ingenious way to attach it to her body. It held the keys to all the doors and all the cupboards, where she kept her most precious silk garments and jewelry, the jewelry she was given as a new bride. The jewelry that she divided among her four daughters, two daughters-in-law, and eight granddaughters before her passing six years ago. She gave me a set of earrings that hang delicately like chandeliers. They are made with pearls, garnets, and rubies and reflect brilliantly off my brightly colored *lenghas* and saris. When I wear them, I think of how many weddings and parties they have attended. But my most prized possession of my grandmother's is her key chain, because now I wear it, hooked onto my waist. As I move, its bells move in a rhythm that comforts me in a way I cannot explain. Maybe I am in awe of its power. I remember how my grandmother held the unique ability to open parts of the house. She was the ruler of that house's treasures, and now I hold the key to mine.

"What do you do for a living?" he asks innocently.

"I work in a hospital," I say. (I don't think strangers should be privy to my personal life, so I am purposefully vague.)

"Oh, so are you a nurse?" Of course he thinks that. This is my standard response from the average white American man. Always assuming I fit the stereotype of a woman.

"What do you do for a living?" This time asked by an Indian man.

"I work in a hospital," I say.

"Of course you are a doctor; all good Indian daughters are." This is my standard response from the average Indian man. Always assuming I live only to please others.

The women on the other side of the room chatter in a rumbling buzz of animated sounds. It takes a while before I hear fragments of their debate. "Poor thing," I hear, and then, "What will become of her?" I see my cousin try to leave the room inconspicuously, but not before I catch a grimace of shame on her face. She is twenty-four and unmarried, an unthinkable prospect to many of our female elders. She has not mentioned any stress to me about this during my summer vacation there. Maybe she is embarrassed, I realize. Maybe she thinks I, a still unmarried twenty-eight-year-old living in the States, will judge her as well. Suddenly, I wonder what they think of me. By now, they must either think I am gay or that I have a sordid past that has blemished my record. I think about my cousin and the pressure that lays on her to find a suitable match. What does she want to do, or has anyone even bothered to ask? A flurry of thoughts come to mind and I want to run to my cousin and comfort her. "You should do what you want to do. There is more to life than getting married." But I hesitate. How can I impose the ideals of an American culture in which she will not live? But how can I allow her to be castigated by her culture for being human? I struggle with the realization that we are sisters, but sisters separated by more than miles.

Everyone *oohs* and *aahs* at this picture, my body painted with intricate patterns of *mehndi*, or henna, as Americans call it. It is the night before my wedding. My family and friends dance around me in a blur of lush colors and sounds. A woman paints curved lines and paisley prints on my hands and feet. She paints the letters of my husband's first name, hidden delicately in the texture of the flowing design. Tradition states that on the wedding night, the husband should look for his name. If he cannot find it, the wife has eternal control of the house. It is a tradition steeped in old thought, where the wife has to win power in the house.

But even in modern times, it makes for romantic foreplay. I had always dreamed of the ceremonial mehndi pattern I would choose, as a Christian girl dreams of her white bridal gown. The origins of this ancient ritual lie in the decorating of the bride, to make her beautiful for her new husband. It is my tradition. It is chauvinistic, some could say. I know they would say that if they did not think the henna was so hip. Now, so many women have adopted the trend of wearing henna tattoos. It makes me angry that they frivolously wear these designs without understanding their origins and then tout their feminine power, as if they are stronger than other women across the world. I suppose they can be selective when they want to be.

It is only a few minutes before my wedding. I am looking out the window, dressed all in red. I thought this day would never come. I chose my own spouse and met with resistance. It seemed hopeless at times. But, eventually, my parents accepted us lovingly, uncon-ditionally, and here I stand. I am weighted down by gold, gold on my arms, gold hanging from my ears, gold on my neck, even on my fingers and toes. There is a gold *tikka* on my middle part and a red *duputta* over that. It is heavy but not a burden. It is what women in my family have done for generations. I wear the weight of my culture and class and enter another cycle of my womanhood. My mother adjusts my *kurtha*. She stands behind me with a beautiful lavender and gold *salwar-chameez*, her face shining brighter than my jewelry. The picture is in black and white, but I can still see all the colors. Every time I look at it, tears enter my eyes. My mother, standing behind me in support; that is where she will always be.

They look so innocent, sitting on the bed, all girlishly joking with each other. It is hard to believe that this is an Indian brothel. They represent all cultures of India, from the fair-skinned Punjabi women of the North to the darker women of Madras. They all wear ornately colored saris and various gold ornaments. They explain their lives to me. They are like any other group of women who have to choose a profession for survival. They are excited to have a visitor, especially one who does not want anything from them but their stories.

It is a hot and humid day in Mumbai, as most are; the women wipe the sweat from their foreheads with the colored borders of their saris. They tell me why they moved to the red-light districts, their individual stories. One young girl tells how her in-laws threw her out because of an insufficient dowry. Wracked with shame and fear, she could not go back to her home. That would spell failure for her younger sister's chance of marriage. Another was beaten by her husband for her infertility, another almost burned by her in-laws for the darkness of her skin. I sit in amazement of the stark honesty with which they tell their stories. They are all so welcoming to me, an outsider in many ways. We sit on the bed and laugh like friends while they explain the inevitability of their arrival to Falkland Road, one of the largest brothel districts in this massive city. The stories continue but all have a common thread. These women, without any education or money, desperate for freedom, survived the only way they could. They chose a path that seemed dark to me, but it paved the way for their independence.

> **They tell me why they moved to the red-light districts. One young girl tells how her in-laws threw her out because of an insufficient dowry. Another was beaten by her husband for her infertility, another almost burned by her in-laws for the darkness of her skin.**

I am here on a medical assignment, to provide HIV education and prevention for Indian sex workers. I ask them if they are scared of HIV. They tell me that they refuse customers unless they bring a condom. Here, unlike in their previous homes, they wield power with a small rubber ring. They express admiration that I am a doctor. But I have more admiration for them. Here they are, a reconstructed family, founded on a mutual understanding of what it takes to claim a life of one's own.

The picture is a sad but common one. It is black and white with no borders. Two women are in the foreground. One lies on an examining table, belly exposed, as the other leads a device over her abdomen. The device slides over cold gel and the ultrasound screen displays the motion of a sometimes amorphous shape through a black and gray haze. But the woman on the table is still. Her face stares intently at the active life on the screen, the life that is nurtured by her womb. Her face is motionless, almost paralyzed with fear. She has dreaded this moment, which for some may have been a time of anticipation and excitement. She torments herself with the question that will follow. Is it another girl?

She already has two daughters at home, which is quite enough for her husband and in-laws. This time they are not taking any chances. She cannot "waste" another nine months in the production of a non-male child. They would choose an abortion instead. Plenty of other families had made this choice, and so would they. They would have an abortion. They, not she, would make this choice with her body. They, not she, would decide to end this process that she had started. As she lies there, demoralized, she wonders how her mother-in-law, in particular, could deny the rights and emotions of another woman, of another mother. She is not just an incubator or a vessel through which a lineage can be sustained. She is a woman. She is a mother. She is a thinking and living being. Her resistance and frustration mount. She vows to break her stillness one day and thus break the chain.

The *burkha* is a black, amorphous cover, leaving only the eyes visible. It drives most Western women crazy. For some reason they always ask me how I feel about it, even though I am not Muslim. I suppose to them I look close enough. Today I sit with two Western women in a café who are disturbed by the *burkha*. I explain to them that it is a tool of oppression in some countries, and in others, some women choose to wear it. They shudder at this thought as they sip their lattés. One is encased in makeup and wears a tight shirt with capri pants. Another wears a midriff shirt and jeans with her hair flowing over her neck and around her face. I explain that many women in the world use the burkha as a symbol of power, as a statement of their value system. Women who wear the burkha refuse to be judged by their body or face. They want to be seen as another being, not as a sexual object. In this way, the burkha can be a tool of empowerment.

The women across from me listen with blank faces and confused stares. They argue that it is their right as women to wear what they want and how they wish to wear it. I agree and feel that this is precisely my point. I realize that these women in front of me are oppressed in many ways by society's perception of what a beautiful woman is. They respond to the abundant images of barely clad women with "perfect" bodies and fine-tuned makeup. They sit before me as conformists to their own cultural values. They sport the latest fashions and revel in their sun-soaked glows. I pity them; their oppression is so subtle they cannot even recognize it.

It is a warm day and the beads of sweat fall down my patient in labor. It is the morning after a twenty-eight-hour shift and I should be home in bed. As a resident, your bed is your best friend and you want to visit it any chance you get. But this patient only speaks Punjabi and the nurses have asked me to stay and help with translation. Although I have not slept for the whole shift and am exhausted, I want to stay and help this woman. I think of how terrifying it must be for her to go through this painful process without the ability to communicate with the medical personnel.

She is near the end of labor and her screams escalate. Her husband is here, but he sits on the opposite end of the room, acting as though he has no idea what his role is. He, too, speaks no English and sits dumbfounded by the intensity of the image before him. I remember my mother telling me that they never allowed men in the delivery rooms and that is why Indian men are not sure what their role is in childbirth. But I cannot empathize with him as he watches his wife yell out: "I am going to die" in our common tongue. I rub her back and think of what must be going through his mind. How can he not comfort her as she agonizes before him? I go over to him and lead him to the bed. I place his hand on her back and show him how to rub her and give her some attention. He looks lost, as if this is not something he has ever done. He obliges me for a while. But when I leave for a minute and return, I see he has found his old seat again, his seat of comfort where he has no obligations.

The nurses remark that it must not be part of his culture to comfort her. I wonder if this is the same culture to which I belong. Is it a culture in which an individual is able to show no consolation to his partner in a time of distress, one in which roles are so segregated that even during one of the most important events of their marriage, he will wait for her to finish her job before he starts his? In response to her cries I hear him mumble under his breath, "You will be fine!" Again, I lead him over to her, place his hand on her body and tell him that he is not to move this time. He should sit here, caress and support her. He stares at me and shows offense at a young woman directing his actions. But he does oblige. How could he not? I am not trying to impose some feminist rhetoric on him. I am merely instructing him on how to be human, and that transcends all cultures.

A child is born in India. She is a beautiful, innocent bundle brought into this world as a testimony to two people's love and commitment. She is the couple's fourth daughter, and they are overjoyed that she is healthy and happy. They were hoping for a son, but they are just pleased to have been blessed with another life. They understand the ability of women to succeed in the home and society, to build strong families, to sustain communities. They appreciate the gift they have given to the world and sing its praises. This is the snapshot I hope to take one day.

Our Hermanitas' Heroes

ANDREA L. PINO

It was February 28, 2016, and I stood backstage at the Dolby The-
atre, waiting to step in front of this year's Academy Award nomi-
nees. I was surrounded by a crew of fifty people who to an onlooker
had nothing in common: visibly queer bodies, a Texas Republican,
a CEO of a corporation, a Harvard law grad, a tenor at the National
Cathedral, and more black and brown folks than there had likely
ever been on the Oscars' stage. Some of them were nervous, some
excited to be in the presence of their lifelong heroes. I felt love. We
were so different, but as the stage lights burned on our faces, as
we began to hear Lady Gaga's words echo in the room, our fingers
enlaced and we walked forward to face the world as survivors of
sexual assault. We were invincible.

I was twenty-four. Women my age and older called me their
hero.

When I was twenty, I had organized with other women to take
on a two-hundred-year-old Public Ivy university where I and dozens
of other students had been raped. With other women, I had gone
after the federal government for failing to make colleges across
the country places that are free of sexual assault and harassment.
At twenty-one, I had started a national organization to end rape
on college campuses. At twenty-two, I had been the subject of an
award-winning documentary that had exposed the campus sexual

assault epidemic to people around the world, and had traveled to forty-six states to meet with hundreds of survivors who wanted to change their campuses after they saw the film.

In a way, I understood why women saw me as a hero, but the word made me hesitate. "Hero" made me think of my abuela Eva, who had been the first to leave Cuba at twenty, and risked everything to bring my abuelo Tony and her siblings to America. Heroes were the feminists I found when starving for a sense of belonging and solidarity after rape. It was Audre Lorde and Gloria Anzaldúa who taught me the power of rawness and of telling your unapologetic truth. It was Catharine MacKinnon who taught me about Title IX and my right to a safe education. And it was reading about other warriors, like Marsha P. Johnson and Anita Hill, that taught me to believe in the strength of my convictions and to never doubt that one person could catalyze a movement.

What did it mean now for me to be a hero? What did it mean to be a hero when I had not always been myself on this journey? When parts of my story had been edited out from my activism by white feminism?

Every morning before school, my abuelito and my hermanita waited for me in his 1989 Toyota Corolla, honking every few minutes to remind me that we would be late. I locked myself in our only bathroom, desperately trying to gel that untamable frizz around my face that prevented my hair from being properly contained. Complementing this mess was the ever-persistent middle button of my white blouse that wouldn't close, thanks to my inflating chest. Nothing could tame the marimacha in the mirror, and certainly not the constraints of a Catholic school romper.

There was never a time I didn't struggle to balance my need for belonging and my insatiable need to question everything. I was never happy sitting in class and repeating oraciones, and when we had to go to confession I never felt the need to apologize for missing misa that Sunday when I had an important episode of *Sailor Moon* to watch. I didn't really let myself process my queerness, but perhaps looking back I knew that I didn't want to be Sailor Jupiter so much as date her.

As a niña I was starving for images of heroes, of mujeres who were free to ask questions without limitation. I had seen glimpses of these heroes in movies, in books, and in video games even, but they weren't Cuban, they weren't marimachas, and they weren't sitting alone in a bathroom dressed in a Catholic school uniform questioning if they felt more trapped in a skirt or in their own community. I would spend years straightening my hair and my body, learning how to speak like the americanas on TV, pretending to like that boy, the one who seemed least unbearable, and questioning if my ideas and accomplishments truly deserved merit.

> **" I had seen glimpses of heroes in movies, in books, and in video games even, but they weren't Cuban, they weren't marimachas, and they weren't sitting alone in a Catholic school uniform questioning if they felt more trapped in a skirt or in their own community. "**

I wish I could say now that I found that sense of belonging when I first sat down at the back of my Women's Studies 101 lecture in college. I hesitated then just as I had when I'd been a niña to look around me and search for other mujeres like me who longed for the tenderness and nurture of communidad. It was 2013—before these same peers posted #MeToo, before feminism was the "Word of the Year" and sexual assault survivors adorned the *Time* cover for Person of the Year. I approached my white women's studies professor about struggling to complete my assignments when I was overcome by my duty to combat campus sexual violence.

In her office—surrounded by the smell of books that I had devoured well before taking Women's Studies 101 when I was most starved for a community, most alone in my pain and my rawness so soon after assault—my professor told me that I didn't understand feminism and that perhaps I should take time off. That was the last women's studies class I ever took.

There were times when I believed that being a hero meant I had a duty to publicly relive my rape in detail. At the same time, I could never make mistakes in my storytelling, because "lives depended on me" to be a perfect victim. At other times in my activism to end sexual assault, I have been the sole voice of color in a classroom, on a panel, or in a nonprofit organization, and I have had white women tell me I speak too fast, too passionately, too angrily. Just like in high school, I have felt the need to be more acceptable. I have added an extra layer of foundation to my face and spoken extra slowly or sat in silence.

How could I be a hero when there were times that I felt like I didn't want to live anymore? When I found myself fixed to a hospital bed, needles digging into the veins on the backs of my hands, liquids flowing in, struggling to circulate life into the shell of a body that would rather die than face the shame of others knowing that even with all I have accomplished, survivorhood can still look like this?

I began to feel that to be a feminist, to be a hero, I had to pass— as a white woman, as a straight woman, as an able-bodied woman.

Sometimes, I believe there isn't a place for my real voice in feminism. Sometimes I feel that the work I do isn't enough, when there are Dreamers, beautiful questioning queer Latinas, and young sur-vivors who won't ever pick up this book because they are trying to survive—luchando to pay their bills instead of taking that unpaid in-ternship at an organization run by some white feminists who mem-orized the word "intersectionality" for Women's Studies 101, but never thought it was important enough to write it into their organi-zational bylaws—trying to pass like I have in a world that only wants our stories during every election, production, or fundraising cycle.

But now I am done letting them take my voice.

White feminism: our stories and our bodies don't belong to you, but your spaces will one day belong to us.

My younger hermanita Angie has always seen me as her Wonder Woman. We are two years apart—23.7 months, to be exact—and it's hard to imagine how things were before we were together. In Cath-olic school one time, an older kid pushed her to the ground to cut in front of her at the water fountain, but I saw him, ran to her side, and hit him with my oversized rolling backpack. In other words, I have never questioned that fighting for what was right was worth the cost, especially if that fight meant making the world safer for my hermanita.

I paused on college so I could stop rape on college campuses in this country. It took me seven years to finish college, and that meant my hermanita became the first person in our family to grad-uate from college. Because of the mujeres who came before and the mujeres who worked alongside me, things are better for her, and that makes all the difference.

The mujeres in my family have always been my heroes. In addi-tion to my abuela Eva, there's my abuela Puchi, who supported my father and uncle as a single mother when the Castro regime imprisoned her husband. Mami has been the breadwinner our entire life—leaving her first year of college to support our family when my abuela had a heart attack. She's held the same office job since 1990, and I wonder if she thinks about what life would have been like if she didn't need to be our hero.

The women in my family raised me with San Lazaro, heladeros, and bodegas that kept our little world closed off, trapped in the immigrant journey, not here and not there. The mujeres in my family taught me the power of resilience, but they also lived their dreams through me. La lucha for me meant staying up an extra five hours to study for the SAT after finishing a night class at the local college, but it also meant keeping my doubts from those who saw their life's work in my success. I didn't call Mami after I was raped, and to this day we haven't talked about it or the fact that I will definitely marry a woman. I'm certain abuela Puchi ya sabe—both about my assault and that I'm queer—but the most we've discussed is that sexism is real, and that she was much smarter than her father ever understood.

Orgullo doesn't begin to describe how my family feels about me, how proud my abuelo is to display my graduation photos and my photo with President Obama on the coffee table at the entryway to his house. They believe in me now as they did when I was a niña, even if they don't know how to talk to me about where my journey has taken me. To them, I am la mujer they've always dreamed I would become—their hero.

Being a hero means admitting that I have lost friends to social justice movements, and I have gained family. I have been betrayed and have betrayed those I love in our work for justice. I have met the woman I love in this activism, but I am still learning to let myself be loved. I have kept secrets from my familia, but I have learned that there is a power in my voice that was carried over from our little islita and that I carry across any sea that stands in my way.

Organizing 101
A Mixed-Race Feminist in Movements for Social Justice

LISA WEINER-MAHFUZ

I have vivid memories of celebrating the holidays with my maternal grandparents. My jido and sito ("grandfather" and "grandmother," respectively, in Arabic), who were raised as Muslim Arabs, celebrated Christmas rather than Ramadan. Every year, my sito set up her Christmas tree in front of a huge bay window in their living room. It was important to her that the neighbors could see the tree from the street. Yet on Christmas Day Arabic was spoken in the house, Arabic music was played, Arabic food was served, and a hot and heavy poker game was always the main activity. Early on, I learned that what is publicly communicated can be very different from what is privately experienced.

Because of the racism, harassment, and ostracism my Arab grandparents faced, they developed ways to assimilate (or appear to assimilate) into their predominantly white New Hampshire community. When my mother married my Jewish father and raised me with his religion, they hoped that by presenting me to the world as a white Jewish girl, I would escape the hate they had experienced. But it did not happen that way. Instead, it took me years to untangle and understand the public/private dichotomy that had been such a part of my childhood.

My parents' mixed-class, mixed-race, and mixed-religion relationship held its own set of complex contradictions and tensions. My father comes from a working-class Ashkenazi Jewish family. My mother comes from an upper-middle-class Lebanese family, in which—similar to other Arab families of her generation—women were not encouraged, and only sometimes permitted, to get an education. My mother has a high school degree and no "marketable" job skills. When my father married her, he considered it an opportunity to marry into a higher class status. Her background as a Muslim Arab was something he essentially ignored except when it came to deciding what religious traditions my sister and I were going to be raised with. From my father's perspective, regardless of my mother's religious and cultural background, my sister and I were Jews—and only Jews.

My mother, who to this day carries an intense mix of pride and shame about being Arab, was eager to "marry out" of her Arabness. She thought that by marrying a white Jew, particularly in a predominantly white New Hampshire town, she would somehow be able to escape or minimize the ongoing racism her family faced. She converted to Judaism for this reason and also because she felt that "eliminating" Arabness and Islam from the equation would make my life and my sister's life less complex. We could all say—her included—that we were Jews. Sexism and racism (and their internalized versions) played a significant part in shaping my parents' relationship. My father was never made to feel uncomfortable or unwelcome because he had married a Muslim Arab woman. He used his white male privilege and his Zionistic point of view to solidify his legitimacy. He created the perception that he had done my mother a favor by "marrying her out" of her Arabness and the strictness of her upbringing.

My mother, however, bore the brunt of other people's prejudices. Her struggle for acceptance and refuge was especially evident in her relationship with my father's family, who never fully accepted her. It did not matter that she converted to Judaism, was active in Hadassah, or knew all of the rituals involved in preparing a Passover meal. She was frequently made to feel that she was never quite Jewish enough. My Jewish grandmother was particularly critical of my mother and communicated in subtle and not-so-subtle ways that she tolerated my mother's presence because she loved her son. In turn, I felt as if there was something wrong with me and that the love I received from my father's family was conditional. Many years later this was proven to be true: when my parents divorced, every member of my father's family cut off communication from my mother, my sister, and me. Racism and Zionism played a significant (but not exclusive) role in their choice. My father's family (with the exception of my Jewish grandfather, who died in his early seventies) had always been uncomfortable that my father had married an Arab woman. The divorce gave them a way out of examining their own racism and Zionism.

Today my mother realizes that her notions about marrying into whiteness and into a community that would somehow gain her greater acceptance was, to say the least, misguided. She romanticized her relationship with my father as a "symbol of peace" between Jews and Arabs, and she underestimated the impact of two very real issues: racism within the white Jewish community and the strength of anti-Semitism toward the Jewish community. At the time she did not understand that her own struggle against racism and anti-Arab sentiment was both linked to and different from anti-Semitism.

For me, the process of grieving the loss of the Jewish side of my family after the divorce led me to realize that their choice was a painful recognition of and rejection of my mother and ultimately our Arabness. I needed to figure out how to not reject my Jewishness, while at the same time learning how to embrace my Arabness on my own terms rather than on those of the adults around me. Today I do not consider myself to be "less" of an Arab because I did not grow up with a direct and explicit understanding of myself as one. I also do not consider myself to be "less" of a Jew because I am half Arab. I consider myself a woman who is working to understand how spoken and unspoken messages have shaped my experiences and political perspective.

MAKING THE CONNECTIONS

My understanding of injustice started with a series of visceral reactions. As a child I remember feeling a pit in my stomach when I sat in temple listening to stories about the Holocaust, or when my mother and her siblings used to talk about being beat up in school because of their "funny" names and hair. I later experienced that same reaction in high school when I learned about slavery in the United States, and then again in college, when I took my first women's studies class and began to understand the impact of heterosexism on my life and the lives of all women. Despite these reactions, however, I did not have the language to articulate why these feelings were so personal to me until I started exploring feminism. Feminism awakened my commitment to fighting injustice.

> 66 Feminism taught me that one can experience privilege and oppression simultaneously and that using my white privilege to try and hide my Arabness was not an honest way to live in the world. 99

Feminism challenged me to see how deeply I had internalized my own assimilation. Feminism taught me that one can experience privilege and oppression simultaneously and that using my white privilege to try and hide my Arabness was not an honest way to live in the world, nor did it guarantee me safety—after all, being Jewish provides no refuge in an anti-Semitic culture.

Audre Lorde's book *Sister Outsider* provided me with a feminist framework for understanding the interconnectedness of oppression and my own identity as a Jewish/Arab-American, mixed-race, mixed-class, lesbian feminist. This book made a particular impact on me because Lorde was making visible and political her perspective as a woman with multiple identities. Before reading this book, I did not understand that my power and my commitment to fighting oppression lay in finding those places where my experiences of privilege and oppression seem to be at odds with one another. Lorde's work and life taught me that I must not be afraid to go to those complex and "messy" places to understand myself, the history of my people, and to learn how to use my identities in a clear and subversive way. Reading *Sister Outsider* was just the first step in helping me to see that this was possible. Figuring out the strategies and politics involved in *how* to do this at the intersections of my own identities has been and will continue to be a lifelong process.

Although feminism has shaped my personal and political perspective, it has also been a sharp double-edged sword in my work as an organizer. Time and again I have experienced being in a "feminist space" where I have been asked or forced to check my full self at the door—my Arabic words, my lesbian ideas, or my Jewish experience. This, to me, is not feminism. I now focus on understanding the interconnectedness of my own identities and the role that oppression and privilege play in my life and work as an anti-racism activist. This has been particularly difficult because many on the "left" uphold the mythology that since we work against "the evils of the world," we are somehow free of racism, sexism, classism, anti-Semitism, ableism, and adultism (the institutional power adults have to oppress and silence young people). After years of anti-oppression training and organizing work, however, I now know that many "progressive" people and organizations are just as invested in either/or dichotomous thinking and in perpetuating oppression in the world.

Six years ago I attended a conference in Boston entitled "Race and Racism in the Nineties." I participated in a workshop about women, spirituality, and anti-oppression work. During the workshop, the facilitators, a white woman and an African-American woman, divided the group into two caucuses: a white caucus and a woman of color caucus. Before breaking up the group, I raised my hand and asked where mixed-race people were to go. This question opened up a flood of questions and challenges toward me. The white women in the room, including the white facilitator, said they felt I should caucus with them because I could pass for white. Most of the women of color concurred with this. I recall feeling confused and vulnerable because I did not anticipate what I would be opening up by calling attention to the dualism that was at play. I also felt angry and hurt because I felt the women in the room responded to me based on my light skin rather than on my experiences or the politics of what I was trying to raise. The discussion proceeded with the facilitators spending ten minutes talking to the group about the privileges of being able to choose—as if I were not in the room. The level of tension in the room was palpable. Bodies stiffened and voices raised a notch.

I was frustrated with myself because I did not know how to handle the "logistics" of putting complex racial issues out in a group in a way that clearly demonstrated in word and deed that I was taking responsibility for my privilege while simultaneously taking an uncompromising stand against white supremacy. Although I had Audre Lorde's words floating around in my mind, I had not yet learned how to apply her teachings to my own experience. Finally, the group resolved that I could "choose" where to go. The feeling in the room was that the situation had been resolved. But it was not resolved for me. I felt alone. I felt that regardless of where I chose to go, it would be the wrong choice. I felt like the illegitimate bastard child that no one wanted or knew what to do with. Many of the women of color were angry with me. Many of the white women felt as if they had made an "antiracist" intervention by challenging me on my racism. Still, as the group broke up into two, I made a choice and walked toward the room that the women of color were to meet in. As I approached the door, it quickly slammed in my face.

On this day "feminism" was extremely painful for all of us in the workshop. Everyone was angry and upset because I did not neatly fit into either the white or the colored framework. No one, including myself, knew how to grapple with the complexity in a constructive way. I struggled to articulate that taking responsibility for my white privilege did not mean I was "admitting" to being white. It meant I was recognizing my privilege and trying to establish my accountability. But in this case, this difference and its complexity were not honored; they were not seen as something necessary to explore. It was also a hurtful experience because I had hoped that I could turn to other women, especially activists, to mentor and challenge me around how to bring my whole self to my work as an organizer. I learned that receiving that kind of support depended on two things: getting clarity about how my experiences of oppression and privilege overlap, and challenging my own assumption that all women activists were automatically going to approach their work with an anti-oppression analysis.

RESISTING CLASSIC SCRIPTS

In talking with other mixed-race activists about their experiences, I have discovered that this is a classic script. This is how racism and internalized racism are often directed toward mixed people. In many activist circles, it has become easier to delegitimize and shut us out, rather than to take on the challenge and opportunity that mixed-race people with anti-oppression politics can present. Our multiple perspectives and commitment to challenging oppression can deepen the discussions about white supremacy and sharpen our tools for challenging it.

Yet the presence and voices of mixed-race people are often deeply feared. We are feared because interracial relationships are still taboo in our culture. We are feared because our mere existence calls into question the status quo and the way that race is constructed in our society. We are feared even by people on the "left" who propose to be working to challenge these deeply rooted beliefs and constructs. We live in a white supremacist culture that banks on dichotomous thinking to keep people divided and fragmented within themselves. Those of us who do not fit into either/or boxes therefore experience an enormous amount of pressure to choose one "side" of ourselves over another. We are not considered whole just as we are. We are taught that these are dualisms: Jewish/Arab, public/private, visible/invisible, black/white, privilege/oppression, pride/shame. But these are false separations that don't exist. They are imposed. My struggle and that of other mixed-race people is to not internalize these dualisms and become paralyzed by a society that rejects our complexity in the name of keeping things simple and easy to categorize.

I have learned many lessons about how important it is to be accountable to those who experience oppression in ways that I do not. Being accountable does not mean I allow my legitimacy to be freely debated by individuals or groups. From my perspective, the question of who is a legitimate person of color (based on their skin color) is misguided. Rather, what is important to me is how individuals and groups use their privileges to challenge oppression. This means that where I experience oppression, I resist it alongside of those who experience that same oppression. Where I experience privilege, I stand in solidarity with those whose lives are being impacted by challenging others who benefit from that same privilege.

Maintaining my accountability is not a choice, but it is certainly fluid. Each situation that I am in calls me to assess myself in relation to the time, place, and company. For example, when I am with a group of darker-skinned people of color, I am very conscious of my privilege and actively take steps to acknowledge it. When I am in the company of white people, I am conscious of my privilege in a different way. I am prepared to challenge the assumption that my light skin makes me an ally in perpetuating racism.

I have come to define accountability in a complex way, one that both takes into account and challenges identity politics. Identity politics have given me the opportunity to define and claim myself as a complex and whole person and to build community with those who share common experiences in the struggle for justice. Yet identity politics, when narrowly defined and used as a tool to divide, have made my ability to maintain accountability a treacherous experience. I often feel pressure to choose one community over another, one part of myself over another. As mixed-race people with multiple identities, this pressure to choose can cut deeply and painfully into our souls. More often than not, I find identity politics to be defined narrowly in progressive circles. This can limit our work to build coalitions and solidarity across communities and movements because this leads us to simply replicate all that we want to eradicate in the world.

For personal and political reasons, this essay on feminism covers racism and other forms of oppression. I have had to make sense of and to develop the tools for challenging why I, as a mixed-race, mixed-class, Jewish/Arab-American lesbian, have been shut out of so many "feminist" spaces. Developing and practicing anti-oppression politics is not just about my own survival; it is about creating a feminist movement that speaks to and represents the experiences of all women. I refuse to be shut out and I refuse to allow other women who do not fit into the mainstream feminist movement to be shut out. Being an antiracist activist is the best way that I know how to honor my mother's experience, to honor my own identities, and to honor women, such as Audre Lorde, who paved the way before me to work for justice.[1]

Many thanks to Lisbeth Meléndez, Cynthia Newcomer, Randi Kristensen, Ana Lara, and Stephanie Morgan for their support, feedback, and excellent editing skills.

Lost in the Indophile Translation
A Validation of *My* Experience

BHAVANA MODY

I had zoned out at some point during the conversation, eyeing the variety of cat food products on his sister's bookshelf. The rest of us were seated on the couch while he was grounded on the floor, waving his arms around, making driving gestures, vomiting gestures, turning, yelling, and dancing....It was more like a game of charades than a conversation, except there was zero audience participation. In fact, I don't think I had been given the opportunity to respond once. The two other women on the couch were *oohing*, *aaahing*, and giggling now and then. But he couldn't evoke a smile from me at this point. His question had left me feeling sick and unimpressionable.

He was an acquaintance from college who was sharing some tales with us about his recent travels to India, where he had been studying Buddhism in the hills of the Northeast region of the subcontinent. He threw around gestures and statements, and for the most part, I had no idea what he was talking about. I wanted to butt in, but there was no room to disagree with him. After all, he had just recently returned, and I hadn't been to India in years. So whenever he looked at me, I smiled and nodded, as if in agreement. I *should* have known what he was talking about, right? I eyed the two other women. Is that what they were thinking?

My pride was on the line here. How come they weren't looking at *me* and asking *me* questions? I wanted to be given the floor. *Yes, I really am Indian. Sure, I know all the Hindu goddesses. Of course I meditate. Well, yeah, I've been to Bodhgaya.* When the truth is, I know about three Hindu goddesses, have tried meditating about twice (and failed), and have never been to Bodhgaya. Yet I didn't want them to think I was void of the Indian experience. So here I was already feeling insecure about my Indian-ness, and then he popped the question.

He smiled at me, his dreadlocks swayed forward, and his crooked teeth poked through his brown wild boar of a beard. I saw his mouth move the first time, but for some reason the words didn't seem real. I almost choked.

"What did you say?" I asked, eyebrows raised. He didn't think he was implying anything when he asked it. He just wanted to be generous with his wisdom, you see.

"Do you know what your name *means*?" He grinned excitedly, eager to share the knowledge. I blinked a couple of times. The other women were eager, too. They turned their heads toward me for the first time, but not their bodies. He was much more entertaining than I was and they wanted to continue the charades-style conversation. I shifted uncomfortably and muttered softly. I suddenly felt shy about talking about myself.

"Yeah, it means like dream or something, I think—" I wasn't finished. I was just starting to recognize the power I held for those few seconds when he snatched it back. They nodded and turned their eyes back on him.

"Your name means 'MED-I-TA-TION.'" He articulated each syllable as if none of us had ever heard the word before. This is when I turned toward the cat food, my eyes welled up with tears, my pride sunk, my Indian-ness disproved. And the white man in front of me carried on.

I can't tell you how many male friends and acquaintances I know, all white, all college-educated, who have traveled, meditated, and studied in India. And each time another white male person tells me about his time in India, I wrestle with a range of emotions, dealing primarily with race and power. I immediately begin to think of my skin color and how I was always different in the United States, but how I'm also different in India.

During my small-town upbringing in Kentucky, I experienced plenty of racism, sometimes in the form of stares and at other times in more blatant forms. So in some way I do take it as a compliment when white men obsess over India. They are actually *interested* in my culture rather than appalled by it. This "interest" is a *huge* step up from my old Kentucky home, where if *I* "acted Indian," I'd be made fun of. That's probably how Indians in India feel about white tourists, relieved by the curious smiles, the cameras, and the sari-shopping. The exotification is a step up from the blatant racism and terrorism that Indians have experienced both in India and in America. It is nice knowing that white men aren't out to get us, right? They're just *interested*. I know their admiration of Indian culture is well-intentioned. I even brag to my parents and relatives about the white men I know.

They are often taken aback but also proud that Americans are so interested in their way of life. "These American boys like wearing robes?"

"These American boys drink chai?"

"These American boys enjoy sitar music?"

"These American boys must be crazy."

Well, no, Indian relatives, Americans are good and they aren't all materialistic, fashionable football players who eat hamburgers and listen to Backstreet Boys and live in mansions. So here I am, on the one hand questioning white men for exploiting my culture. And on the other hand I want them to go to India so they can develop a sense of respect for Indian people.

"It is good your American friends are trying to *understand about you*."

Yeah, that's it. Right there. Uh-huh. This is where the problem lies. My relatives are wrong in assuming my American friends are trying to understand me. Sure, the India-obsessed dudes (to reduce redundancy, I'll refer to these white men as "Indophiles") who go to India understand more about the "third world," Hinduism, yoga, and whatnot, but do they really understand actual Indians (including me)? How do they treat actual Indians in this country? Like I mentioned before, I wasn't always treated so kindly.

As an Indian-American woman, my identity was and still is challenged repeatedly. In rural Kentucky, I wanted so badly to fit in. But it was difficult for my blond, blue-eyed neighbors to get past the fact that I was dark, that my parents had accents and dressed "funny," and that our house was painted a bright blue, the shade of an eighties-style satin prom dress. I was *odd* and that identity stuck. Somehow, I made it through my years in that town, through preteen battles with my parents about wanting to try cheerleading instead of math team, and through being made fun of because my grandfather had a braid and wore "sheets."

I spent most of my time at home, sometimes feeling socially inept and other times simply enjoying the Indian-ness. I loved my mom's soft *rotis* she made regularly, and my dad's old Hindi movie music he played on Sunday mornings. I loved playing games using seashells with my grandmother and singing *bhajans* with her at night. Sometimes I would parade around my room wearing a *salwar* dress and lots of bangles.

The funny thing is, aside from the folks in my Indian home in Kentucky, I wasn't really comfortable among other Indians. I detested going to India, where I felt invaded with my relatives' comments on how I spoke, ate, dressed, and studied. When I was in India, I longed to be back in Kentucky, where I could listen to my Indigo Girls songs on long country drives or sit in my own room and read or write without interruptions, dreaming of being an actress or part of the Peace Corps.

You'd think I'd have had a sense of peace among other Indian Americans, but this was not the case either. I reluctantly attended Indian gatherings in the bigger cities with my parents, awkwardly wearing *chaniya cholis* and tripping on the *garba* dance floor. I was intimidated by the other Indian-American girls my age, who dressed and danced beautifully. I would stand there holding my *choli* skirt up because I didn't tie it right, while they glided and gossiped in their friend circles, discussing their bright futures in medicine and engineering.

Eventually, I landed myself in a small liberal arts college in Ohio, where I learned to feel a sense of power in my oddness. It was a school that was predominantly white, so there was no such thing as ethnic studies or Asian studies. I was lucky enough to have a Black studies class. But during my first year of college, nothing upside-downed my world as much as Women's Studies 101. I learned that maybe I wasn't so odd after all, because maybe, just maybe, patriarchal social constructions had caused the various forms of discrimination I'd experienced all my life, both as a woman and as a person of color. The other women in the class connected with me; we had a shared understanding. I was overjoyed. I embraced my new friend, *feminism*.

But as I delved deeper and deeper into feminism, something was still missing. Although I was understanding more and more about gender and oppression regarding women's issues, I still hadn't come to terms with the racism I experienced and my Indian-American identity. And because there was no one to have a shared experience with, I threw it on a back burner and poked at it from time to time. For example, I drew parallels in my anthropology classes, learning about other cultures, particularly women in other cultures. Independently, I read about women in India and decided to write my thesis on that topic. When I interviewed Indian women, and they nodded their heads at me in ways that only *I*, being Indian, would understand, I felt reconnected to the culture and tradition I had always felt so distanced from. I couldn't wait to go back to India and be with my family there. In my thesis I explored ethnicity and gender repeatedly and, thanks to feminism, I could question and critique various social constructions.

And so I know something is very wrong with white men telling me this and that about India. But I don't have an official theory from which to critique them. Although I understand exotification and discrimination and where it comes from, sometimes I feel too shocked and tongue-tied to say anything. I get pissed because I don't think my experience as an Indian-American woman is understood, just as the experience of Indians in India is grossly misinterpreted. When I do say something, everyone thinks I am overreacting because nothing comes out logically.

One time I was seated with a couple of Indophile friends, and the two were exchanging stories about train riding in India. I was very attentive while they were talking because I really like trains in India. I can see how train riding in India can be enjoyable, but I'm not sure how much of a *crazy* adventure riding on a train is. The two friends kept gabbing about this and that—imitating the vendors and discussing all the CRAZY times on the trains. And then discussing all the CRAZY times in some city. All the CRAZY craziness and CRAZY adventure of travel in India. Usually, when I go to India, I see my family. Nothing terribly CRAZY. When I was seated with the two Indophiles, I felt like I had to justify why I'd never done anything as CRAZY as they had while in India. What was my hang-up? Then I realized that "CRAZY" was a judgment: what they saw as so CRAZY was just the same-old same-old for most Indians, including my family, living their everyday lives.

I can't say I've ever had a wild adventure in India. It's very difficult for me to travel in India, as I am rarely allowed to leave the house alone. In most cases girls and women cannot travel long distances unaccompanied because it is important to be associated with a man, as a wife, a daughter, a cousin, or a niece. What these Indophiles didn't seem to understand was what a privilege they had to be able to roam all over India. Women cannot travel as independently as men. And Indian women can travel even less independently. We do not limit ourselves but are limited by societal constraints that white men do not have to deal with. The few times when I was alone, I encountered a great deal of harassment. Most of my family in India (men and women, but especially the women) have not seen anything in India outside of their home state of Gujarat.

During this same conversation, both men mentioned how they *only* rode third-class trains, where the "real" Indians are. As if "real" Indians are poor and cannot be middle class or rich. I admire that they acknowledge the poverty that exists in India, rather than turning a blind eye to it. But I do not like how they glorify it. As if they're way too tough and way too poor to sit among the weenies in the air-conditioned first-class train. Well, I guarantee that if those third-class passengers had the choices my Indophile friends did, they'd be happy to be weenies. I didn't say anything, but I thought to myself how I'd be much less irked if my friends had swapped a first-class ticket with a third-class passenger—that way, both could have had a unique, once-in-a-lifetime experience. After all, we all know Indophiles can afford four extra dollars.

There was also a lot of talk from these guys about how great village life is. *Milking cows, eating mangoes, laughing all day, la, la, la.* I, too, believe in simple living, but there is a difference between *simplicity by choice* and poverty. Most Indian villagers are of the latter group. Admittedly, I had a similar perception of village life once, too. Then I hung out with my family in the village for an extended period of time. They are dealing with alcoholism, domestic violence, illness, lack of education, and so on. The truth is, most of the people who live in Indian villages are suffering miserably. On the surface, though, when language barriers are thick, it may seem that village people are always smiling. Also, what Indophiles don't always see when they hang out with the cheerful, "hard-core" fellas in the villages is that those who suffer the most are the women, those who work the hardest are the women. But they don't talk it up with the women.

> **Something just ain't right about the glorification of poverty by those who have a $2,200 airplane ticket in their hidden chest pouches.**

This is the real *India,* they seem to say. As if poverty makes it more real. Something just ain't right about the glorification of poverty by those who have a $2,200 airplane ticket in their hidden chest pouches. So that leaves the Indophiles with a very romantic perception of Indian culture. Few of these enlightened white men are aware of India's complex history and social structures; nor are they familiar with the racist stereotypes, harassment, and violence that Indians and other people of color face daily within the United States.

Dude, chill out... Indian people are interested in our sicko culture, so why can't we learn all the beautiful things about theirs? It's about sharing, not commodifying. You see, people say that to me all the time. *Indians come here and are taking advantage of the motels and the tech companies. They love to listen to the Backstreet Boys and eat at McDonald's. Why is it any less ethical to go to India and take bits of their culture and religion?* This is when my eyes go big and I start shouting about power and who's got the power and how the wrong people are getting empowered, but nobody seems to get what I'm saying.

I don't think that white men see themselves in a constant position of power. It's just an equal exchange to them. They aren't the ones who are dealing with discrimination, stereotypes, and colonialism. It has never been an equal exchange. South Asian immigrants provided the technical and medical expertise the United States was begging for, particularly in the sixties and seventies, and currently in Silicon Valley. Americans benefit from highly trained professionals without having to spend money educating them. In most cases Indians leave their homeland and come to the United States to make a new life for themselves. Americans go to India to check it out. They've got that ticket in their chest pouch, remember? So the exchange is not equal at all.

Since this most recent obsession with India has begun, I can't say that the lives of most Indians have improved. We have no greater political voice in the United States, even though all our gods and goddesses are in all the head shops and henna is sold at beauty salons everywhere. While we deal with the reality, the white men have chosen to deal with the fantasy. The fantasy of India. And that's exactly what it is. Ask any nonresident Indian if the India they know is the same as the India the white men know. I guarantee the two experiences will be as paradoxical as chai in Orissa and chai in Oregon.

I called my mom the very next morning after that horrible evening of charades and asked her about my name. "It means 'dream' or 'good dream,' right?"

"Yes, it does." Sigh of relief.

"It doesn't mean 'meditation,' right?"

"Well, yes, it does."

"What?!?!"

"It also can mean 'emotion' or 'thought' or 'wish.'..."

"But, Mom, I want to know what it means exactly."

"*Dhiku*, your name means many things. It is very difficult to translate to English." Right on, Mom. You heard it. Aw yeah. Another deeper sigh of relief.

Some things just can't be translated.

TALKING BACK, TAKING BACK

A Native American Feminist's Guide to Survival

NATANI NOTAH

I was born in 1992, about five hundred years after Christopher Columbus sailed the ocean blue. While Native activists were protesting the upcoming quincentennial of Columbus making contact with the first peoples of the Americas, I popped out of my screaming mother in an underfunded urban hospital in Southern California. I was brought home to the west side of San Bernardino, and I grew up learning how to protect myself on the streets and in the classroom. My introduction to the history of Indian residential boarding schools in the United States was not from any textbook, but in my family's living room. My father didn't talk much about his experiences at these schools, but there is one story he told my siblings and me that is worth more to me than any fancy degree.

My father's face lit up as he recounted the day when he stole all the nun's paddles. The paddles were used to beat the children when they spoke their Native language, talked back to authority, or acted out of line. So one day my dad decided to take all the paddles from the front of the classroom, run outside, and throw them onto the schoolhouse roof. With pride, he said it took the nuns the rest of the day to get them down. Even now I can imagine all the students cheering him on, and I find comfort in the possibility that at least for an afternoon, nobody got beaten.

I was not sent to a boarding school like my father, but my own journey with education has not been easy. Starting in kindergarten I learned that I was not the same as all of my peers. I was on the playground when Harrison ran after me, pinched my butt, smacked his hand to his mouth in a repetitious war whoop, and danced in circles around my tiny, shaking body. I was six years old, and a white boy had attacked me for my sex and my race for the first time. This taught me to always watch my back.

Hearing my father talk about his rebellions in boarding school helped me to understand that I come from a long line of Diné people fighting for freedom and equality. Stories like my father's have carved me into the strong woman I am today. I had these stories before I knew what feminism was, but they have informed my interpretation of what it truly means to call myself a feminist. To be a feminist means I actively advocate for the well-being of men, women, and two-spirited individuals. To be a feminist means I respect our connection to Mother Earth and believe in the value of every living being.

> " Hearing my father talk about his rebellions in boarding school helped me to understand that I come from a long line of Diné people fighting for freedom and equality. "

When I recall the times in my life that I have been called Pocahontas, squaw, redskin, injun, and prairie n•gger, it has honestly been hard to respond to such hatred. Do I call them out on their racism or ignore them? What would my father do? In these instances I find myself falling back on my Diné understanding of balance being paramount to the interconnection of everything. This means that I don't meet hatred with hatred, but rather I respond with compassion and a learned understanding that individuals who are capable of spreading such negativity are actually a part of larger issues. I often assess what that person's intentions might be, asking myself if it feels like an ignorant "mistake" or if they are trying to hurt me. When I was younger, I struggled to quickly respond out of fear of confrontation and ended up remaining silent and frozen in place. Later on, I realized that physically and emotionally distancing myself was the key to feeling safe again. This usually looked like gracefully excusing myself in the middle of the conversation, walking away, and not returning. However, in recent years I have worked on using my voice to calmly call out offenders, with the hope that generative dialogue will take place.

While blatant racial attacks aren't directed at me every day, they are inscribed in government mandates, such as Title VII, an educational policy that is meant to "support the efforts of local educational agencies, Indian tribes and organizations, postsecondary institutions, and other entities to meet the unique educational and culturally related academic needs of American Indian and Alaska Native students." Although this policy is meant to help Native youth, like the Indian boarding and missionary schools it was founded on problematic ideas of white superiority and goals of "killing the Indian, saving the man." Policies like Title VII perpetuate white savior complexes that are detrimental to the well-being of Native communities everywhere. I experienced this firsthand in my freshman year of high school, when I would meet once a semester with my school district's Title VII director to go over my grades and talk about college plans. Finally, my senior year rolled around, and college applications were due soon. He asked me where I was planning to apply, and I mentioned four universities in California and a couple of Ivy Leagues on the East Coast. He noted the names on a copy of my stellar transcript and promptly dismissed me from the meeting.

The next day I was called into the office of my assigned high school counselor. I sat down in a chair across from her and asked why I was there. She proceeded to tell me that she had been contacted by the director of Title VII and there were some serious concerns about my college plans. The next thing I knew, she was talking about how I should really be applying to the adult school downtown, because my current choices for colleges were far-fetched. I sat there in silence, listening to a white woman regurgitate the words of a white man who fundamentally believed I wasn't good enough to get into a four-year college. I left that meeting being reminded again of my position in this country. On the car ride home, I wept into my hands as my big brother consoled me. He insisted that they were wrong and that I should apply to where I wanted to no matter what anyone else said. A few months later, I accepted my admission to Cornell University and declined all the other offers.

Over the course of the next four years of college, I learned a lot, including the art of unlearning. In my sophomore year, I took an introductory course on feminist, gender, and sexuality studies and found hope in the conversations that were taking place, but also noticed a lack of Native representation. It wasn't until my senior year, when I enrolled in an Indigenous arts course, that my struggles as a Native American woman were affirmed. The first assigned reading was Walter D. Mignolo's *The Darker Side of Western Modernity: Global Futures, Decolonial Options*. I remember my head spinning as I struggled to get through the density of the text. The language was extremely difficult to comprehend, but as I flipped through the pages I discovered terminology like "colonization" and "decolonization," which defined and challenged the foundations of the Western patriarchy in which I was living. This simultaneous process of learning and unlearning the history of systems of oppression of people like me via education was tricky. However, the time I spent doing this work has been crucial to my growth.

It was during my undergraduate years that I also worked on my mental health, fighting the negative voices that told me I wasn't good enough. These same voices also tried to convince me to take my own life. In my dorm room I would cry as waves of pain blurred my vision. I would think about the circumstances of the recent years: the overwhelming hurt that accompanied the untimely death of my grandmother from breast cancer, the heartbreaking death of my beloved father from kidney cancer, and the abandonment by my fierce mother. These extreme losses had hit my family one after the other and at the time they occurred I didn't know how to process them. Thankfully I didn't inherit this trauma. I also inherited a strength inside of my DNA. It is through my connection to my ancestors, my spirituality, and my gifted ability to make art that I found my grounding again and fought my suicidal thoughts and depression.

Now I am in my second year of a master of fine arts program in art practice. Through mixed-media artwork I turn historical trauma into testaments of beauty that explore the impacts of colonization from the perspective of being a Native American feminist and woman. Although I am grateful to be making artwork that challenges Western ideologies, the problematic issues in higher education still exist. At times it feels like a pressure being placed on me by peers to speak on behalf of all Native nations, because I am the only Native person in the classroom. Other times, the issues look like the day a white professor sent me an email asking if I needed academic help, even though I was getting straight A's. It hurt, too, the time a white colleague insisted that the only reason I did well during my in-class critique was because people were afraid of offending me. I cringe at the times that people have insisted that the only reason I got into college in the first place was because I was Native American, since, "You know, they have to fill a quota." Racism in higher ed today also takes the form of a text-message GIF from another white colleague equating my artistic practice to that of a monkey stealing.

This constant bombardment of racist comments and actions is exhausting, but through my feminist research into the violence against Indigenous women and girls, I find conviction to keep fighting to make this world a more just place through the visual arts. Although I don't have it all figured out, and I still struggle with owning my worth, I have more tools now to acknowledge that outsiders' attacks on my race, sex, gender, and culture do not define me. Nor will their jealousy, negativity, or hatred stop me from striving to meet my goals in an educational system that was designed to beat people like me. As a practicing Diné feminist, artist, writer, student, and educator, I am choosing to honor the resilience I came from.

The impacts that colonization had and continues to have on my family are numerous, but we are not alone with our stories. Native American people are the descendants of genocide. We continue to face civil rights violations on a daily basis but the most powerful ways we can respond to this adversity is through challenging the systems that were put in place to defeat us. This means infiltrating all facets of society, including education, to break it down and constructively build it back up to include Native stories of survival and success. By defying all expectations and thriving, I believe there will be a shift in consciousness that will wake the masses up to the utter importance of Native knowledge, art, and imagination.

Heartbroken
Women of Color Feminism and the Third Wave

REBECCA HURDIS

This essay isn't just about an adopted, woman of color feminist; rather, it is a story about how I came to believe that I was worthy of all of these identities. It isn't just a story about feminism or solely about adoption. It is an exploration of where the mind stops and the heart follows. It is too easy to distract myself with ideas about "deconstruction" and "critical analysis," terms that lack the emotional depth to explain my experiences. The struggle is not to find one place where I can exist, but to find it within myself to exist in all of these places, uncompromisingly. To live a life of multiplicity is as difficult as it is to write about it.

All of my life I have been told the story of when my mother held me in her arms for the first time. It was late at night at the airport in Newark, New Jersey. My mother, father, and two brothers, along with my grandparents and uncle, were all waiting in the terminal lounge for my plane to arrive from Seoul, Korea. There were other families also waiting for their new babies to be brought off the plane. My mother tells me that she watched in anticipation as all the escorts walked off the plane with small bundles of Korean babies. Each time they walked toward her, they would pass by, giving the babies to other families. My family grew anxious and nervous as the flow of people exiting the plane grew sparse. My chaperone and I were the last to deplane. The woman walked toward my family and placed me in the arms of my mother. I was six months old. I clung to her, put my head on her shoulder, patted her back, and called her "mother" in Korean. The year was 1975. The day was Mother's Day.

Growing up in a transracial adoptive family, I was often confused by the images of the "normal, nuclear families." We didn't look like any other family I saw. I couldn't comprehend how I could love my family, feel accepted by them, and believe that I belonged to them as much as my phenotypically white brothers did. Yet every time I looked in the mirror, my reflection haunted me, because the face that stared back was not the same color as my family's. This awareness was reinforced by the sometimes brutal questions of others. I constantly had to explain that I really was my brother's sister. He was not my husband but truly my brother. I was not the foreign exchange student who just never left. Embarrassed by the attention, I tried to ignore the differences. I took the negativity and dissociation I felt and began to internalize the feelings. I fooled myself into thinking and acting the role of a "good little Asian saved from her fallen country and brought to the land of salvation." I began to believe the messages about being an Asian girl and about being adopted. This compliance was one of the only ways I learned to gain acceptance and validation as a child. I realized that my identity was being created *for* me, not *by* me.

When I was ten years old, we moved from a progressive city in Maryland to a small town in Connecticut. Aside from the infamous New England fall foliage, the only color I saw was white. I suppose it wasn't such a radical change for the rest of my family, because they didn't need the difference and diversity I required for spiritual survival. I quickly realized the key to acceptance was to not be too ethnic, or ethnic at all. To be accepted, I had to grasp and identify with whiteness, completely denying my Asian self. I spent my teenage years running away from myself and rebelling from the stereotype of the "good, cute little Asian." The only images of Asian Americans that I saw came from the television. I accepted the misrepresentations as real and accurate because our town only had a few people of color to begin with. I always thought they were the exceptions to the stereotypes. We were the "fortunate ones," and we self-perpetuated the lies about ourselves and about our people.

> **I realized I was entitled to feeling something other than apologetic. I could be angry. I could be aggressive. I could be the opposite of this little china doll that everyone expected me to be.**

I fooled myself into believing that life was so great. I was accepted and had all of the things I thought made me just like everyone else, yet I couldn't understand why I still carried around a sadness. I was playing out the script that had been given to me, yet I kept feeling as though I was in the wrong play. When I would talk to my friends about it, they wouldn't and couldn't understand. I was told that I was making too big a deal out of being Asian, and besides, I *was* just like everyone else. They thought I just worried too much. My friends went so far as to convince me by telling me that "I wasn't really Asian. I was white." But the truth couldn't be denied, just as the color of my skin couldn't. They thought that because we were friends they were entitled or allowed to nickname me "Chinky." They tried to justify it by saying it was only a joke. My boyfriends were ashamed they had an Asian-American girlfriend.

They assumed they had a right to physically, mentally, and sexually abuse me because they thought they were doing me a favor by lowering their standards to be with a woman of color.

I came across feminism as a first-year student at Ohio State University. I was extremely depressed at the time. Everything—my created identity, the world of whiteness that I knew, the denial of my race—that I had worked so hard at repressing and ignoring throughout my life was finally surfacing and emerging. I no longer had the validation of whiteness to protect my false identity. The world that I had understood was changing, and I was confronted with defining myself without the associations of my family and friends. I was forced to step outside of my white world, shedding my blinders to find that I wasn't white and that I had never really been so. The only illusion was the one I had created for myself, the one that had found acceptance. But I was beginning to realize the cost of this facade.

Yes, I had a large circle of white friends and boyfriends throughout high school. Despite their acceptance, however, I was simultaneously cast as the other. I was undeniably Asian. I was the subject and the object. I was the china doll and the dragoness. The contradictions and the abuse confused me. How could my friends and boyfriends love me, yet in a heated argument spit out "chink" at me? How could they respect me, yet sing the song that had been popularized from the movie *Full Metal Jacket*, "Me So Horny"?

My first women's studies course focused on the history of the women's movement and the social context and contemporary issues facing feminism today. We looked at issues ranging from violence to sexual orientation, women-centered spirituality, representation in music and film, and body image. I began to recognize my extensive history of sexual, mental, and physical abuse with boyfriends, and I started to comprehend the cycle of abuse and forgiveness. I was able to begin to stop blaming myself and shift the responsibility back to those who had inflicted the abuse. Initially I had disconnected the abuse from racism, even though it was heavily intertwined and simultaneous. It was just too large for me to understand, and it was still too early for me to grapple with race. I still was thinking that I just needed to become the "right" kind of Asian American and then everything would make sense.

I know that for a lot of women of color, feminism is perceived as being a white woman's movement that has little space for or acknowledgment of women of color. I understand how that is true, but back then, this class became a catalyst for change and healing. It was a major turning point in my life, where I was able to break my silence and find empowerment within myself and for myself. Women's studies offered me a place where there was validation and reason. I was uncovering and understanding how my own internalization was tied to ideologies of racism and sexism. Although the analysis of racism was somewhat limited in these courses, it served as a lead for future interests. Women's studies and feminism were a stepping-stone toward striving for a holistic understanding of myself.

Initially I identified my experiences as being part of a larger discourse and reality. I named the abuse and trauma of my past and could therefore heal from it. I proudly began calling myself a feminist. I viewed feminism as, broadly, the eradication of sexism, racism, ageism, ableism, and heterosexism. It was a social and political commitment to a higher vision for society by resituating women from the margins into the center. I began recognizing and naming what I believed was sexism. The summer after my first women's studies course, I returned home and wrote a dramatic letter to the Congregational church of which I was a member. I earnestly asked them to remove my name from its list because "I did not want to support or be affiliated with a patriarchal institution such as a Christian church." I felt this act was a rite of passage, my initiation into the feminist movement.

But I left college feeling as though there was something missing from this feminism. Professors would talk about Black feminism or women of color feminism, but merely as another mark on their feminist timeline. Little time was dedicated to really examining the intersection of race and gender. Back home, I went to my local New Age store (which also doubled as the feminist bookstore) and stumbled upon *This Bridge Called My Back: Writings by Radical Women of Color* (edited by Cherríe Moraga and Gloria Anzaldúa). It was the first time I had found a book that had the words "women of color" as part of the title. It was as if I had found the pot of gold at the end of the feminist rainbow. Even though I didn't find myself completely represented in the book—specifically, because none of the contributors had been an adopted child—I did find my thoughts, anger, and pain represented through the eloquent voices of other women of color. Their writings incorporated race and sexuality.

Reading this anthology, I realized I was entitled to feeling something other than apologetic. I could be angry. I could be aggressive. I could be the opposite of this little china doll that everyone expected me to be. Given my background, this book was life-changing. It represented one of the first moments where I could claim something that was mine; something different from my parents, my friends, my community; something other than whiteness. I remember sitting at the town beach on a hot and humid August day, flipping through the book, my mind exploding and expanding. As I sat there frantically reading, I recall looking up at the sun, closing my eyes, and thanking the goddess that I had found this work. Through this discovery I had found that I was not alone. Not only was I feminist, but I was a woman of color feminist.

What makes my relationship to women of color feminism different from most other women of color is how and why I entered the conversation. I began looking at race through gender, where most have the reverse experience. This idea of entry point is crucial. I call myself a woman of color before I call myself an Asian American. It reflects how I have come to see myself and how I understand my own identity. The term "women of color" seems broadly inviting and inclusive, while "Asian American" feels rigid and exclusive. Women of color feminism took me from being a victim to being a warrior.

I am now in an ethnic studies graduate program trying to explore if women of color are within feminism's third wave, and if so, where. I began this project as an undergraduate, but I had hit a wall. It was difficult locating voices that represented Generation X or third-wave women of color feminism. Not much had been written, as our voices were just beginning to emerge. I found women of color feminists in alternative places, such as zines, anthologies, magazines, and pop culture. I felt frustrated that our voices were deemed not "accredited" enough to be represented in the mainstream.

I held a certain expectation for Jennifer Baumgardner and Amy Richards's book, *Manifesta: Young Women, Feminism, and the Future*. This book markets itself as being *the* text for the third wave of feminism, and I had high hopes that it would address issues of race, gender, and class sexuality. Instead, I found the specific history of white (privileged) women. This is a great book for the white college woman who has recently been inspired by feminism and wants to know about the past and how she should contribute to the future.

Yet this history is complicated by the fact that the authors do not honestly acknowledge that this is their intention. Rather, they assert that this book is a history of all women, dropping the names of such women of color as Rebecca Walker and Audre Lorde.

I found it astounding that there is no extensive discussion of women of color feminism. This indicates that Baumgardner and Richards feel as though this is a separate issue, a different kind of feminism. It is as if their work is the master narrative of feminism, with women of color feminism as an appendage. I had hoped that they would consider such books as *This Bridge Called My Back* and Audre Lorde's *Sister Outsider* as groundbreaking, as they are deemed by most Generation X women of color. These books were life-changing to me, not only because their critiques have historical value, but also because what these writers were saying in the 1980s was still relevant in the 1990s. *Manifesta* is successful in creating momentum for young white women's activism through the attempt to move feminism out of academia and back into a social and political movement. But the book's greatest contribution was that it raised a need to create a lineage for women of color feminism.

Is it possible to construct a feminist genealogy that maintains inclusivity? Does feminism still exist for women of color, or is it just a "white thing"? Are Generation X women of color participating in feminism? These questions propelled me to think further about the connections as well as the separations between women of color and feminism. In the exploration of the third wave of women of color feminism, I talked to several women of color professors and students at the University of California at Berkeley. Their responses and our conversations together were incredibly helpful. These women challenged me to further think about my own conceptions surrounding feminism.

I had expected that, as women of color, most of these students would also identify as women of color feminists. I believed the two terms to be synonymous. Instead, I found a rejection of the word "feminism." I hear many women of color refer to themselves as such, yet they make the distinction that they are not claiming a feminist identity. Although many of the women support and stand in alliance with women of color feminism, there is still a lapse in their chosen identity. Many report to have read the popular and pivotal texts within women of color feminism and have felt moved, but their "empowerment" only goes so far.

What is it about the word "feminism" that has encouraged women of color to stand apart from it? Feminism has been indoctrinated into the academy through the discipline of women's studies. It has moved out of the social and political spaces from where it emerged. Women's studies have collapsed the diversity that was part of the feminist movement into a discipline that has become a homogeneous generality. For women in the third wave, then, one needs to have the academic training of women's studies to be an "accredited feminist." Once race is added to the complexity, many women of color feel as though the compromise or negotiation is just too high a price to pay to be called a feminist. For women of color, participation in women's studies and feminism still causes splintering in our identities.

Many women believe that there is a certain required persona to be a feminist. In the ethnic studies course "Women of Color in the U.S." at Berkeley, for example, students expressed feeling that they didn't have enough knowledge or background to be able to call themselves feminists. The students' comments reflected how many women of color find it difficult to access feminism. Often the response is that "feminism is a white women's thing." Whiteness in feminism comes to represent privilege, power, and opportunity. It rarely positions women of color as being as legitimate as the identities of white women. The field of women's studies has been accurately accused of treating race as a secondary oppression by offering courses about race that are separate from the central curriculum, while the field of ethnic studies feels more comfortable as a place to discuss race and gender. But even in ethnic studies, women's experiences and histories still remain on the margins. Like women's studies, they, too, have had problems integrating gender into the analysis of race.

Women of color often feel that women's studies is a battlefield where they are forced to defend their communities and themselves. Women's studies, the academic endeavor of feminism, has a history of relegating women of color to second. When women of color raise issues of race in these classrooms, the response from other students is often defensive and loaded with repressed white guilt. For young women of color, there is a sentiment that we must find a central identity that precedes all others. We are asked to find one identity that will encapsulate our entirety. We are asked to choose between gender, class, race, and sexuality and to announce who we are first and foremost. Yet where is the space for multiplicity?

Although I am a self-proclaimed woman of color feminist, I struggle with being an "authentic" woman of color feminist. Even though I realize it is self-defeating, I worry that other women of color will look at my feminism and judge it as being socialized whiteness and an effect of adoption. The roots of my feminism are connected to my adoptive mother, although I am uncertain whether she would identify as a feminist. She was a woman who wouldn't let us watch *The Flintstones* or *The Jetsons* because of their negative portrayal of women, yet she unquestionably had dinner on the table every night for her husband, sons, and daughter. Most important, she raised me to believe I could be whoever I wanted to be and a strong woman. If feminism has been bestowed to me from my adoptive mother, then I choose not to look at it as another indicator of whiteness or of being whitewashed. Rather, I see it as a gift, one that has shown me not the limitations of mainstream feminism, but the possibilities of women of color feminism. People sometimes question my attachment to feminism. Despite the criticism, it has served as a compass that helps me navigate away from paralysis into limitless potential.

One of the reasons that my project is now at a standstill is that the conversation has changed. In the 1970s and 1980s, women of color feminists seemed to be in solidarity with each other. Their essays showed the racism and classism within mainstream feminism, forcing mainstream feminism to be accountable. Today, however, women of color are focused on the differences that exist among us. When we try to openly and honestly acknowledge the differences between us, we become trapped in difference, which can result in indifference.

Women of color feminism has currently been reduced to a general abstraction that has flattened out difference and diversity, causing tension between women of color. Instead of collectively forming alliances against whiteness, women of color now challenge the opposing identities that exist under the umbrella term "women of color." It raises questions about entitlement and authenticity. It tries to suppress the heterogeneous composition of women of color feminism by trying to create a unifying term. Yet the differences of class, racialization, and sexuality have arisen and persisted, challenging assumptions that all women of color are in solidarity with each other. We all come with backgrounds and histories that differ from one another, and despite knowing this, we still maintain this ideal and creation of the authentic "woman of color." The one that is the right class, the right race, the right sexuality. We must refuse to be reduced to an abstraction. We must address the conflicts that have begun to fester and cause paralysis instead of fostering change. But that also means we need to revitalize women of color feminism so that those actions can begin to take place.

I see women of color feminism at this moment of indifference. I see the backstabbing. I hear the gossip. I feel the tension. We use our words like fists to beat each other down and beat each other silent. It is not pretty and certainly not productive. When do we recognize that the moment has come to move forward? I wish I had some solution, a way to "use our difference to achieve diversity instead of division." But we know that clichés are just clichés. They don't provide us with the fairy-tale endings. They don't make us feel better or more hopeful. More often than not, I think clichés just annoy us and leave us sarcastic.

It is crucial to explore and expose the problems of women of color feminism, but we also need to be wary of what we are willing to sacrifice. I think a new, third space is being created in women of color feminism. Those of us who are not easily recognized and acknowledged as women of color are coming to feminism as a place to discuss the implications of invisibility. We are pushing, expanding, and exploding ideologies of multiplicity and intersectionality. We come as transracial adoptees, women of mixed race, bisexuals, refugees, and hundreds of other combinations. For us, women of color feminism continues to be a living theory and a way to survive.

It's Not an Oxymoron
The Search for an Arab Feminism

SUSAN MUADDI DARRAJ

> I see no reason to say that the Arab woman is less intelligent and
> energetic and sincere than the [W]estern woman.
>
> —Ghada Samman, 1961

My father is a feminist, although he would probably never admit it.
It is difficult to even write the two words "father" and "feminist"
next to each other in the same sentence (despite the nice allitera-
tive sound). I can imagine him hearing it and shrinking away from
the word, shaking his head vehemently and saying, in his thick
Middle Eastern accent that all my girlfriends find so charming,
"No, no, no, not me, thank you." And yet, despite his denial, my
father has helped me form my own unique feminist identity more
than that other F-word—Friedan.

I remember sitting in a feminist theory class in graduate school,
feeling strangely unmoved by the words of Betty Friedan and the
second-wave feminist writers. I understood their struggles and
respected their courage—there was not a doubt in my mind that
it took a lot of courage to resist Western patriarchal demands on
women's lives. But these were not representative feminists. In *The
Feminine Mystique*, Friedan expounded on the woes of being a mere
housewife, but it seemed there was a certain level of class privilege

285

that accompanied her position. The role of a "housewife" usually developed when there was a man to support the family, when he could do it all on his own salary. Although my mother swept the floor and cooked most of our meals, I realized that housework was not her only "work." She also worked full time in the business that she and my father ran together.

Sitting in that class, with other women who expounded on the oppression of housework, I dared once to ask, "Who will do the housework then?" Seventeen pairs of eyes turned to me, and I continued: "If men don't do it and women don't do it, who will? It has to be done. Do you propose that we hire *other women* to come and do it? Other women who clean people's homes because they have the opportunity to do nothing else?"

Silence greeted my question, as I had expected. I realized then that most of the women in the class were upper-middle and middle-class white women—and I felt like a complete outsider. Perhaps they could understand Friedan because her brand of feminism spoke directly to their experience. But it didn't speak to mine. I didn't view housework as a mark of oppression. There was a certain sense of pride placed on a clean, welcoming home, and both my parents had always placed value on it. That was why my father spent his weekends trimming the lawn and sweeping the walkways, and why my mother mopped the kitchen floor and wiped the windows until they sparkled. It was why my brothers and I were marched off to various rooms every Saturday morning, armed with furniture polish and dust rags. We *all* did housework. No, this version of feminism did not appeal to me. But then again, what version did? For a long time I thought that this was the *only* brand of feminism that existed. If that was true, I certainly wasn't a card-carrying member.

Furthermore, I didn't like the way this feminism viewed people like my mother and grandmothers and aunts—and me, for that matter. I was tired of turning on the evening news, eager to learn news of the Middle East, and seeing women clad in heavy, black robes, their eyes lowered but barely visible behind the slits in their face veils as they scurried past the television cameras. I have been to the Middle East. I am an Arab Christian, and I know many Arab Christian and Muslim women. Some—but definitely not all—of my Muslim friends veil themselves, as do a few of the older, conservative Christian women, especially before entering a church. Why did Americans equate Muslim women with veils so completely, and why did the cameras seem to pick out only these women?

The answer was an uncomplicated one: because this was the quaint vision of the Middle East with which America felt comfortable. This vision included heavily robed and mustachioed sheiks, belly dancers, tents, camels, and—of course—veiled women. This vision was, to use an orientalist cliché, a desert mirage, concocted by the same Hollywood producers who had created Rudolph Valentino (*The Sheik*).

American feminists, like the rest of the nation and the Western world, had accepted the flawed image of the Middle East and Middle Eastern women without question. "Of course, they [meek and silent Arab women] are oppressed; *we* [liberated, assertive Western women with voices] must help *them*." I have heard similar statements (with the notions in the brackets implied) from white American feminists who wanted to save their Arab sisters but not to understand them. They wanted to save them from the burden of their families and religion but not from the war, hunger, unemployment, political persecution, and oppression that marked their daily lives and that left them with only their families and religion as sole sources of comfort. The tone of white Western feminism—with its books about "lifting the veil on Arab women" and Arab women "lifting the veil of silence"—was that Arab feminism was nothing greater than an amusing oxymoron.

> **❝ I felt betrayed by a movement that claimed to create a global sisterhood of women, but it seemed that the Arab woman was the poor and downtrodden stepsister in this family. Where was my feminism? ❞**

The apparent hypocrisy and condescension that white Western feminists held for Arab women confused me. I felt betrayed by a movement that claimed to create a global sisterhood of women, but it seemed that the Arab woman was the poor and downtrodden stepsister in this family.

Where was my feminism?

It was my father who first taught me "feminism," who told me that I could do anything I wanted—achieve any goal, reach any height—and that he would support me in that climb. I don't remember ever feeling that my culture—and in my mind my father embodied that culture almost completely—stood in my way, although others thought my culture was a jungle of patriarchal pitfalls.

One day my father told me a story that rocked my world. It was that of Djamila Bouhired, an Algerian woman who had played an instrumental role in the Algerian resistance against the colonial French forces. It was one of those stories that he and his generation had heard about while growing up in Palestine, nations away from Algeria, though the story stirred them nonetheless. Bouhereid had been captured by the French and tortured in unspeakable ways, but she had refused to divulge essential information about the resistance. The torture continued until it finally killed her. He told me the story during one of our many marathon conversations that usually lasted through the night, while we sat at the kitchen table, sipping coffee and eating oranges. I became obsessed with Bouhereid's story and tried to find out everything I could about her. Unfortunately, there was very little information about her—or Arab women in general—available in English.

My futile search was not a complete failure, however, only the opening of a new door. I came across the names of other Arab women I had heard of: Huda Sha'rawi, the founder of the Egyptian Feminist Union, who had called for the ban of the veil at the beginning of the twentieth century; Mai Ziyyadah, a feminist writer and a contemporary of Sha'rawi, who called for men to free women in order to free themselves; even Khadijah, the first wife of the Prophet Muhammad, who had financed his travels, owned a lucrative business, and been the first convert to Islam. I searched the Internet for information on more modern Arab women: Hanan Ashrawi, a chief spokesperson for the Palestinians; Leila Ahmed, a feminist and scholar who wrote about Arab women with accuracy, honesty, and pages of solid research; and Fatima Mernissi, who sought to rediscover Islam's valuation of women.

I also searched for something that neither the Internet nor the library's shelves could offer me: a real, hard, searing look at the lives of modern, everyday Arab women. I saved my pennies and, armed with my notebooks and pens, traveled to Egypt, Jordan, and Palestine over the course of a few years. I met women in my family and made some new friends. One summer, I spent three months in the West Bank, in the city of Ramallah, and studied at Birzeit University. Ramallah and Birzeit were a mere half-hour taxicab ride away from Taybeh, the small village where my parents grew up and where my grandmother and several aunts, cousins, and uncles lived. Although I was thrilled to spend time with my relatives, I also wanted to meet and interact with Palestinian college women, and I met quite a few and listened to their stories. At many points and on many occasions I felt like I was looking into a mirror at what I would have been like had my father and mother never left the political oppression and insecurities of Palestine.

One woman, a twenty-four-year-old student, told me how it was a struggle to get to the university every day, not because her father wouldn't permit it (for he actually encouraged her), but because she had to take a multi-passenger taxi in which she had been groped many times by the male passengers. Another woman, also in her mid-twenties, described how her parents were proud that she had been accepted at the university, but she often skipped semesters because money usually ran low. It was a choice of buying textbooks or letting her younger siblings go without meat for several months. She estimated that at that rate it would take another six years to finish her bachelor's degree. Another woman, who veiled herself, explained to me how as a religious person she felt compelled to educate herself for her own betterment and for that of her family.

It struck me that many of the women whom I met could be considered feminists, perhaps not by the standards of the white Western feminism that I had encountered in my feminist theory class, but by the standards of a different feminism—one that allowed women to retain their culture, to have pride in their traditions, and to still vocalize the gender issues of their community. These were women whom I considered feminists because they believed in the dignity and potential for upward mobility of every woman; they wanted to erase class lines between women; they worked so that they could have choices in their lives and not be channeled into one way of life.

I realized upon my return to the United States that fall that, more than ever, I longed for a feminism that would express who I was and what my experiences were as an Arab-American woman. Feminism was within my grasp, but I discerned several obstacles that blocked my path. The chief one was the seeming universality of white Western feminism, which appears to leave no room for other visions. This caused various conflicts within me. Another obstacle to voicing my own feminism to white Western feminists was that of the various traditions in my Arabic culture that were indeed the markings of a patriarchal culture. Many feminist texts and discourses on the Middle East highlighted such traditions, although most modern-day societies, including that of the United States, can be accurately described as patriarchal.

One such tradition is that Arab parents are usually referred to by the name of their eldest son. Thus, a couple whose eldest son is named Abdallah would be referred to socially as Im Abdallah (mother of Abdallah) and Abu Abdallah (father of Abdallah). I am the eldest child in my family, but my parents are called by the name of my brother, who is a year younger. There is generally an emphasis on having at least one male child in Arab families, and the boys are often named after their grandfathers; my brother Abdallah was given the name of my grandfather Abdallah. As a woman, this certainly bothers me, and it strikes a sour note with many Arab women. After all, why the big deal about boys? What is so disappointing about girls? It seems to me that American feminists overly criticize this tradition, however, while forgetting that it is no different from American boys being named David Jr. or Jonathan So-and-So III. As far as I can remember, American girls aren't dubbed Michelle Jr. or Jennifer IV, unless they are European monarchs, but this point does not occupy chapters in Arab feminist texts on the West.

Another unfairly beleaguered custom is that of the traditional Arabic marriage, which has wrinkled many a conversation with my American feminist friends. In the Middle East and among Middle Easterners living in other parts of the world, when a couple decides to get married, it is expected that a *toulbeh* will take place. During the *toulbeh*, the potential bridegroom arrives at the home of the potential bride, escorted by several members of his family. The bride's family waits, and members of her extended family wait with them. The eldest male of the groom's family requests the bride's hand from the eldest male in her family. When the expected "yes" is announced (because the question is a formality, after all), the two families celebrate their upcoming union. Of course, this is a patriarchal tradition, one in which a woman is viewed as a person who should not answer for herself. Again, is it different than in American culture, where it is considered a sweet gesture and a romantic leftover from traditional times for a man to ask for the bride's hand from her father? And don't fathers still walk their daughters down the aisle and "give them away"? The endless explanations of Arab wedding customs that I had to offer my American feminist friends, however, would have led one to think that it was utterly barbaric.

In the aftermath of the events of September 11 and with the conflict in Afghanistan, the same stilted media coverage would make anyone think that *every* Middle Eastern woman saw the world from between the peepholes of her burqa's face netting. These traditions are usually used to create a picture of the Arab world as a *1,001 Nights*-like land of wicked and despotic sultans and silenced and imprisoned harem girls—women who need the West to enlighten, educate, and save them. (But Scheherazade, a Muslim Arab woman and the heroine of *1,001 Nights*, saved herself and her countrywomen, so it doesn't make sense to me *why* Arab culture is attacked as antiwoman, as if no other culture had gender-oppressive traditions of which to be ashamed.)

These naming and wedding traditions, and others like them, made me second-guess my professed need to find a feminism that suited me. After all, on one level I liked these traditions—they were deeply embedded in my culture and in myself as a person. When I got married, my husband's eldest uncle asked for my hand from my eldest uncle. Did that mean I wasn't a feminist? Some of my friends, upon hearing this, wrinkled their noses in disgust and shook their heads sadly at me as if to say, "Poor thing! She's just condemned herself to a lifetime of constant pregnancies, Little League games, and soap operas." My God, I thought, was I being kicked out of the club before I had even officially joined?

This experience—feeling emotionally torn between my culture and what white Western feminism told me I had to be—relates almost inversely to another conflict that obstructed the recognition of my feminist identity: America's exoticism of Arab women. Although we were considered veiled and meek, we were simultaneously and ironically considered sultry, sexual, and "different." People, especially white feminists, were often intrigued by my "exoticness" and asked me silly questions, like whether Arab women knew how to belly-dance or whether I knew of any women who lived in harems. I was also frequently mistaken as a Muslim, because many people couldn't conceive of an Arab Christian (although Arab Christians and Muslims have long allied themselves against the pervasive stereotypes that threaten to categorize us both). They wanted to know if I had ever ridden a camel, and if I would have an arranged marriage, and would my husband be taking other wives as well? If people in general, and feminists in particular, knew so little of my culture, what was the hope that I would be seriously received as a feminist?

Some Muslim women see no contradiction between feminism and Islam. In her book *Palestinian Women: Patriarchy and Resistance in the West Bank*, Cheryl Rubenberg studies Palestinian women who live in the camps and villages of the West Bank and highlights the phenomenon of the Muslim Sisters (Ikhwat al-musilmat).[1] Sometimes called "Islamist feminists," the Muslim Sisters believe that Islam gives women full rights but that the religion has been corrupted by men to suit their patriarchal agenda. One Muslim Sister whom Rubenberg interviewed said that their mission is to bring people back to the true Islam, which historically allowed women the right to be educated, to work, to participate in public life, and to own property. According to the Sisters, however, Islam has been perverted by men's patriarchal ambitions in the centuries since the Prophet Muhammad's death. Because of anti-Muslim sentiments (which are inextricably linked to anti-Arab sentiments) and the general misconceptions of Islam in the West (that all Muslim men are terrorists with long beards, and all Muslim women are battered and wear veils), it would be difficult for a Western, non-Muslim person to understand the desire of Arab Muslim women to retain both their religion and their sense of feminism.

Another conflict that threatened my development of a feminist voice was my split vision—my ability to thrive in American culture but to also appreciate Arab culture. Further, it was my frustration with white Western feminists who took up issues like keeping one's name after marriage, but who sniffed at Arab women, who had always kept their names, and whose biggest problem was how to afford bread for dinner.[2] I was living in America, land of the free and home of the brave, while cousins in the West Bank were throwing stones at Israeli tanks and working extra jobs to help my aunts and uncles pay the bills. While I was hopping into my car to work every day, perhaps stopping for my morning coffee, they were walking to the taxi stop to see if a car was available and willing to drive them around the roadblocks that the Israelis had set up—all just to get to class on time for a final exam. Even worse, it was US money and foreign aid to Israel that kept Palestinians locked in a seemingly hopeless situation that robbed them of their futures.

I think that I had a guilt complex as a result of this split vision: I loathed having to write papers on the "Angel of the House" theory and the imagery of women trapped behind wallpaper, while Arab women were dealing with issues of physical survival.[3] Although I admired the work of white feminists and respected the ways in which they overcame their own obstacles, those were not my obstacles. I could not focus on the complexities of white Western feminist theory when I knew that Arab women faced very different issues.

And I returned once again to my initial question: Where did I fit in all this?

A few years ago, through a strange set of coincidences, I found an answer. I had started reading the work of Black feminists, such as bell hooks, who took on Betty Friedan full force. She challenged the relevance of Friedan's ideas about housewives to Black women, who have always had to work. Her work led me to Gloria Anzaldúa, who led me to Barbara Smith, and the list grew. I was heartened by the fact that Black women and other women of color had the courage to carve a feminism of their own out of the monolithic block that was generally accepted as "feminism."

About this time I caught up with a friend of mine, an assertive and lively Arab woman from San Francisco, who was visiting when I lived in Philadelphia. I was twenty-four. It was a gloriously sunny day in the city, and we decided to go out. We sat in a coffee shop on Philadelphia's hip South Street section and talked about the way that we both felt locked out of feminism and the lack of relevance that feminism seemed to have for our lives. We also talked about the way that analyses of Arab women's issues seemed to be largely conducted by white Western women.

"But it's white Western feminism that doesn't relate to my life," I interjected.

"True," she agreed. "There is actually a group of Arab women who deal with gender issues—their association is called AWSA, the Arab Women's Solidarity Association."

"Arab feminists?" I asked, unbelieving.

"Yeah. I think that you can call them feminists." She gave me the website information, and I checked it out immediately upon my return home. I found out that AWSA is a network for Arab women, meant to provide support and to serve as the basis for the Arab women's movement. It was founded by Nawal el-Saadawi, an Egyptian doctor and leading feminist. That sunny Philadelphia afternoon initiated my awareness of AWSA members, who were scholars, artists, writers, and everyday women who felt that gender issues in the Arab world and among Arabs in other countries should be discussed and diagnosed by a circle that included Arab women themselves.

Another life-changing event occurred around this time: I met the man I eventually married. As an Arab woman, romance had never been easy because of the strong cultural taboo on dating. I often watched movies and television shows in which girlfriends chatted with each other (usually while doing each other's hair at slumber parties) about the good looks of a new boyfriend, the disappointment of a blind date, the elation over a romantic dinner, or the pain of a breakup. I could never chat so easily about romance because it was a distant, remote experience, one that I knew only vicariously through television, films, and books. Furthermore, it was difficult to meet American men who were not entranced by my "exoticness" (probably the most ridiculous comment I've ever heard) and the aspects of my culture that they didn't understand (such as not showing someone the bottoms of my shoes or genuinely enjoying time with my family, etc.). I also met some Arab men who, ironically, thought I was too "Americanized": my unaccented, perfect English littered with slang; my tendency to wear boots and blue jeans; and my refusal to spend more than three minutes on my hair and makeup testified to that, I suppose, not to mention my vocalized interest in pursuing my career and my (equally vocalized) lack of desire to have children for a long time.

But meeting my future husband was an eye-opening experience. I felt that I finally had met someone who could understand and even relate to my split vision. Not only was he kind and caring, but he respected my intellect, my career goals, and my opinions. In other words, he allowed me to be myself—and comfortably so. When, over dinner, I mentioned to him the topic of feminism—a word I had uttered to few men, save my father—he said that I didn't strike him as a feminist. I asked why not, and he offered me an interesting response: "Well, I guess I'm thinking of 'feminists' as what I see here in the States. And they seem largely self-involved. But you care about all kinds of issues, not just the ones that affect you. And I think that you consider the concept of family to be above that of the individual."

I pointed out that women have traditionally been reared to ignore and neglect themselves for the sake of others (i.e., children, husbands, in-laws, etc.). This included Arab women. Women in general had also never had the opportunity to focus on their own development and their own goals. But I also realized that he was thinking of traditional, American, white feminism when he said that, and I explained that I felt there might be another kind of feminism out there, one that appealed more to women like me, who wanted to be feminists and spouses and mothers.

I could see that he was intrigued by what I was saying, and he admitted that this conversation had redefined feminism for him. "Besides," he asked casually, "why does there have to be a choice between feminism and family? I think a woman can have both."

He was right.

I knew at that point that with the recent riveting conglomeration of coincidental events in my life—my interest in Black feminism, the AWSA and the discovery of a possible Arab feminism, and meeting my future husband—something exciting was happening. My feminist self—my own version of feminism—was emerging.

It required no great sacrifice of my Arab heritage, no shame at my close ties to my family, and no compromise of my own needs. It involved two of the most important men in my life—my father and my husband—unlike the ways in which I saw American feminism making a conscious split from male influence. (I should also mention here that although my father and husband are the two best men I personally know, they are not rare examples of Arab men— their mentalities are not unusual in the Arab world, despite what CNN says.) There was no need to define independence as living in isolation from my family and making decisions without their support and advice. There was no imperative to shake my head at the thought of having my own family and being a mother. I could be a feminist in a way that suited *my* life, not in a feminism that would mold me to its ideal shape. After all, wasn't feminism supposed to be about making my own choices?

So here I am—an Arab-American feminist. I am happily married. I work. I write. I have three children. I read the newspaper every day.

I call my congressperson about US foreign policy issues that negatively affect Arab women. I follow the news in Palestine and Israel religiously, on both American and Arab news channels (thanks to satellite technology). I cringe first and take action second whenever I come across hackneyed "exotic" portrayals of Arab women. I eagerly read the ever-growing body of work being produced about Arab women. This lifestyle is what feminism means to me now, although I once thought that I would never use this word to describe myself.

Most important, once I realized my own version of feminism, I found myself better able to understand white Western feminism and the many outer storms and internal divisions it has had to weather. Now that I have my own foundation, I see the need for a cross-cultural feminist dialogue, especially after the September 11 attacks on the United States, which have led to an overthrow of the Taliban and an intensified interest on the part of Americans to understand Islam in general. As that interest expands to include the issues of Muslim women and Arab women, it should be clarified that any resulting dialogues must be inclusive of Arab voices in order to be successful. I applaud American feminism for attempting to bridge an intimidatingly wide gap, but that bridge must be rooted in firm ground at *both* ends of the divide. It should no longer be possible to write about Arab women with any aura of expertise or authority without *first* knowing what Arab women need and want.

Angry Transsexuals

LEXI ADSIT

"YOU'RE RAAAACCCIIIISSSTTTT!!!!!!"

"I just don't understand why we're spending millions upon millions of dollars for rights of the privileged few when there's thousands of queer and trans youth that are homeless."

"Just a heads up: _____ _____ is problematic as **** and here's what they said..."

These are just a few of the examples of various call-out posts I have written in my time. When I was in high school and my early years of college, I was one of those people who got into a lot of Internet arguments. Whether it was about race, queerness, being transgender, or capitalism, I would fight tirelessly from behind my keyboard. I would rip people apart, whether they were people I had gone to high school with or friends of friends that I barely knew, for posting articles or opinions on anything from same-sex marriage (at the time I was against "assimilatory politics and tactics") to whether capitalism was good or bad (obviously bad).

Sass, snark, anger, and righteousness were all there to guide and empower me. I was beginning to enter what some might call the Social Justice Warrior fervor. I was beginning to understand the world and be angry at its structures of power that had failed me and my communities and reproduced a system that exploited every aspect of our lives. It wasn't just me, either. Almost an entire generation of young folks (primarily queer and trans young folks of color, in my experience) used what is now named "call-out culture" and taught us how to name and reveal problematic people. It was an outlet, a way of coping with a world that treated us like shit, and our way of striking back against people with more privilege than us.

As I struggled to write this essay, I kept thinking about call-out culture as something that happened exclusively on Facebook and other social media, but some of my most fiery Sagittarius-rising call-out moments happened offline. It wasn't until I saw other ways of engaging with these topics and learned how exhausting and unproductive it was to call someone out that I started to change my approach.

In 2007, I fell in love with an organization and gave them three years of peak organizing and labor, working for free to conduct workshops at high schools across Northern California providing support for my fellow queer and trans youth who were trying to organize around LGBTQ issues. I quickly climbed the ladder of leadership, ran a leadership training retreat, and was eventually invited to be on the board of directors as a youth member. I and many youth participants had a very different vision of how the organization should operate and envisioned an organization that offered more opportunities to queer and trans youth and didn't exploit us to help pass laws or work as program staff without compensation. However, when I brought these issues up, I was accused of failing to complete my duties as a board member, an attack that left me shaken and crying. It was at this point that I turned to call-out tactics.

In 2010, I resigned from the board of directors and called for the executive director's resignation and accountability to the constituents of the organization by the board. In 2011, I also resigned from an internship at a research center, because I was fulfilling the role of what I believed should have been a paid staff position and did not feel the organization was doing enough for the community it was researching. These two situations are private examples of how race, class, and gender came into play as I navigated organizations and nonprofits that consistently worked around issues of queer and trans people of color.

Was it worth it? Probably not, but it made me feel better than almost anything. I would joke to my friends that it was time for me to join another organization so I could resign or call them out. Granted, at the time, in 2010 and 2011, I was nineteen and twenty years old. I had barely experienced work and didn't fully understand how nonprofit organizations were intentionally built after the social movements of the 1960s as an alternative to mass movements. I didn't know that organizations just can't shift the way they operate in their day-to-day without significant investment and push from numerous stakeholders. I learned hard lessons about nonprofit operations, missions, funding, and adults' investments in capitalism and hierarchy.

As I learned more about the revolutionary history of queer and trans communities, my fervor and anger grew. How could we be so compliant in a system that continually marginalized and disposed of us? How could we wake up our siblings who had turned to nonprofits as the only solution to these social issues?

At the time, I didn't know it, but in 1973 Sylvia Rivera took over a stage at the Christopher Street Day Parade (also known as Pride), angry and calling out people left and right. She participated in the

Stonewall Riots in 1969 and carried its revolutionary torch until her passing in 2002. In her speech "Ya'll Better Quiet Down," Sylvia was trying to get the attention of Pride-goers and recruit them to support incarcerated queer and trans folks. She did this with a hoarse and anguished voice, an angry appeal to uneducated masses. Sylvia Rivera was twenty-two years old in 1973 and understood the world in an intersectional way akin to the Combahee River Collective.

Fast-forward forty years, and young queer and trans people of color still carry that same anger and righteousness. Unsurprisingly, queer and trans folks, especially Black, Native, and other folks of color, are being exploited in the very organizations and social structures that are meant to push for our liberation and equality. In many of my daily interactions, I still witness, at minimum, microaggressions of racism, transphobia, classism, ableism, or some other form of problematic behavior and, at most, outright expressions of hatred against a marginalized group of people. It shouldn't shock us that as trans women of color we use every tool in our box to appeal to the masses for the right to survive and thrive.

However, are transsexuals always angry and burning bridges? No. We learn from our previous actions and anger. Sylvia Rivera went on to found Street Transvestite Action Revolutionaries (STAR), a house that offered space to previously incarcerated gay and trans folks and sex workers. She went on to become a huge advocate for trans rights, and even on her deathbed met with the Empire State Pride Agenda to negotiate inclusion of transgender people in their structure and goals. This was one small example of Sylvia's evolution into an advocate and her work to transform community organizations to ensure a lasting legacy for her community.

I am grateful that I found ancestors, elders, and peers who saw and validated me for who I was and affirmed my experience as a translatina and as a transracial adoptee and who helped me find mothers I didn't know I had. They deeply impacted my approach and helped me change my ways as I went from exposing and disposing to exposing and holding. I first learned of Sylvia Rivera through my work as president of my gay-straight alliance, and after having gone through countless call-outs, I got older and I got tired. I got tired of putting so much energy and my own fire into battles that more often than not isolated me from the community members and friends I had worked with. I really began to feel the loneliness of my former actions when I had to find my first full-time job out of college. The network that I would typically rely on was nonexistent and I had to start from scratch.

I learned a hard lesson about disposability, and how important it is, as someone who is already marginalized, to value allies, even imperfect allies, if I wanted to succeed. So I shifted my perspective. I learned, I asked for help and support, and, most importantly, I worked to heal those inner demons that had plagued me since childhood.

In middle school I had picked up social cues from pop culture, my friends, and my obsession with Jennifer Lopez. I was this fat baby brown femme who had been assigned male at birth and so people policed my gender expression as they saw fit. When two eighth graders followed me home, peppering me with questions like "Why are you walking like that? Why are you carrying your binder like that? Why are you dressed like that?" I remember so clearly, coming home from school, picking up a kitchen knife and going into my closet and running it flat against my forearm. The cold steel gave me goose bumps and I could imagine taking the sharp edge against my skin and red liquid oozing out. I wanted to have a body that wouldn't draw so much attention, that wouldn't be a target, a body that wouldn't take up so much space. I wanted to be thin, white, and a girl. I wanted to cut the brown, fat, and male features away.

At the time, I didn't realize that this is internalized racism, fatphobia, and cissexism. I didn't know that, even though it was unintentional, being adopted and raised in a primarily white family and community led me to resent my body for being fat, brown, and hairy. Everyone had different features than I did and could access some semblance of happiness while I was struggling with my sexuality, my gender, my expression, and what I now perceive as race and gender performances.

We're living in a time when our organizing and community relationships are the most important things keeping us alive. We aren't the ones who should be choosing whether someone can be a part of our groups or not. We should do better, and we should be better. We need to drastically transform our realities and the ways in which the state perpetuates its harm. We cannot perpetuate the violence that the state continues to inflict upon generations of our communities. It's time we disrupt these cycles.

> **We're living in a time when our organizing and community relationships are the most important things keeping us alive.**

Feminism needs to be rooted in the intersections and engagement of race, class, gender, ability, citizenship, and what Audre Lorde called "difference" in order to continually examine the privileging of other identities or groups and work to undo them for our communal liberation and the creation of a world that allows us to live, learn, and adapt from our mistakes. I need feminism because collectively we are greater than any individual, and now, more than ever, this country needs a moral compass. I need feminism because I need support holding myself accountable and learning from my mistakes. I need feminism because trans women of color are being murdered for existing, and the feminism I need is one that is rooted in the experiences of those who are marginalized and disposed of.

I hope we can undo the violent legacies of capitalism and imperialism. I hope we can undo the violent legacies of genocide against Black and Indigenous communities. I hope we can learn to humanize people and admit to our mistakes. I hope we can become better neighbors, healers, and community members. I hope we are willing to stay and fight for what our communities deserve. I hope we can take this one breath at a time.

Falling off the Tightrope onto a Bed of Feathers

DARICE JONES

I lived my life for a long time on a tightrope, trying to find my middle ground, to please my audience of parents, friends, teachers, and bosses, trying to look good doing it and come out on the other side unscathed. In my little block of Oakland, California, it was not okay to be all that I was. There was too much contradiction involved. I am African (American), Christian-raised but Tao-embracing, invested in the plight of Black men but my life partners are to be women, raised working class but with a middle-class education, peace-bound but activism-prone, and a feminist whose politics are centered around all life—not just the lives of women. Part of learning feminism for me has been learning that you can't be what people want you to be—and learning how to do better than just survive when you fall.

I didn't grow up with "feminism" as an important word. In fact, I didn't come to hear a working definition of it until a college professor created one for me. She said feminism is simply the idea that women should be free to define themselves. A feminist is someone who espouses that belief. I would add that feminism is also about putting that belief into action and working on your own internalized sexism. A feminist is not just someone who envisions a different world, but someone who creates a life that will change it.

I can see feminism at work in every area of my life, as I went from a teething ring to an eyebrow ring. In the late seventies, my early years, I watched my mother and her mother stomping out a ground for me to walk on. Full-time working full-time mothers with full-time investments in their communities and churches is the only image I ever had of the women closest to me. So media images of "stay-at-home" moms never penetrated my psyche. They were as fictional to me as Saturday-morning cartoons. Most of the images I saw in magazines, on television, and in movies were of white middle-class women, but working-class African-American women were my reality; mothers, aunts, cousins, teachers, even my Girl Scout instructors were Black women on a mission to make good in the world.

> "Media images of "stay-at-home" moms never penetrated my psyche. They were as fictional to me as Saturday-morning cartoons."

As early as I can remember, I knew the bar was high. I was expected to conquer any challenge presented to me at school, to excel in extracurricular sports and music, and to be a young leader in our church. These expectations were implicit in the way our family operated. My mother taught me and my four sisters to read as soon as we could speak, and she made us teach each other. That passing down of learning, child to child, laid the groundwork for our deep, close relationships as sisters.

The relationship between my parents was filled with examples of the feminist ideal in action. While we all lived together, until I was twelve, I saw my parents as two equal superpowers, one never bowing to the other. They seemed to have a respect for each other stronger than romance or love. My father, who passed away a couple of years ago, was a big man, intimidating to many because of his size, but a man of heart to those who knew him best. My mother is a tall woman, and people responded not to her size but to her presence, her voice, the way she takes over a room just by walking in. So while movies, TV shows, and commercials portrayed women as weak and emotional and men as strong and stoic, the Jones residence was one in which a couple's home was their castle, and the king was more likely to cry than the queen.

When my parents separated, the two equal pillars that had held up my world into adolescence were shaken. When the dust settled, my mother was left holding up the earth, on her own. After working anywhere between ten- and sixteen-hour overnight shifts as a nurse, our mother would come straight home and drive us to swimming, tennis, craft, or drama lessons. My father lived in the same city and was involved in our lives, and although he never worked an overnight shift, every single ride to every single lesson, my entire life, was given to me by my mother. She made it clear to us that learning was essential to living. Maybe the even greater message was that a woman's choices, actions, and goals were not necessarily dependent on the support of a man. With my mother at the helm of our family, I just assumed that they weren't.

Although my home was a haven for a girl with ambitions and dreams like mine, our Pentecostal church was the first place I encountered a challenge to my right to fully explore my potential. I was thirteen. It was the first place where I saw people close to me reinforce those media images of women "in their places" that I had so easily dismissed in early childhood. The more deeply involved I became in the church, the less sure I became about my right to a full, free, explosive, untamed life. Even though I had been raised in the Pentecostal church all my life, it had been peripheral for me, at best. With hormones raging, acne taking over, body blossoming, and grown men looking, I needed something to define me other than those things. I chose the church. That choice would later determine my responses to my African ancestry, education, friendship, relationships, sexual violence, and sexual identity. And if feminism had a face, she would have frowned; if eyes, she would have cried; if hands, she would have slapped that thirteen-year-old me before I ever internalized the church's position on women.

The story of Adam and Eve reveals the church's view on women. The woman in the story is created specifically to meet the man's needs. He is made from earth; she is made from him. She manipulates him, and her trickery is his downfall. She is smart enough to fool the man, but too dim to realize the scope of her actions. She is disloyal to her partner and conspires with the creature who has the most to offer. All of the suffering she endures, she brings upon herself, including the pain of childbirth and the death of one of her sons. In short, women are inferior, manipulative cheats whose main purpose in life is to bear children and please men. This was not considered an insult to women in my church but a fact of life.

My parents' reaction to my newfound faith only reinforced that I had made a good choice. I remember the day my father, who was not a religious man, got all dressed up to see me sing the lead in our choir. Similarly, my mother, who never blinked an eye when I brought home the expected A on my report card, seemed to take a sense of pride in my loyalty to the church. So while the United States' politics around women in the 1980s were generally a time for marked advance, I was headed back in time with a destination that was literally biblical. Despite the fact that I had recognized the importance of Geraldine Ferraro being chosen as the nation's first female vice presidential candidate, Whoopi Goldberg's Academy Award nomination for *The Color Purple*, and even the rise of several popular television shows with female leads, my teenage heart was numb to every image but one. The image imbedded in my head through no less than three church services a week: Jesus Christ hanging on a cross, giving his life for sins I had committed. For this I had to pay with my soul, and the men who led my church would show me the way.

The lessons came in many ways. All of our ministers were men. They sat in a raised pulpit above and away from the congregation. They were in charge of all the messages to the congregation. Admonishments to women to stay in their places as outlined in the Bible were commonplace: women, obey your husbands; and single women, obey your preachers. Never wear pants because the Bible says a woman should not dress like a man. Choose a profession becoming a Christian; my broadcast focus was out because I'd have to wear makeup. Always forgive—even cheating, lying, abusive partners. And for God's sake, young women, get married and be fruitful—the younger the better. Don't be gay, period; it is an abomination in the eyes of God.

With admonitions flowing, rushing over the pews like water over a fall, teachings about our African ancestry were notably missing. I was grown before I heard of the Diaspora. I was grown before the feeling was real to me that there must be more to God than rules that, if broken, led to eternal punishment. The feeling that sometimes whatever spirits moved people to sing and rock and love and look inside must have a woman's face. Some of the God in me must look like me and move like me and soul like me. But Pentecost had no time, room, or interest in telling a little curious girl with an open heart that she was a daughter of the Goddess Osun. Osun is a representation of a creative force in the universe that is not male, coming directly from our African sisters and brothers but not found at all in our teachings—not even as an alternative "God view" to be dismissed. When I started studying African religions on my own, in college, I realized that I was both shocked and comforted by representations of spirit that put forth a need for a balance between female and male energy in life; it felt closer to right than the male-dominant philosophies that permeated Christianity.

What you don't know can hurt you deeply. This sin of omission and ignorance committed by the church kept me as far away from my sisters and brothers in Africa as the miles between us. The internalized racism presented to African Americans as part of the United States' ongoing system of oppression of thought, history, and culture against us—beginning with the transatlantic slave trade and continuing today with the prison-industrial complex—was so deeply ingrained that children even used the words "Black" and "African" as insults to each other. No one was rushing to offer other images of Africa besides those found in the *National Geographic* books that lined the shelves in both the school and public libraries. Exacerbating the ignorance about our history was the apathy that pervaded it. Our only passion was God. As a result, we weren't even Christians of action like Martin Luther King Jr. and his cohorts; we were Christians of criticism and isolation and passivity.

The constant image of one God with a male face only perpetuated the sexism that was so accepted that I never even heard it called by its name. I took in silent messages as I watched the twentysomething couples struggle with the church's heavy-handed tenets and old-world views of male and female roles. The women were always encouraged to acquiesce in any disagreements, while the men were encouraged to show strength by keeping their families in line. Men whose wives seemed to conform were openly rewarded with higher posts; men whose wives were less obedient were slower to rise up the church hierarchy. Divorce was one of the greatest indications of spiritual weakness, so the few married women whose husbands were not in church were encouraged to wait them out, let God handle it, and at all costs, stay.

But my greatest lesson about the value of women in the church's eyes was a personal one. One of those pulpit kings took off his crown and robe and stepped down from his dais just long enough to rape me. God had allowed my teenage body to blossom too soon. When I confided in my trusted women in the church, they told me my salvation depended on me forgiving him. Years later, when I told our pastor, he told me that the preacher had much more to protect and much more to lose if the news became public. He was a man with a family. I was just a girl. I was a girl too afraid to tell my parents. I was a girl too warped by the fear of losing what felt like the only real relationship in my life—that with Jesus—to leave the church right away. So I paid with my soul, and feminism prayed for eyes to cry for my enslaved little Black soul. What she got was an eleven-year struggle from that dusty road of Bible stories, church sermons, and women who walked behind to a place where I would rather walk alone with eyes open to the world than in a shadow just to feel like I had some company.

The journey was by no means smooth. Although 1980s politics had failed to touch me, the politics of the 1990s held me in a suffocating embrace. It was in this last decade of the century that all my cultural, religious, and political contradictions came to a head. The world was battling over a woman's right to choose, and I was confronted with my own obligation to do so. It wasn't a choice about my body, but my mind, and everyone seemed to want a piece. To practice our religion, one had to filter every thought, every move or emotion, through the Bible. It was a constant checking and rechecking against biblical tenets and the church's interpretation of those doctrines. The older I became, the more I came to question the teachings. The more I questioned, the more I was reprimanded for being weak in spirit. Mention of other belief systems brought reproach, and instead of exploring questions fully, I was encouraged to put my faith in God and wait for answers from him. It was a way to keep people in line and quiet. The discussion was to be confined to prayers between you and God, preventing you from having discussions with each other.

This narrow view of my spiritual possibilities and total lack of acknowledgment of our forefathers' and foremothers' beliefs eventually put me on a path away from Christianity. As I started college in 1992, the church was still teaching that pride was a person's downfall, but African-American pride was calling my name. The more time I spent with my young sisters and brothers seeking knowledge about our spiritual possibilities, the more I realized how stifling the church was for a woman with questions. It disturbed and at the same time invigorated me to learn that ours was one of the only religions on earth that lacked powerful images of women as gods.

It is no surprise that the Christian United States continues to show open contempt for its female population through its dissemination of wealth, which keeps working-class women and their children last. African-American women and their children are barely in the running. By 1990 a woman's right to choose was being openly attacked by terrorist murderers, while woman-battering and rape laws laid down sentences that belittled the crimes. As a rape victim—who could have easily become a teen pregnancy statistic as a result—I found the politics of the time grating on my spirit.

If that wasn't bad enough, there were weekly news reports of women, mostly African-American women, cheating the welfare system. These images were constant and so incessant that they became normalized as a representation of the average low-income African-American mother. Single African-American women were commonly represented as teen mothers who either abandoned their babies or smoked crack until the babies were born with a multitude of birth defects. Similar news stories about white women were more forgiving and left the audience with questions rather than judgments: What is our country saying when a young woman has to deceive the government about how many kids she has just to get enough support to take care of one child? Where have we gone wrong when a young woman is so afraid that she leaves her newborn to be found by a stranger? When the subject of the same stories were African-American, reporters spun them in a way that inevitably left the audience outraged, no questions asked. The shoddy journalism supporting a racism that lived so deep in the average American consciousness that it went unspoken was painful. It was like being slapped across the face with the hatred that our high school history classes had tried to convince us died after the civil rights struggles of the 1960s. It was a different kind of hurt than the everyday encounters with people who showed contempt for my brown skin, because it was being mass marketed as the truth. I felt as if they were daring viewers to even think about questioning it.

The control over these racist messages about women was totalitarian. Goliath stood firm. Another blow to my spirit was the fact that representations of women I knew, the woman I was becoming, were lacking. Who would write their stories, who would tell their tales, who would produce news reports asking questions about their plight? I wavered on the tightrope between religion and spiritual freedom, finally choosing to follow my spirit. My spirit motivated me to choose a journalism major in college, and I began to ask questions for African-American women at work.

Angela Davis, the 1960s activist and professor at the University of California in Santa Cruz, came to speak at a rally on campus. I was expecting for her to light a fire under all of us, encouraging us to take our fight for a more egalitarian society to the streets! What she said, with a mellow vibe and tone that can only be attributed to older, wiser Black women who've been down roads and seen things we never will, was that our activism was not to mirror the activism of old. This generation faces the challenge of defining activism in a United States that no longer responds to sit-ins and marches. She suggested that our strength would come from building coalitions with other people of color and like-minded folks.

But first I had to build coalitions with the different parts of myself. The sexism within the African Student Alliance on my campus (which mirrored the kind of sexism I'd witnessed in my church and in my local African-American community) was pushing out the feminist me. At the same time, I found feminist groups so desperate to hang on to some credibility in the mainstream, pushing against my focus on African heritage and pushing to keep the door closed to the closet behind which I hid my love for women. It seemed less and less likely that I would find a place in the world to fully be myself. I worried that the definition of feminism that one of my college professors had so eloquently laid out would never become a reality for me.

Of course, it was my mother who set me straight. She told me to stop worrying about what people said and to do what I was here to do. She told me I was an artist, and she said it with pride in her voice. With that, I began to put pen to paper, paint to canvas, voice to air, and break down all the systems of thinking and accepted ways of being that excluded some part of myself. I found that while what my mother thought of me was paramount to my spiritual survival, what the world thought no longer mattered. Though I didn't share her religious fervor any longer, I still respected her more than any other person.

I didn't know any other woman who'd worked a graveyard shift in various hospitals for more than twenty years to feed, clothe, and care for five hungry girls. She'd worked overnight so she'd be home when we got out of school. I had never encountered any other woman who would share her meager supply of groceries with the single mother across the street, or spend the small amount of free time afforded her, a woman with five daughters, sitting with the elderly folks in our church and taking their blood pressure. She was even willing to challenge our church on some of its interpretations of the Bible and didn't force us to follow those interpretations, as most parents in the church did. When my father moved out, she continued to maintain the household without blinking an eye (at least I never saw her blink). Somehow she created time to go back to college and attain various certificates to further her nursing career. I'd spent my entire life face to face with a feminist powerhouse who offered neither explanation nor apology, and the effect went deeper and was more motivating than reading any book on feminist theory. She taught me an abiding love for self and for humanity—and she taught by example. So I went to work.

I created a cable-access show called *Point of View* to discuss politics. A local show, it aired in four nearby Bay Area cities. For every negative representation I saw of people of color, I wrote a show that allowed us to shine. For every report I read that asked no questions about the plights of African-American women, I created a show and asked the questions myself. The walls between me and effecting change in the politics of oppression, racism, and sexism that pervade the United States were starting to crumble. I wrote, produced, sang, painted, and created ways to say, "We are here. We are diverse. We are good." I knew I was on the right path when a man approached me in the BART train station and told me he'd taped and shown my Black History show to a group of students at a seminar he gave in Sacramento.

The momentum created by following my mother's lead and becoming a woman of action gave me the strength to slowly open the doors to my closet. My passivity in loving had created such a stark contrast to my passion in every other area that I could no longer ignore it. Spoken word provided a platform for me to be honest about falling in love again and again with women. My love of women was the one area in my life where fear of judgment, reprisal, and loss still ruled me. Not only had I been raised in a religion that preached that same-sex love was abominable, but I had grown up in a community with strictly defined male and female roles, and in a country that openly and lawfully discriminated against same-sex couples. Even feminists seemed obsessed with not being characterized as lesbians. What would it mean about my overall identity if I acknowledged this truth about my makeup? What doors would close? What would my mother think?

I found that just as my questions about our religion had not gone away, and just as my need to seek out my heritage had not been assuaged, in the same way that the need to tell the stories of African-American women had risen to the top, so would my orientation reverberate through my spirit and force its way into my voice, my paintings, my writing, and my reality. As the 1990s ended and the twenty-first century began, I reached a kind of wholeness. I sat with the woman who had given me all the tools and examples I needed to be strictly myself. I drank coffee and ate eggs and looked into the eyes of the woman who made feminism real for me when I didn't even have words to describe it. I told her that I was in love, that it was not a fad, that I planned to spend my life and raise children with another woman. She didn't accept it. Because of her, I knew she didn't have to. I was free to define myself.

How Sexual Harassment Slaughtered, Then Saved Me

KIINI IBURA SALAAM

The New Orleans streets of my adolescence were a bizarre training ground where predatory men taught me that—in public—no part of me was safe from comment. At ages twelve and thirteen I was trained to keep my guard up by voices shouting lascivious phrases at me. Clothes were inconsequential, yet I inferred that the miniskirts and tight jeans of my preteen years would worsen the verbal attacks. Repeated lewdness can do that to you. The constancy of male aggression hammered in the suggestion that something bad could happen to me.

INDOCTRINATION

Catcalling men are often a monumental challenge for adult women to navigate; for an adolescent, catcallers can be downright terrifying. After a time, the simple act of walking past a group of men unnerved me. The abrupt break in conversation as their eyes crawled over me announced that my body had their attention for a few seconds. These were not casual appraisals, nor were they a simple appreciation of the female form. They were loud (though silent) proclamations that informed me of the entertainment and sexual titillation I provided them, just by walking by. By the time my breasts and hips grew in, tense interactions with men on the street became normal. Not easy to deal with, not acceptable, not invisible, but expected.

I was never taught techniques to protect myself from the whispering lips of adult men. In the absence of safety, I developed tactics to handle the pressure.

1. If there is a group of men ahead, cross the street.
2. If there are groups of men on both sides of the street, choose the older ones. They might find you too young and let you slip by without comment.
3. Do not make eye contact.
4. Do not make any verbal or physical motion that can be perceived as an invitation for conversation.
5. If someone speaks to you politely, speak back while staring straight ahead.
6. Keep moving.

Sometimes my tactics could not buy me escape. If I was stopped by a red light or waiting at a bus stop, I was easy prey for the next level of intrusion. Under the pretense of polite interaction between strangers, men often launched into proprietary interrogations. "What's your name?" "How old are you?" "Where do you live?" "Do you have a boyfriend?" These inquiries paved the way for forced conversations. To my ears the questions were staccato demands that chafed my self-control and independence. The men delivered these queries as if my participation in the conversation and the choice of whether or not I would be carted off was completely up to them. If I resisted the interaction, I was seen as abnormally hostile or angry without reason. I would answer their questions in a terse, sullen manner, looking around for a possible exit. I hated my compliance. I wanted to destroy the assumption that their interest in me eclipsed my own disinterest. I wanted to smash the expectation that I would supply details about my personal life. I wanted to obliterate my own paralysis, my own inability to comfortably remove myself from their proximity.

Without knowledge of feminist doctrines and theories, I knew there was something wrong with catcalling. I don't remember the word "feminist" being used in my house, yet my parents injected the same power, pride, and self-governance into my and my sisters' upbringing as they did in my brothers'. When my mother would go away on her Black women's retreats, my sisters, brothers, and I shared equal household duties. Decorating the walls of my childhood home were prints proclaiming, "If it's not appropriate for women, it's not appropriate at all," and "Women Hold Up Half the Sky," which was a print of the cover art from my father's book of the same title. My home environment convinced me that feminism is the natural result when women are taught their worth.

As an adolescent, no one taught me that catcalling was anti-woman, yet I instinctively felt that it squelched my autonomy and personal power. I quickly discovered the only pass card I had to convince men to leave me alone was being possessed by another man. Hostility or disinterest on my part only resulted in surreal arguments about my right to say no. I could fabricate names and phone numbers or I could make up boyfriends or husbands, but I couldn't simply say no without a fight. Having to lie to protect my legitimate disinterest was ridiculous to me. The men could continue with their pathologies, but the woman I wanted to be wouldn't bow to their demand. Some mornings I woke up adamant. I'd swear to myself, If a man hits on me today, I will not lie. My disinterest is worth something and they are going to respect me. On one of those days a young man approached my friend. She smiled and demurred and told him she was married. He turned to me and said, "What about you?"

"What about me?" I asked.

"You married too?"

"No."

"You got a boyfriend?"

"No."

"Well, give me your phone number," he said.

This is the approach of men on the street. They cast a wide net, fishing for a response. Who the woman is, is irrelevant. Catcallers see the street as a grocery store where they can shop for entertainment, titillation, and interaction, but this is my life. I have to deal with every joke, invitation, and comment thrown my way. Multiple catcalls become a deluge of harassment that quickly overwhelms.

"You don't even like me," I told him. "You like my friend."

"That don't mean nothing," he said to me. "Stop being so cold. Give me your number."

I refused. With each rejection he grew more belligerent, pulling out the anger that keeps women in line. I feared the verbal attacks that might follow my refusal to give away access to myself. I feared the male anger that was always seething under the surface of men's solicitous remarks.

"See," the young man said, "that's what's wrong with Black people today. Black women don't have time for the Black man."

I grabbed my friend's hand and walked away, once again angry at the male intrusion into my life. I was upset that I couldn't stand on a corner without getting into a fight about sex and race. The men of my youth habitually positioned female disinterest as a hostile act of emasculation or genocide, while their harassment was defended as healthy male behavior. I will always remember the drunk vagrant who—when my sister refused him—said, "You must like white men." What warped psychology would jump to such a conclusion? When my sister's choice not to date an alcoholic is considered a rejection of Black men as a whole, the relationship between men and women can only be seen as fractured.

By the time I reached college, I was fraught with anger and questions. I wondered who set up this predator and prey relationship. I wanted to know how I could walk by and not be judged by men. The questions clouded my mind. Do men gain power from making me feel unsafe? Do they get off on treating me like a pet or a toy, a non-human entity to play with, just because I happen to pass by? Is it fun? Does it ever work? Do they ever wonder what catcalling feels like to me? Do they ever get bored with acting out the same old tired roles? What are men asserting about themselves by catcalling? And how can I opt out?

> **❝ Catcallers see the street as a grocery store where they can shop for entertainment, titillation, and interaction, but this is my life.... Do men gain power from making me feel unsafe? Do they get off on treating me like a pet or a toy, a nonhuman entity to play with, just because I happen to pass by? ❞**

THE SLAUGHTER

During my junior year of college I went to the Dominican Republic to study Spanish. A few weeks after my arrival, I went to an outdoor concert with some friends. When we arrived, a man grabbed me and started dancing a merengue with me. His laughter told me he just wanted to have fun. Giggling, I joined in. It was exactly how I imagined a street party should be. Loud music, laughing crowds, strangers dancing together. My friends and I moved on into thicker crowds. As we paused momentarily, trying to determine how to get closer to the stage, a hand reached out and squeezed my vagina. My head snapped in the direction of the hand, but I was surrounded by a crowd of blank faces. I couldn't tell who had molested me.

I might have written it off as the type of assault you can expect in a rowdy street crowd. But it happened to me again at an upscale dance club in Santiago. My friends and I were squeezing past a row of men on our way to the bathroom when another hand reached out and touched my vagina. When I made it to the bathroom, I told my friend about the abuse, and she said, "Yeah, he did it to me, too."

After a few months hanging out in the clubs, I realized these sexual intrusions were partly tied to race. My two white women friends were always the first asked to dance, then the Chicana woman, followed by Black friends with perms. Eventually I identified two types of men who would dance with me: the pity partners and the molesters. The pity partners saw that I had barely danced all night and, out of the kindness in their hearts, took me out on the dance floor. Invariably these men would comment, "Oh, you dance so well!" but at the end of the song, they would walk me back to my seat and never return for another dance. The molesters were men who used the closeness of the merengue as an excuse to press their bodies against mine. I would push them away, keeping my arm locked, struggling to hold them at a distance for the duration of the song. If they were too insistent, I would have to leave the dance floor before the song was over.

Interviews with my girlfriends revealed that the level of abuse I—the only Black woman with natural hair—was suffering was unique. Each of them had had one or two experiences that bothered them, yet all levels of harassment happened to me. The boys on the corner saying, "Comb your ugly hair!" The guy reaching out of a passing bus to touch my hair. The man who stopped by the side of the road to pee and decided to turn around and display his genitals to me and my friends. The ancient tradition of throwing berries at a woman when she passes, to show that you think she is beautiful. Just as skin color is an easily identifiable marker for unequal treatment, my natural hair singled me out for sexist disrespect.

My fashion sense died in the Dominican Republic. I began to experiment with using my wardrobe to make me invisible. Baggy T-shirts and oversized pants became the order of the day. Although I understood that clothing does not cause sexual abuse, I hoped bigger clothing could stop it. I needed to believe I had some control over my own safety. But when a man reached out and casually squeezed my breast through a big, shapeless T-shirt, I learned that these acts were beyond my control. My hand shot out in retaliation, but I hit only air. The man walked on, as if molesting a woman while passing her in the street was an everyday occurrence.

When I relayed this story to my host mother, she said, "He must have thought you were Haitian." My host mother's dismissive remark revealed the Dominican belief that nationality (Haitianness) was a legitimate explanation for abuse. Haitian women were the only other adult women I saw with natural hair during my entire nine months in the Dominican Republic. (I was in the city of Santiago in 1992; apparently in later years study-abroad students made links with Black women's groups in the capital who identified Black and had natural hair.) I had unknowingly installed myself into a country whose hatred for all things African was infamous. My body learned of this hatred as my boundaries were crossed again and again and again.

My last clash with a Dominican man happened at three o'clock in the morning. My friend and I had made the questionable choice of walking down a deserted side street on our way home from a club. We heard footsteps behind us and immediately stepped to the side. A man walked by, rubbing his hand along my friend's arm as he passed. We had become so accustomed to Dominican men taking liberties with our bodies that we were not alarmed by this. Anger flared, we talked about how fucked up the men were, but we didn't think for one moment we were in any danger. We were wrong.

After the man reached the corner—in hindsight I realize he was probably checking to see if there would be any witnesses—he made an about-face and confronted us with a gun. "Don't scream," he demanded. Everything else he said was a blur. My Spanish comprehension evaporated as my mind scrambled to make sense of the assault. He continued mumbling as my friend and I backed away. "Leave us alone," I repeated in a flat voice over and over again. We backed into a corrugated metal fence. The man pulled the shoulder of my top down to my elbow, exposing my breast. My gaze fell to his pelvis. I noticed his fly was open and his penis was dangling. Although my spirit was battered by the myriad of molestations I had suffered during my time in the Dominican Republic, I was not so defeated as to not fight back. I kicked, pushed, did what I could to let him know he wouldn't violate me while I was alive. We struggled until the man stopped fighting. He stared into my eyes, then turned and walked in the other direction. My friend pulled me toward home and we ran.

My host family was not helpful. "If he didn't shoot, he wasn't going to hurt you," they said. "He must not have had bullets in the gun." I wondered if that was true. I wondered how many women he had raped with a bulletless gun.

When I got back to the United States, my teachers noticed I was quiet and withdrawn. My mother's friend said I looked shorter. I slept more and smiled less. When I faced emotional challenges—the same challenges I had previously surfed gracefully—I found myself breaking down into tears. I returned home hysterically afraid of walking too close to men on the street. What I needed then was a feminism that could cover me with a protective cloak. I needed a feminism that could return my body to me. I needed a feminism that would nestle in the hearts and minds of men. Any political movement is only as advanced as the individuals it represents. Ultimately, the successes of feminism can only be measured by individual women's quality of life. My quality of life on the street was low, and I needed a practical application of feminism so the streets would once again be safe for me.

SALVATION

In the years after my nine-month stay in the Dominican Republic, I climbed out of my pit of fear and entered into an angry stalemate with men on the street. I viewed the sexual abuse in the Dominican Republic as a more extreme expression of the verbal harassment I had become accustomed to on US streets. The molestation was certainly more painful than catcalls, but the verbal and physical violations in the Dominican Republic and the United States both hinged on men's relationship to women as objects for gratification.

After I left college and grew into womanhood, my old avoidance tactics became too cowardly for me to stomach. Rather than lying about my phone number or my relationship status, I learned to say, "I'm not interested." As a grown woman, I understood what I did not know as a teen: I am not bound to respond to men's overtures. Accusations of meanness left me unmoved, and I refused to engage in any unsolicited conversation. Freed of my adolescent compulsion to be kind to strangers, I enforced my own agenda with a stubborn willfulness. Rather than cross the street in avoidance, I would plow straight through groups of men, offering a loud "Good morning" or "Good evening" as I walked past. The men were often shocked into silence. By the time they got their game together, I had already passed them by. Despite my new protective tactics, the old rages still owned me. My behavior still consisted of premeditated defensive acts aimed at dismantling male aggression, and random men still had the power to ruin my day.

Four years after my return from the Dominican Republic, miniskirts were no longer part of my wardrobe, and most of my warm weather tops were T-shirts rather than tanks. With a suitcase full of modest clothing, I traveled to the city of Salvador in Brazil's northeastern state of Bahia. From the moment I arrived in Bahia, I was immersed in a culture that exuberantly embraces skin exposure. Rather than cover up their bodies in an attempt to avoid harassment, Brazilian women display an over-the-top sexiness. Many Brazilian girls and women dressed modestly, but I was amazed to see little girls trained in sexy dress from girlhood. In Bahia, fatty flesh was displayed as proudly and blatantly as well-muscled limbs, and even pregnant women sported string bikinis.

After days of fruit and heat, I fell in step with the trend. Especially on beach days, I would wear thigh-bearing shorts and skirts and little triangular halter tops. On one such day I walked past a group of men, my bare legs uncovered, my braless breasts jiggling. Without being consciously aware of it, I was on the alert, waiting for some comment to trail after me as I passed. But I heard nothing; not one word, not even a whisper. Their silence rocked my world. In the quiet of the moment I caught myself thinking, "If I am dressed like this, how can they let me slip by without comment?" Through that renegade thought, I was shocked to discover some small, dark corner of my heart where I was holding on to self-blame. My indoctrination of woman as victim had been more complete than I had imagined.

The Dogon, the ancient West African astronomers, philosophers, and mystics, believe there are multiple levels of knowledge.

For a concept to be fully integrated into the human psyche, it has to be learned, they say, from the front, the side, and the back. From the front I understood that I was not responsible for men's decisions to harass me. It was an intellectual knowing that had no practical proof. From the side I had gathered quantifiable experiences in the Dominican Republic that destroyed any argument that clothing caused sexual harassment. Now, here I arrived to the back, to the heart of the matter. On the most profound level of knowing, I learned I could be a woman—covered or uncovered—and move through the world without censure. I felt the burden of being a desirable thing slipping from my fingers. The blame of causing chaos on the street and the shame of creating deviant behavior in men disappeared.

The slaughter I had unknowingly walked into in the Dominican Republic was being soothed by an equally unexpected gift. These Brazilian men—with their sexist presumption that I should walk around exposed—helped to free me of the expectation of abuse. The false responsibility I had been nursing for men's behavior began to wash away. Even in the following days, when a large group of boys yelled, "Hey, look, a girl all alone," during a street festival; even as the low whispers of *gostoso* (sexy, literally "tasty") fluttered by my ears as I wandered the streets of Bahia—I recognized street harassment as men's drama, not mine. I acknowledged it as something I am forced to navigate, but never again would I take the accountability, pain, and anger home with me.

By the time my cousin came to visit months later, I had totally embraced the Brazilian style of dress. "You look cute," she told me, her eyes taking in my bare skin with surprise. "I could never dress like that." I told her about the men in the calm neighborhood of Santo Antonio, where I lived. Though I had heard tales of extreme harassment in neighborhoods farther from the center of the city,

I raved about the freedom I experienced on the streets near my home. In response, she grunted noncommittally, a sound that told me she believed my words, but the reality of it just could not sink into her body. Later, at the house, she went through my clothes. Looking at the pieces of cloth held together with strings, she said, "I would love to be able to wear this." "Put it on, wear it, nobody's gonna bother you," I said. She thought about it for a second and shook her head. "No, that's all right." She put on a T-shirt instead.

Wandering through my Brazilian neighborhood that afternoon, we entered into a passionate conversation about something—family, art, love—and we strolled past a group of men. Though we were entrenched in a conversation, my cousin stopped abruptly and said, "They didn't say anything!" I could tell by the wonder and incredulity in her voice that she, too, had never imagined she could walk past a group of men and not be harassed. Her surprise at being granted freedom was a moment of painful validation. Her expectation of abuse was so immediate, so adamant, that it substantiated my historical anger about catcallers. Her reaction showed me that my fixation on the issue was neither exaggerated nor unwarranted. At the same time, it was heartbreaking, because it meant the force I had to muster up just to walk down the street is required not just of me as an individual but of a whole society of women. Suddenly I imagined legions of women futilely employing defensive motions to navigate the sexually hostile environments of the streets in their cities. The next day, my cousin wore that halter top.

RECONCILIATION

Just as there are women who travel to the Dominican Republic unscathed, there are women who travel to Brazil and suffer extreme violations. There is no Shangri-la, no magic safe space to heal women's wounds of harassment. As feminists, we need to approach catcalling from the front, from the side, and from the back. It's not enough to condemn men's behavior—we must also heal our past hurts, remove our assumptions, and create positive forms of interactions. As women, it is essential that we share our harassment stories with our children (male and female), our sisters, our brothers, our parents, and our lovers. Our brothers are potential catcallers, our husbands may have molested girls as teenage boys, our daughters may need a context for the aggression they are forced to thwart in their public lives. Our stories are healing: they tell us that we are not alone. Our experiences are instructive: they point to options for managing the fear and diverting the aggression.

Today I can identify exactly what catcalling is and how it functions in women's lives. At its most basic level, catcalling is sexual harassment. Verbal assaults, invitations, and compliments are opportunities for men to demonstrate who is predator and who is prey. One catcall yanks a woman out of the category of human being and places her firmly in the position of sexual object. While men readily admit to the assertive flirtatiousness of catcalling, they fail to acknowledge the veiled aggression that often accompanies the act. Depending on a woman's response, catcalls can go from solicitous to angry. There is often a violent edge lurking under the surface causing women to question their safety. When a man screams (or whispers) something inappropriate to a woman, the harassment inserts itself into her consciousness, whether she interacts with the catcaller or not. With intrusive overtures, catcallers assume the right to engage a woman in a sexual fashion without her permission. This presumptuous crossing of intimate and sexual boundaries is a painful disempowering force. Relentless catcalls destroy women's power to define their own parameters for public interaction. Rather than face the world on their terms, many women walk the streets burdened by anxiety, discomfort, and fearfulness.

The reality of the situation is dire, yet since my return from Brazil, I have ceased to think of men as the enemy and myself as the victim. I prefer to think of the catcallers as individuals who choose to yell and rub their groins and aggressively pursue conversations with me. Male expectations and verbal aggression still anger me, but my mental stress is significantly diminished. Rather than try to block their ignorance, I float beyond it. I know now without a doubt that male aggression is not caused by me.

I am aware that men don't consider the cumulative effect of unwelcome sexual comments. Instead, they focus on their individual moment of interaction, insisting that they were just being men. I take a similar attitude when dealing with them now. My responses to catcalls are based on my feelings and the man's attitude. If a man asks me my name, I might say "No," refusing to enter the game. If he seems rational, I might reason with him. "Look," I may say. "You had your choice of whether or not you wanted to talk to me. Shouldn't I have a choice of whether or not I want to give you my number?" If I have the time, and they seem gentle enough, I might enter into a philosophical conversation. When I once refused to give a man my number, he asked, "Why you being so mean?" I said, "You don't want me to give you my number just to be nice, do you? Don't you want me to actually like you?" He thought about it, and said, "Yeah, I guess so." I guess men get caught up in the game, too.

Just as often as women get caught up deflecting the attack, men get caught up pursuing the goal. An ideal interaction with a catcaller snaps him out of his gender-based assessment of me as an object and informs him that I am a human being. Sometimes with a few words, a man can be reminded that I am not that different from him. I, too, would like to choose who I interact with, sit in silence if I feel like it, and make friends based on my interest, not because of the force of their aggression. Should a feminist force rise to transform the streets into a safety zone, that force would need to reeducate men. It would need to teach them that every women is not a flirtation waiting to be fulfilled, or a conversation waiting for an introduction; nor do we exist to respond to every invitation or overture. Women are individuals with desires, preferences, prejudices, and pet peeves. And we want as much control over our own interactions as men demand for themselves.

The Black Beauty Myth

SIRENA J. RILEY

For those of you well versed in the study of body image, I don't need to tell you that negative body image is an all-too-common phenomenon. The issue of young women's and girls' dissatisfaction with their bodies in the United States has slowly garnered national attention and made its way into the public discourse. Unfortunately, the most visible discussions surrounding body image have focused on white women. As a result, we presume that women of color don't have any issues when it comes to weight and move on. As a black woman, I would love to believe that as a whole we are completely secure with our bodies. But that would completely miss the racism, sexism, and classism that affect the specific ways in which black women's beauty ideals and experiences of body dissatisfaction are often different from those of white women.

To our credit, black women have often been praised for our positive relationships with our bodies. As a teenager, I remember watching a newsmagazine show about a survey comparing black and white women's body satisfaction. When asked to describe the "perfect woman," white women said she'd be about five foot ten, less than 120 pounds, blonde, and so on. Black women described this ideal woman as intelligent, independent, and self-confident, never mentioning her looks. After the survey results were revealed to the group of both black and white twentysomethings, the white women stood, embarrassed and humiliated that they could be so petty and shallow. They told stories of starving themselves before dates and even before sex. The black women were aghast! What the hell were these white women talking about?!

I was so proud. I went around telling everyone about the survey results. I couldn't believe it. Black women being praised on national television! There they were telling the whole country that their black men loved the "extra meat on their bones." Unfortunately, my pride also had a twinge of envy. In my own experience, I couldn't quite identify with either the black women or the white women.

In my black middle-class suburban family, we were definitely expected to be smart. My family didn't work so hard so that we could be cute and dumb. I'd expressed interest in medical school, and I got nothing but support in my academics. As I was raised by a single mother, independence was basically in my blood. But in a neighborhood of successful, often bourgeois black families, it was obvious that the "perfect woman" was smart, pretty, and certainly not overweight. As a child, no one loved the "extra meat" on my bones. I was eight years old when I first started exercising to Jane Fonda and the cadre of other leotard-clad fitness gurus. I knew how to grapevine and box-step as well as I knew my multiplication tables. I now have a sister around that age, and when I look at her and realize how young that is, it breaks my heart that I was so concerned about weight back then.

Still, I consider myself lucky. I had an even temper. That made me no fun to tease, since I wouldn't give the perpetrator any satisfaction by reacting. Plus, I had good friends who would be there to have my back. But despite this support, I was a very self-conscious middle-school girl. And that's where I gained the most weight, sixty pounds in the course of three years. Because hindsight is twenty-twenty, it is easy to understand why I put on so much weight then. My mom got married when I was ten years old. The next year she had my first little sister, and then another sister was added when I turned fourteen. I love them, but that's a lot of stress for a little kid. My single-parent, only-child home had turned into a pseudo–nuclear family almost overnight. My grades started slipping and the scale started climbing.

Enter my first year of high school. Being an overweight teenager, I don't need to describe the hell that was gym class. To my relief, I only had to take one year of gym, and then never had to do it again. Plus, in high school I had options. In addition to regular gym, there was an aerobics dance class and something called "physical training." Now, considering that Jane Fonda and I were well acquainted, I wanted to take the aerobics class. But when I went to register, the class was full. I guess I wasn't the only one who'd had it with the kickball scene. I was left with either regular gym or this physical training class. I decided that I'd played my last game of flag football and opted for the latter.

Physical training turned out to be running and lifting weights. And when I say weights, I mean *real* weights. None of those wimpy three-pound dumbbells. We were lifting heavy weights and learning professional weight-lifting moves. Well, it worked. By sophomore year I'd lost over forty pounds. The thing is, I didn't even know it. Remember, I had only enrolled in the class to get out of regular gym. I'd thought it might be nice to lose some weight, but that wasn't what I was concentrating on. After all, I'd been doing exercise videos since I was a kid and I'd only managed to gain weight.

How did I not notice that I'd lost weight? Well, I was completely out of touch with my body. I didn't want to live there. I don't even think I really considered it a part of *me*. No one ever said anything good about it, so I just pretended it didn't exist. I basically swept my body under the rug. All I was wearing back then were big baggy jeans and sweatshirts, so most of my clothes still fit despite the weight loss. People had been asking me for several months if I'd lost weight before I noticed. They were also asking me how I did it, as if I knew. While back-to-school shopping before my sophomore year, I decided to just see if I could fit into size 10 jeans. Not only did those fit me, I could even squeeze into a size 8.

Ironically, it wasn't being overweight that really screwed up my body image and self-esteem, it was *losing* weight. All of a sudden I was pretty. No one had ever really told me that I was pretty before. So if I was pretty now, then I must have been ugly then. My perception of myself before my weight loss was forever warped. I ripped up pictures of myself from middle school. I never wanted to be fat again! Boys had never really been interested in me before, but now guys were coming out of the woodwork. Family I hadn't seen in years just couldn't believe it was *me*. Some even told me they'd always known I'd grow out of my "baby fat" to become a beautiful woman. At fifteen, this was my introduction to womanhood. I had dates now. I could go shopping and actually fit into cool clothes. I was planning for college and looking forward to my new life as a pretty, smart, successful, independent black superwoman.

For a few years, I actually did eat and exercise at what I'd consider a comfortable rate. But after that year of intense exercising, it was impossible to completely maintain my significant weight loss. I just didn't have the time, since it wasn't built into my schedule anymore. I settled in at around a size 12, although at the time I still wanted to be a "perfect" size 8. This actually was the most confusing time for me. I kept telling everyone I still wanted to lose twenty pounds. Even my family was divided on this one. My grandmother told me I was fine the way I was now, that I shouldn't gain any weight, but I didn't need to lose any more. She didn't want me to be fat, but thought it was good that I was curvy. Meanwhile, my grandfather told me if I lost twenty more pounds, he'd give me $1,000 to go shopping for new clothes. And my mom thought my skirts were too short and my tops too low-cut, even though when I was a child she had prompted me to lose weight by saying that if I stayed fat, I wouldn't be able to wear pretty clothes when I grew up. What the hell did these people want from me?

I wasn't overeating, and my self-esteem had improved, but for all the wrong reasons. I thought I was happier because I was thinner. In reality, I still hadn't made peace with myself or my body. Over the years I gained the weight back, but not before dabbling in some well-known eating disorders. I had a stint with bulimia during the second semester of my first year away at college, but I never got to the clinical stage. I pretty much only made myself vomit when something bad happened, not on a daily basis. I didn't binge on huge amounts of food. I'd eat two bowls of Lucky Charms and the next thing you know, I'd be sticking the spoon down my throat. This was not at all like the bulimics I saw on those after-school specials. They were eating sheets of cake, loaves of bread, sticks of butter, anything and everything they could get their hands on. That wasn't me.

Then I started compulsively exercising. I mean, I couldn't think straight if I hadn't been to the gym that morning. And even after I went to the gym, all I could think about was how great it was going to be to work out tomorrow. I would also plan my whole day around my food. It wasn't necessarily that I was dieting, but I was always aware of when I was going to eat and how much I was going to eat. I was completely obsessed.

Around my junior year in college, I finally realized that something was wrong. I just couldn't take it anymore, so I started seeing a counselor on campus. At first I didn't tell her about my encounters with bulimia, but any trained therapist could see right through me. One day, she asked me point-blank if I'd ever had an eating disorder, so I told her everything. I realized then that what I had been doing was considered disordered eating. I also realized that inherently I knew it wasn't right, since this was the first time I had breathed a word about it to anyone. I had never even tried to articulate it. I decided not to exercise or worry about what I ate until I got through therapy.

Throughout my course of therapy, I was in three body-image and eating-disorder therapy groups with other young women on my campus. I was always the only black woman. The memory of that television news survey I had seen as a teen comparing body-image issues for black and white women stayed with me over the years. Looking at the other women in my therapy groups, I had to wonder if I was an anomaly. I had read one or two stories in black women's magazines about black women with eating disorders, but it was still treated like a phenomenon that was only newsworthy because of its rarity.

I was a women's studies major in college, and body image was something we discussed almost ad nauseam. It was really cathartic because we embraced the personal as political and felt safe telling our stories to our sister feminists. Whenever body image was researched and discussed as a project, however, black women were barely a footnote. Again, many white feminists had failed to step out of their reality and see beyond their own experiences to understand the different ways in which women of color experience sexism and the unattainable beauty ideals that society sets for women.

Discussions of body image that bother to include black women recognize that there are different cultural aesthetics for black and white women. Black women scholars and activists have attacked the dominance of whiteness in the media and illuminated black women's tumultuous history with hair and skin color. The ascension of black folks into the middle class has put them in a unique and often difficult position in which they have tried to hold on to cultural ties while also striving to attain what the white bourgeois has defined as the American Dream. This orientation permeates not only their capitalist and materialist goals but body image as well, creating a distinctive increase in black women's body dissatisfaction.

White women may dominate pop-culture images of women, but black women aren't completely absent. While self-deprecating racism is still a factor in the way black women view themselves, white women give themselves too much credit when they assume that black women still want to look like them. Unfortunately, black women have their own beauty ideals to perpetually fall short of. The representation of black women in Hollywood is sparse, but among the most famous loom such beauties as Yara Shahidi, Halle Berry, Jada Pinkett Smith, Nia Long, and Angela Bassett. In the music scene there are Beyoncé, Janelle Monáe, Lauryn Hill, and Janet Jackson. Then, of course, there is model Naomi Campbell and everyone's favorite cover girl, Tyra Banks. Granted, these women don't necessarily represent the waif look or heroin chic that plagues the pages of predominately white fashion and entertainment magazines, but come on. They are still a hard act to follow.

In addition to the pressure of unrealistic body images in the media, another force on women's body image can be men's perspectives. In this category, black men's affinity for big butts always comes up.

Now, I'm not saying that this is a completely false idea—just about every black guy I know has a thing for the ass. I've heard both black guys and white guys say, "Damn, she's got a big ass"—the former with gleeful anticipation and the latter with loathsome disgust. Of course, dwelling on what men find attractive begs the question, why the hell do we care so much what they think anyway, especially when not all women are romantically involved with men?

Indeed, many songs have been written paying homage, however objectifying, to the black behind. "Baby Got Back," "Da Butt," and "Rumpshaker" are by now old standards. There's a whole new crop of ass songs, like "Shake Ya Ass," "Wobble Wobble," and everyone's favorite, "The Thong Song." But did anyone actually notice what the girls in the accompanying videos look like? Most of those women are models, dancers, and aspiring actresses whose full-time job it is to make sure they look unattainably beautiful. So what if they're slightly curvier?

Now that rap music is all over MTV, the rock videos of the eighties and early nineties featuring white women in leather and lace have been replaced with black and Latino models in haute couture and designer thongs. Rappers of the "ghetto-fabulous" genre are selling platinum several times over. Every day, their videos are requested on MTV's teen-driven *Total Request Live* (*TRL*) by mostly white, suburban kids—the largest group of consumers of hip-hop culture. It is the latest mainstream forum for objectifying women of color, because almost all of the ghetto-fabulous black male rappers have the obligatory video girls parading around everywhere, from luxury liner cruise ships to mansions in the Hamptons. If this doesn't speak to the distinctive race/class twist that these images add to the body-image discussion, I don't know what does.

The old mantra "You can never be too rich or too thin" may have been associated with the excessive eighties, but some of that ideal still holds true today. Obesity is associated with poverty, and in our society, poverty is not pretty. Being ghetto-fabulous is all about going from rags to riches. It includes having money, house(s), car(s), clothes, and throngs of high-maintenance women at your disposal. It's an ironic twist to the American Dream, considering that many of these rappers claim to have attained their wealth not with a Puritan work ethic but through illegal activity.

Overweight women of color aren't included in these videos because they aren't seen as ghetto-fabulous, just ghetto. (Not that I'm waiting for the day when *all* women can wash rappers' cars in cutoffs with twelve of their girlfriends, but you get the picture.) Talented comedienne Mo'Nique, star of UPN's *The Parkers*, is representative of this idea. She is a full-figured woman whose character, Nikki, has a crush on a black, upwardly mobile college professor who lives in her apartment building. Through his eyes, she seems uncouth and out of control. For the audience, her sexual advances are funny, because she's loud, overweight, and can't take a hint. He squirms away from her at every turn and into the arms of some slim model-type.

The professor in *The Parkers* views Nikki the same way that many middle-class people view overweight people: as greedy. But in the show we get to see it through a black lens—the greedy ghetto woman with no class, talking loud, wearing bright colors and tight clothes. I'm sure that in true sitcom fashion, the professor and Nikki will eventually get together, but well after we've had our fun at Nikki's expense.

For the past few years, a popular black R&B radio station in Washington, DC, has had a contest where it gives away free plastic surgery every summer. You know, to get ready for thong season. Needless to say, the average contestant is a woman. At first it was just breast implants and reductions, but now they've expanded to liposuction and even pectoral implants for the men. That hasn't had much impact on the demographics of the participants. Despite the expanded offerings, the contestant pool remains overwhelmingly female. In order to win the "prize," you have to send in a letter, basically pouring out all of your insecurities, to get the DJs to see why you need the surgery more than the other contestants do. Sick, isn't it? Anyone who thinks that black women are oblivious to body insecurities needs to listen to some of these letters, which, by the way, pour in by the thousands. The one thing they have in common is that all the women really want to "feel better about themselves." Even in this black middle-class metropolis, somewhere these women got the idea that plastic surgery is the way to go. Clearly, it is not just white America telling them this.

Sexism has played a starring role in every facet of popular culture, with men by and large determining what shows up on TV and in the movies, and the fact is that they've fallen for it, too. I have male friends and relatives who buy into these unrealistic beauty ideals and feel no shame in letting me know where they think I stack up, so to speak. Just yesterday, for example, my grandfather decided to make it his business to know how much weight I had gained in the past few months. Now, I'm old enough and secure enough to know that his and other men's comments have nothing to do with me, with who I am. But when I was growing up, these comments shaped the way I saw myself.

I've consciously decided to treat my body better by not being obsessed with diet and exercise and not comparing myself to anyone (including my former self). When I'm eating well and exercising regularly, I'm usually in the size 12 to 14 range. This is okay with me, but I know for a fact that this is another place where many white women and I don't connect. As much as we get praised for loving our full bodies, many young white women would rather be dead than wear a size 14. They nod their heads and say how great it is that we black women can embrace our curves, but they don't want to look like us. They don't adopt our presumably more generous beauty ideals. White women have even told me how lucky black women are that our men love and accept our bodies the way they are. I've never heard a white woman say that she's going to take her cue from black women and gain a few pounds, however. In a way it is patronizing, because they're basically saying, "It's okay for you to be fat, but not me. You're black. You're different."

In this society we have completely demonized fat. How many times have you had to tell a friend of yours that she isn't fat? How many times has she had to tell you the same thing? Obviously, when people have unrealistic perceptions of themselves it should not go unnoticed, but in this act, while we are reassuring our friends, we put down every woman who is overweight. The demonization of fat and the ease of associating black women with fat exposes yet another opportunity for racism.

> **The demonization of fat and the ease of associating black women with fat exposes yet another opportunity for racism.**

If we really want to start talking more honestly about all women's relationships with our bodies, we need to start asking the right questions. Just because women of color aren't expressing their body dissatisfaction in the same way as heterosexual, middle-class white women, it doesn't mean that everything is hunky-dory and we should just move on. If we are so sure that images of rail-thin fashion models, actresses, and video chicks have contributed to white girls' poor body image, why aren't we addressing the half-naked black female bodies that have replaced the half-naked white female bodies on MTV? Even though young black women slip through the cracks from time to time, I still believe that feminism is about understanding the intersections of all forms of oppression. It only works when we all speak up and make sure that our voices are heard. I don't plan to wait any longer to include young women of color in a larger discussion of body image.

Can I Get a Witness? Testimony from a Hip-Hop Feminist

SHANI JAMILA

I used to think I had missed my time. Thought I was meant to have come of age in the sixties when I could've been a Panther freedom fighter, challenging the pigs alongside Assata, Angela, and Kathleen. Oh, but I went deeper than that. I saw myself reading my poetry with Sonia, Ntozake, Nikki, and June...being a peer of Audre, Alice, and Paula Giddings...kickin' it with revolutionary brothers like Huey, Haki, and Rap...all while rocking the shit out of my black beret. When she needed advice, I would've *been* there for Patricia Hill Collins as she bounced her preliminary ideas about *Black Feminist Thought* off me. Now can't you see the beauty in this? I would have been building and bonding with a community of artists and activists that had this whole vibrancy radiating from its core, and so many of my role models would've just been crew.

I know right now some of y'all are probably like, "Okay, this child's on crack...that decade was not all that!" But don't front. When you heard the stories of your parents, aunts, uncles, and family friends—or even if you just watched some TV special talking about the mystique of the sixties—didn't it ever make you wonder what happened with our generation? Who were our revolutionaries? What sparked our passions so high that we were willing to risk our lives to fight for it? Where was our national Black Arts Movement?

It seemed natural that we should have one—after all, we had flavor for days...high-tops and Hammer pants, jellies and Jheri curls bear witness to that! And as an African-American child coming of age in the first generation to endure the United States post-integration, I can *definitely* testify that we had our own struggles: AIDS, apartheid, affirmative action, the prison-industrial complex, and underdeveloped inner cities are only a few examples. As I grew up, these were the things that would run through my mind while I cut out collages from *Right On!* and wonder what happened to us. Seemed like coping with issues like these would've hyped us up enough to create our own culture of resistance. The glossy pages trying to stick to the walls of my room competed futilely with the vibrations emanating from my spastic MTV imitations as Power 99 FM's bass blasted. I danced around the images of Public Enemy and Queen Latifah that decorated my floor, rapping all the lyrics to "Fight the Power" as I mourned our inactivity.

As I got older, I realized what I'd missed in my youth. Largely due to globalization and growing technology, in addition to some banging beats and off-the-chain lyrics, we'd had an *international* Black Arts Movement shaping our generation. As a kid, I didn't recognize hip hop as a vibrant and valuable sociocultural force—I just thought the culture was cool. I loved the music but never conceived of it as a revolutionary outcry. After all, I'd learned in school that activism was a concept confined to the sixties...so even though I felt empowered by the Afrocentric vibes and in-your-face lyrics, it seemed like the culture came a few decades too late for a critical context. In fact, individuals and organizations whose work challenged me to think critically about Black people at all rarely even entered the public school curriculum. In my high school's halls we were taught a very narrow and revisionist view of world history that boiled down to this: white was right, Africa was an afterthought. In addition to the massive amounts of potentially empowering information that was erased by those messages, a holistic history just was not taught.

Not only were my people not reflected in the syllabi, but I didn't see a proportionate reflection in the faces of my classmates, either. As one of only three Black faces in the honors program, all of whom were middle-class females, I often questioned why our representation was so disproportionate. The subtext shouted that the reason wasn't a deficiency in the newly integrated school system, but rather the failings of people of color. We were tacitly taught that our token presence proved racism and sexism were over, so the problem must have been our peers' inability to achieve. I knew this wasn't true, but as a child I was often frustrated because I didn't know how to prove it, as was often demanded that I do.

See, my generation came of age with the expectancy that we could live, eat, and attend school among whites. Race and gender were no longer inscribed in the law as automatic barriers to achievement, making the injustices we encountered less obvious than those our predecessors had faced. But the issues didn't go away. Instead, we found that an adverse consequence of integration and the "gains" of the sixties was an even more heavily convoluted notion of race and gender oppression. Economic class stratification has also continued to evolve as a serious complication.

The paradox of the Black middle class as I experienced it is that we are simultaneously affirmed and erased: tokenized and celebrated as one of the few "achievers" of our race, but set apart from other Black folks by our economic success. It is the classic divide-and-conquer technique regularly employed in oppressive structures: in this case, saying that Black people are pathological—but you somehow escaped the genetic curse, so you must be "different." These lessons were regularly reinforced with camouflaged compliments, such as, "Wow, you're so pretty/smart... are *both* of your parents Black?" Other times the insults would blaze brazenly, like the comments made by the white girls in my Girl Scouts carpool when we drove by a group of Black children playing in their yard: "Ooooh, Mom! Look at the little niglets playing on the street!" Their snickers echoed in a familiar way that suggested they'd shared this joke before. As the pain and rage began to well up within me, their dismissive comments also gathered force: "God, like, don't be so sensitive, Shani. We're not talking about *you*. You're different." I waited expectantly for the adult in the car to tell her children they were out of line and to apologize. She said nothing. I began to wonder if I was overreacting. Maybe it wasn't such a big deal. Maybe I *was* different. Maybe I thought too much.

Over the years I learned how to censor myself and adapt to different surroundings, automatically tailoring my tongue to fit the ear of whatever crew I was with. Depending on the composition of the crowd, the way I'd speak and even the things I'd talk about were subject to change. White people automatically got a very precise speech, because I knew every word out of my mouth was being measured and quantified as an example of the capabilities of the entire Black race. Around Black people I slipped into the vocabulary I felt more comfortable with, but remained aware that I was being judged. This time it was to see how capably I could fall back into "our talk" without sounding like a foreigner, if I could prove that my suburban upbringing and elitist education had not robbed me of my authenticity as a Black woman.

Passing this litmus test meant the most to me. Because if the daily trials weren't enough, when the flood of college acceptance and rejection letters began pouring in, and I got into schools my white "friends" weren't admitted to, all of a sudden the color they didn't see before came back fierce. My GPA, test scores, extracurricular activities, and recommendations were rendered irrelevant when they viciously told me the only conceivable reason I was getting in over them had to be affirmative action. I realized the racial logic being used against me was something that pervaded all class spheres. Whether we were seen as a beneficiary of affirmative action or in terms of the imagery of the welfare queen (whose depiction as a poor Black woman defied actual numerical stats), we were all categorized as niggers trying to get over on the system.

While most of my memories from childhood are happy ones, I also remember a constant struggle to find a sense of balance. For every "reward" token status bestowed, it simultaneously increased the isolation I felt. I didn't think there were many people who could understand how and why I was struggling when by societal standards I was succeeding. I worried that I was being ungrateful because I knew so many who had come before me had given their lives in the hope that one day their children could have the opportunities I'd grown up with. Despite the public accolades I received for my accomplishments, until I went to college I felt shunned by whites and suspected by Blacks. I was looking for a place to belong.

In 1993 I took my first steps on the campus of Spelman College, a Black women's space in the middle of the largest conglomeration of historically Black colleges and universities in the world. This is not your typical institution. One of only two colleges of its kind surviving in the States, Spelman is a place where Black women walk proud. Our first address from "Sista Prez" Johnnetta B. Cole told us so. As is characteristic of speeches to incoming first-year students, she instructed us to look to our right and look to our left. We dutifully gazed upon each other's brown faces. She spoke:

"Other schools will tell you one of these students will not be here in four years when you are graduating. At Spelman we say we will all see to it: your sister *better* be at your side when you *all* graduate in four years!" Loud cheers erupted—we were our sisters' keepers.

At Spelman I learned new ways of learning, thinking, and challenging. It was in this place that I was first introduced to a way of teaching that was unapologetically rooted in Black women's perspectives, that addressed the reality of what it meant to be at the center of intersecting discriminations like race, class, and gender. My formal education about my people began to expand beyond Malcolm and Martin. I learned about activists like Sojourner Truth and Maria W. Stewart, journalists and crusaders like Ida B. Wells, preachers like Jarena Lee, freedom fighters and abolitionists like Harriet Tubman, scholars like Anna Julia Cooper, poets like Frances Ellen Watkins Harper, and community leaders like Mary Church Terrell. Here our core courses were titled "African Diaspora and the World" and "Images of Women in the Media." The required reading on the syllabi included books like Paulo Freire's *Pedagogy of the Oppressed*, Frantz Fanon's *The Wretched of the Earth*, and Patricia Hill Collins's *Black Feminist Thought*. In these books and classes I found the answers to questions I didn't even have the language to ask with the education I'd received in high school.

This is what made attending a historically Black college such a turning point in my life. I don't want to romanticize my collegiate experience to the point where it was like I opened up a book and suddenly became some sort of guru, but being exposed to this community of scholars and activists did give me a framework for my feelings. The value of having my thoughts nurtured, legitimized, and placed into a historical context, in addition to the power of being surrounded by sisters and brothers who were walking refutations of the stereotypes I'd grown up with, gave me a space to blossom in ways I couldn't have imagined. I felt validated and affirmed by the idea that I no longer had to explain why Black folks were different from the purported standard. Instead of being made to justify what mainstream society perceived as deviance, I was supported in the effort to critically challenge how societal norms even came to be. I loved that when we would discuss slavery, an integral part of the conversation was slave revolts—Black resistance had finally entered the curriculum. It was the first time I saw people reflective of myself and my experiences both inside and outside of the classroom. Living and learning like this was revolutionary for me. It changed my life.

> 66 The value of having my thoughts nurtured, legitimized, and placed into a historical context gave me a space to blossom in ways I couldn't have imagined. 99

Of course, being on an all-women's campus, gender was also a regular topic of conversation. I was part of some beautiful dialogues where brothers would share the struggles they'd endured excelling academically that they hadn't faced when they'd shone in the more "acceptable" realms of sports or music. Sisters would relate back with testimonies of feeling forced to choose between our Blackness and our womanhood—a choice as impossible, a professor pointed out, as choosing between our left and right sides. In stark contrast to the race debates, however, these moments of raw honesty took place on a slippery slope. Gendered analyses were not granted the same sense of universal urgency attributed to analyses of race. Rather, they were received with suspicion. Many people perceived the debate over gender dynamics as a way to pit Black folks against each other. In heated conversations my peers would choose camps, placing race, gender, and class in a hierarchy and declaring loyalty to one over the other. Protests would be peppered with frequent warnings that Spelman was notorious for inculcating crazy mentalities in its students. We were told we'd better watch our backs, before we turned into one of those (gasp!) feminists, too.

Yup, the dreaded F-word continues to be so weighed down by negative connotations that few people are willing to voluntarily associate with it. Hurled out like an accusation, it is enough to make many sistas start backpedaling faster than the stats on violence against women. The reluctance to be identified with something perceived as an internally divisive force inside historically oppressed communities is understandable. Many feminists of color felt it, too, which is largely why Black feminist theory and womanism emerged. Unfortunately, much of what Black feminism really stands for has been stereotyped or obscured by school systems that don't devote time to Black women's intellectual traditions. A sad consequence has been that in addition to having something designed to advance our people become a tool of division, millions of people have been kept in the dark (so to speak) from a wealth of really important information and support networks.

Because of all the drama surrounding the word "feminism," there are mad heads who identify with feminist principles but feel conflicted about embracing the term. But let's examine what it really means. At root, Black feminism is a struggle against the pervasive oppression that defines Western culture. Whether taking aim at gender equity, homophobia, or images of women, it functions to resist disempowering ideologies and devaluing institutions. It merges theory and action to reaffirm Black women's legitimacy as producers of intellectual work and to reject assertions that attack our ability to contribute to these traditions. In stark contrast to the popular misconception that Black feminism is a divisive force that pits sisters against brothers, or even feminists against feminists, I view it as an essential part of a larger struggle for all of our liberation. Our fight for freedom has to be inclusive.

Of course, my understanding of Black feminism is rooted in theoretical texts written decades before I was first introduced to them in college. Many of these theories remain relevant, at the very least as an essential historical base. However, for any movement to maximize its effectiveness, it has to be applicable to the times. It is incumbent upon us as hip-hop feminists not to become complacent in the work that has come before us. We have to write our own stories that address the issues that are specific to our time. For example, some people think it's an oxymoron when I juxtapose a term like feminism alongside a genre of music that has been assailed for its misogyny. It seems obvious to me, however, that just as the shape of what we're fighting has changed, we need to examine how we as a community of activists have changed as well. Hip hop is the dominant influence on our generation.

Since my birth in 1975, four years before the first rap single achieved mainstream success, I have watched the hip-hop movement, culture, and music evolve. I mark important events in my life by the hip-hop songs that were popular at the time, linking my high-school graduation with the Souls of Mischief's album *93 'til Infinity* and my first school dance with the song "It Takes Two" by Rob Base. My ideas of fashion have often been misled by hip-hop artists like Kwamé, whose signature style resulted in the proliferation of polka dots in American schools around 1989. My taste in men has also been molded by hip-hop aesthetics. I entered my love life interested in brothers who were rocking Gumbies like my first boyfriend. As I got older, I discovered my own poetic voice, and I cannot begin to place a value on the amount of inspiration I got from this musical movement and the culture it birthed. I am a child of the hip-hop generation, grounded in the understanding that we enter the world from a hip-hop paradigm.

Those of us who embrace feminism can't act like hip hop hasn't been an influence on our lives, or vice versa, simply because claiming them both might seem to pose a contradiction. They are two of the basic things that mold us. However, we must not confuse having love for either one with blind defense. We have to love them enough to critique both of them and challenge them to grow—beyond the materialism and misogyny that has come to characterize too much of hip hop, beyond the extremism that feminism sometimes engages in. As women of the hip-hop generation, we need a feminist consciousness that allows us to examine how representations and images can be simultaneously empowering and problematic.

We have to engage with the rap lyrics about women and the accompanying images found in video scenes. A friend, Adziko Simba, once told me, "It seems bizarre to me that we Afrikan women have reached such an 'enlightened' point that we are defending our right to portray ourselves in ways that contribute to our degradation.... Did Sojourner Truth walk all those miles and bear her breast in the name of equality so that her heirs could have the right to jiggle their breasts on BET?" I completely feel her, though I don't think the role of feminism is to construct "proper" femininity, or to place limits on how women are able to define and present themselves. I think doing so is actually antithetical to the movement. Teaching women not to be sensual and erotic beings, or not to show that we are, is diminishing and subverts the locus of our own uniqueness as females. Why shouldn't we be able to celebrate our beauty, sensuality, sexuality, creative ability, or eroticism? They are all unique sites of women's power that we should not be taught to hide, or only to display when someone else says it's appropriate. On the flip side, we shouldn't support each other to the point of stupidity. We have to demand accountability from each other, no doubt. We need to be cognizant of the power in this music and of how we are representing ourselves on a global scale and on the historical record. These examples demonstrate how wide open the field is for sisters of the hip-hop generation to address the constantly shifting space women occupy. But these areas of concern should not be solely relegated to the Black feminist body of work. Hip-hop activists, intellectuals, and artists all need to take a leading role in confronting the fragmenting issues our generation deals with.

So, yeah, I used to think I missed my time. I thought the flame lighting the hearts of activists had been snuffed, *Survivor*-style. But liberating my definitions of activism from the constraints and constructs of the sixties opened up my mind to a whole new world of work and progressive thought. Now I draw strength from the knowledge that people have been actively combating sexism, racism, and other intersecting discriminations for a long time. Many of those icons I respect are still on the scene actively doing their thing for us. That knowledge is my ammunition as I join with them and my peers to continue fighting those battles and the other fronts unique to our time. We can't get complacent. The most important thing we can do as a generation is to see our new positions as power and weapons to be used strategically in the struggle rather than as spoils of war. Because this shit is far from finished.

Acknowledgments

Gracias: Bushra Rehman for making me laugh and always making my heart more compassionate; Marta Lucia, Adelina Anthony, and Angie Cruz for giving me my first home as a Latina, a writer, and a queer woman through the organization they founded, Women in Literature and Letters (WILL); Cherríe Moraga for your faith in this project the first and second time around; Gloria Anzaldúa for the power of your vision; Cristina Tzintzún for penning an unforgettable title that came to define the book; Leslie Miller for first proposing that we needed this book; Marcia Gillespie for inviting me to write for *Ms.* when I was barely out of college; and Gail Collins for the chance to learn so much about women's history in the United States.

Thank you: Hedgebrook and MacDowell for residencies that gave me the time to write about feminism more than fifteen years ago; the Barbara Deming Memorial Fund for financial support during the first edition of this book; Miami University in Ohio and its College of Arts and Sciences and Department of English for a research leave that supported my work on this second edition.

Gracias: Ayesha Pande, our agent, for pushing this second edition forward, and Laura Mazer for believing it was time.

Thank you to the friends who supported Bushra and me during the wild ride of creating the first edition and working on this second one: Kristina Lovato-Hermann, Keely Savoie, and Alice Sowaal.

A special thank you to Eugenia González Rosa, Thom Vernon, Char and Traci for giving me spiritual guidance and sustenance.

Gracias a mi hermanita, Liliana Hernández, y mi familia—Alicia Hernández, María de Jesus Sosa, Dora Capunay y Rosa Sosa. Gracias a mi padre, Ygnacio Hernández, y mi tío José Capunay. Thank you, Zami, because a writer must always thank her cat. A special shout-out of gratitude to my sweetheart, Frankie Clark.

Thank you to the readers who loved the first edition enough to make this second one possible, and to the contributors who worked so hard to create, once again, the book I needed to read.

—Daisy Hernández

Thank you: Daisy Hernández for your friendship, brilliance in mind and spirit, and sharing the journey of *Colonize This!* with me; Cherríe Moraga, for your foreword and your vision; Gloria Anzaldúa for your words and spirit; and all the writers of *Colonize This!* both past and present.

Thank you to my family, both chosen and of origin, who taught me how to be a radical woman; special love to my parents, siblings, nieces, and nephews, Rosina Rehman Perowsky, Ben Perowsky, Sa'dia Rehman, Andrea Dobrich, Anastacia Holt, Adele Swank, Chamindika Wanduragala, Chitra Ganesh, Diedra Barber, Kristina Lovato-Hermann, Rekha Malhotra, Saba Waheed, Sally Lee, Stas Gibbs, Yvette Ho, and all my friends from Two Truths.

Thank you to the collectives that changed my life, especially the South Asian Women's Creative Collective, Women in Literature and Letters, and the Asian American Writers' Workshop. Thank you to the Barbara Deming Memorial Foundation and Norcroft, which supported work on the first edition. Thank you to Dr. Ann Raia and Dr. Barbara McManus and all my professors at The College of New Rochelle for sowing the seeds of feminism in my mind.

Thank you to Leslie Miller for pursuing the idea for the first edition with us, and Angie Cruz for suggesting we work together. Thank you to Ayesha Pande and Laura Mazer for helping bring a second edition into the world.

—Bushra Rehman

Notes

Foreword: "The War Path of Greater Empowerment"

1. Cherríe Moraga and Gloria Anzaldúa, eds., *This Bridge Called My Back: Writings by Radical Women of Color*, 2nd ed. (New York: Kitchen Table, 1983). The first edition of the book was published in 1981 by Persephone Press in Watertown, Massachusetts; it was reissued in a fourth edition in 2015 by the State University of New York Press in Albany.

2. This sentence refers to an essay in the first edition of *Colonize This!* by Cecilia Ballí titled "Thirty-Fight."

3. This sentence refers to an essay in the first edition of *Colonize This!* by Ijeoma A. titled "Because You're a Girl."

4. This sentence refers to an essay in the first edition of *Colonize This!* by Pandora L. Leong titled "Living Outside the Box."

5. This sentence refers to an essay in the first edition of *Colonize This!* by Patricia Justine Tumang titled "*Nasaan ka anak ko?* A Queer Filipina-American Feminist's Tale of Abortion and Self-Recovery."

Introduction to the First Edition

1. Audre Lorde, "A Litany for Survival," in *The Black Unicorn* (New York: Norton, 1978, reissued in 1995). Used with permission of the publisher.

browngirlworld: queergirlofcolor organizing, sistahood, heartbreak

1. Staci Haines, *The Survivor's Guide to Sex: How to Have an Empowered Sex Life After Child Sexual Abuse* (San Francisco: Cleis Press, 1999), 121.

#SayHerName: The Day Utopia Came Home

1. Dan Baum, "Legalize It All: How to Win the War on Drugs," *Harper's*, April 2016.

2. Reagan's statements have been quoted often in subsequent years; see, for example, Josh Levin, "The Welfare Queen," *Slate*, December 19, 2013.

3. The Combahee River Collective Statement, April 1977.

4. Audre Lorde, *A Burst of Light and Other Essays* (Mineola, NY: Courier, Dover, 2017 [1988]), 130.

Love Feminism but Where's My Hip Hop? Shaping a Black Feminist Identity

1. Cheo Coker, dream hampton, and Tara Roberts, "A Hip-Hop Nation Divided," *Essence*, August 1994, 62–64, 112–115; Eisa Davis, "if we've gotta live underground and everybody's got cancer /will poetry be enuf?—A Letter to Ntozake Shange," in *Step into a World: A Global Anthology of the New Black Literature*, ed. Kevin Powell (New York: John Wiley and Sons, 2000), 380–384; Eisa Davis, "Sexism and the Art of Feminist Hip-Hop Maintenance," in *To Be Real: Telling the Truth and Changing the Face of Feminism*, ed. Rebecca Walker (New York: Anchor, 1995), 127–142; Joan Morgan, *When Chickenheads Come Home to Roost: My Life as a Hip-Hop Feminist* (New York: Simon and Schuster, 1999); Tara Roberts and Eisa

Nefertari Ulen, "Sisters Spin the Talk on Hip Hop: Can the Music Be Saved," *MS Magazine*, February/March 2000, 70–74; Eisa Nefertari Ulen, "What Happened to Your Generation's Promise of 'Love and Revolution'? A Letter to Angela Davis," In *Step into a World: A Global Anthology of the New Black Literature*, ed. Kevin Powell (New York: John Wiley and Sons, 2000).

2. Tricia Rose, *Black Noise: Rap Music and Black Culture in Contemporary America* (Middletown, CT: Wesleyan University Press, 1994).

3. June Jordan, "Where Is the Love?," National Black Writers Conference, Howard University, 1978 speech, published in *Essence*, September 1981, and *Civil Wars* (New York: Touchstone, 1995).

Bring Us Back into the Dance: Women of the Wasase

1. Louis Karoniaktajeh Hall, *Warrior's Handbook* (Ontario: L. K. Hall), 10.

Echoes of a Mother: Black Women, Foster Care, and Reproductive Rights

1. P. R. Lockhart, "The Untold Story About Black Women and Abortions," *Mother Jones*, October 6, 2016.

Dutiful *Hijas*: Dependency, Power, and Guilt

1. The term *marianismo* refers to La Virgen Maria (the Virgin Mary).

2. Rosa Maria Gil and Carmen Inoa Vazquez, *The Maria Paradox: How Latinas Can Merge Old World Traditions with New World Self-Esteem* (New York: Perigee Books, 1997), 8.

3. Julia de Burgos, *Roses in the Mirror: Translated Poems of Julia De Burgos* (San Juan, Puerto Rico: Ediciones Mairena, 1992); bell hooks, *Black Looks* (Boston: South End Press, 1992); Angela Davis,

Women, Race and Class (New York: Vintage, 1981); Assata Shakur, *Assata* (London: Zed Books, 1987).

4. bell hooks, *Feminist Theory: From Margin to Center* (Boston: South End Press, 1984), 24.

5. Here the term *Americanas* refers to the values of *blanquitas* (white women), who are assumed to divorce themselves from their families.

6. Louis Uchitelle, "Lacking Pensions, Older Divorced Women Remain at Work," *New York Times*, June 26, 2001.

Femme-Inism: Lessons of My Mother

1. Joan Nestle's words originally appeared in "The Femme Question," in *The Persistent Desire: A Femme-Butch Reader* (Boston: Alyson Publications, 1992).

2. Judith Roof, "1970s Lesbian Feminism Meets 1990s Butch-Femme," in Sally R. Munt, ed., *butch/femme: Inside Lesbian Gender* (London: Cassell, 1998), 27.

Migrant Organizing: A Retelling

1. Audre Lorde, "Learning from the 60s," in *Sister Outsider: Essays and Speeches by Audre Lorde* (Berkeley, CA: Crossing Press, 2007), 138.

2. Chandra Talpade Mohanty, "Under Western Eyes: Feminist Scholarship and Colonial Discourses," *boundary 2*, vol. 12, no. 3, and vol. 13, no. 1, On Humanism and the University I: The Discourse of Humanism (Spring-Autumn 1984): 333–358.

Organizing 101: A Mixed-Race Feminist in Movements for Social Justice

1. Another version of this essay appears in *Fireweed: A Feminist Quarterly of Writing, Politics, Art and Culture*, issue 75 (May 2002).

It's Not an Oxymoron: The Search for an Arab Feminism

1. Cheryl Rubenberg, *Palestinian Women: Patriarchy and Resistance in the West Bank* (Boulder: Lynne Rienner, 2001).

2. In Arabic culture women traditionally keep their family names when they marry. Their children assume the names of their fathers, but women are considered to be members of their original families always. This is unlike the Western tradition of marriage, in which a woman is symbolically "given away" by her father to her husband's family.

3. The "Angel in the House" is a theory put forth by Virginia Woolf in her essay *A Room of One's Own*, first published in 1929 (London: Hogarth Press; New York: Harcourt Brace). For Woolf, the Angel in the House is the epitome of Victorian womanhood, whose image haunts her as a writer and attempts to stop her creativity. The angel therefore represents womanhood in an era in which "feminine" women were uneducated and uncritical of their own oppression. The "wallpaper" allusion refers to Charlotte Perkins Gilman's story "The Yellow Wallpaper," in which a woman goes mad when her husband restricts her ability to write. It was first published in the *New England Magazine* in January 1892 but is frequently reprinted in anthologies.

About the Contributors

Lexi Adsit is a fierce, fat, and femme translatina woman born and raised in the San Francisco Bay Area. She has helped organize groundbreaking projects such as the Queer Yo Mind Conference at San Francisco State University, the International Trans Women of Color Network Gathering, and the first all-trans women of color comedy show *Brouhaha*. Her writing has been featured on Salon, on Autostraddle, and in the new anthology *Trap Door: Trans Cultural Production and the Politics of Visibility*. You can find out more about her work and get in touch with her at lexiadsit.com.

Paula Austin is Afro-Caribbean and proudly (although maybe not as loudly) still femme-identified. An assistant professor in the History Department at California State University, Sacramento, she specializes in African-American, gender, and urban histories of the nineteenth and early twentieth centuries and is currently working on an intellectual and social history of young, Black, poor, and working-class Washingtonians in the interwar US capital. She is also proud to have contributed "Femme-Inism: Lessons of My Mother" when she was still officially a "young" woman of color. Her mother is now gone, and the essay in this anthology stands as an homage as well as a reminder that structures of oppression are not the only things that define us. Every day we generate and regenerate spaces inside and in spite of those structures for our liberation.

Siobhan Brooks is an associate professor of African American studies at California State University, Fullerton. She received her PhD in sociology from The New School. Brooks's work explores the intersections of sexuality, race, gender, class, and mental health among LGBTQ urban-identified Black women. She is the author of *Unequal Desires: Race and Erotic Capital in the Stripping Industry.* Her work was published in the anthology *Black LGBT Health in the United States: The Intersection of Race, Gender, and Sexual Orientation.* She is currently working on a book that explores the impact of hate crimes on Black and Latinx LGBTQ families.

Sayeeda Copeland is a native of Harlem, a writer, and a mother. Her poem "Pregnant with Haiti's Prayer" won "Best of the Bronx" in the 2010 Random House Creative Writing Contest. Currently residing in the Bronx she is a part of Las Raices, a writing group of women dedicated to bringing awareness of cultural changes in the borough. She enjoys studying the work of her favorite authors: James Baldwin, Langston Hughes, Maya Angelou, Toni Morrison, and Sister Souljah. She is currently creating a line of journals to encourage other people to fall in love with writing as much as she has.

Susan Muaddi Darraj is associate professor of English at Harford Community College in Bel Air, Maryland. A 2018 USA Ford Fellow, she is also a lecturer in the writing program at Johns Hopkins University and a faculty member for Fairfield University's master's in fine arts program. Her collection of short stories *A Curious Land: Stories from Home* won the 2016 Arab American Book Award and an American Book Award the same year and was shortlisted for a Palestine Book Award. She is also the author of *The Inheritance of Exile* and lives in Baltimore, Maryland.

Erica González Martínez, a lifelong advocate for social justice, led digital inclusion and innovation work at the New York City Council and is the former executive editor of *El Diario-La Prensa*. She is committed to a #justrecovery for Puerto Rico and is working on a criminal justice project that looks at the experience of the Puerto Rican community. Erica currently serves as a board member for the Women's Media Center and is a judge for the Aronson Awards.

Sonia Guiñansaca is a queer migrant poet, cultural organizer, and activist from Harlem by way of Ecuador. Named as one of the "Up and Coming Latinx Poets You Need to Know" by Remezcla, she is the 2017/2018 artist-in-residence at the Hemispheric Institute of Performance and Politics and a US Future Leaders Delegate for the British Council. She has emerged as a national leader in the undocumented/migrant artistic and political communities, cofounding and helping to build some of the largest undocumented organizations in the country and coordinating and participating in groundbreaking actions. She founded some of the first creative artistic projects by and for undocumented writers/artists. Currently, she is the managing director of CultureStrike.

Kahente Horn-Miller (Kanien:keha'ka/Mohawk) is an assistant professor in the School of Indigenous and Canadian Studies and codirector of the Centre for Indigenous Research, Culture, Language and Education at Carleton University. Her community-based research centers on Indigenous membership and citizenship, Indigenous womanism, Haudenosaunee and Kanien:keha'ka culture and philosophy, Indigenous participatory democracy, rematriation in practice, embodied knowledge, and storytelling/performance. Her work is about putting Indigenous theories into practice. She challenges others to learn about themselves as human beings, fostering relationships that go beyond the written word, the classroom, and the research setting to reconnect us to the realities of reinvigorating Indigenous traditions in the modern world.

Rebecca Hurdis received her PhD in ethnic studies from the University of California, Berkeley, in 2009. She has been an adjunct professor at the University of California, Santa Cruz, and California State University, Monterey Bay. Most recently, she was the executive director of a residential program for homeless pregnant women. She has lived in the Santa Cruz area for the past twenty years. Above all, she is grateful for how women of color feminism continues to shape, inspire, and guide her commitment to creating a more equitable community and society.

Soyon Im has been published in the *New York Times* and the *Seattle Times*. She is a photographer and writer and is inspired to create modern stories of old-fashioned love.

shani jamila is a teacher, traveler, hip-hoppian, and cultural worker. She is a proud graduate of Spelman College and holds a master's degree in African diaspora cultural studies from the University of California, Los Angeles. She has visited or lived in more than twenty countries, including a year in Gabon, Central Africa, where she taught more than three hundred students and cosponsored an intercontinental book drive to found a school library. She is also the recipient of a Fulbright Fellowship that allowed her to spend a year studying women's activism in Jamaica and Trinidad. Her work on hip-hop feminism has been the subject of international colloquia and has received extensive radio, television, and newspaper coverage. In addition, she has performed her poetry in

North and South America, Africa, and countries throughout the Caribbean. As artist, academic, and activist, shani's drive is to reach and reflect her people.

Darice Jones, aka DJ, based in Oakland, California, is a writer and director. In the mid-2000s, she co-published a Bay Area queer zine called *PussyTown*. Jones completed her first feature film, *She Wasn't Last Night*, in 2009. She was able to showcase the black lesbian project internationally to receptive Afri-Queer audiences. Through her small indie film organization Griot Soul Films, she is currently in development on three new projects: *Love Letters to Black Children* (a short-form web series), *Resonance* (an Afrofuturist feature fantasy), and *The Seven Codes* (an urban TV fantasy series). She has also continued her storytelling through novel writing and poetry. In addition to her creative works, DJ is development director at Brava! for Women in the Arts, a San Francisco nonprofit theater organization.

Jamilah King is a journalist who writes about race and gender. She is currently the race and justice reporter at *Mother Jones*, and her work has previously appeared in the *Washington Post*, the *California Sunday Magazine*, *Mic*, and *Colorlines*. She currently lives in Brooklyn.

Sandra Kumwong, a junior in the Macaulay Honors College at Hunter College, is majoring in sociology with minors in chemistry and biology. She is also a health educator and a co-coordinator for the Peer Health Exchange chapter at the college, a former intern for Planned Parenthood of New York City, and a full-spectrum doula for The Doula Project. You can find her in a yoga studio, hiking around New York, demonstrating how to use an internal condom, or waitressing. As a proud, vulgar daughter of Thai immigrants, she hopes to further health access for all people by taking stigma and shame head on.

Stella Luna is a graduate of the Chicano/Chicana studies program at Arizona State University. She is recognized as an activist and grassroots organizer for women and children living with HIV. She has spent the past twenty-seven years changing the face of HIV to help end the stigma related to the disease. She gave birth to her daughter, who is HIV negative, in 2003. Stella's son, who was born with HIV, is now healthy, engaged, and a new father. Both his fiancée and his baby are negative. So Stella is a grandmother! Today her mission is to encourage HIV women not to be afraid to experience all that life has to offer.

Luna Merbruja is a Mexican-Athabaskan multidisciplinary artist and writer. She is the author of *Trauma Queen* and *Heal Your Love* and has been published in *Nerve Endings: The New Trans Erotic* and *The Resilience Anthology*. Currently she is a project adviser for Mirror Memoirs and a book editor for biyuti publishing. You can find her work archived at luna.merbruja.com and follow her on social media @LunaMerbruja.

Bhavana Mody lives in Novato, California, where she indulges in hikes and long bike rides in the redwoods and near the Pacific Ocean. For her primary job she teaches elementary school environmental science in English and Spanish at a dual-immersion public school in Napa. Since writing her essay for the first edition of *Colonize This!*, Bhavana has made several visits to India, deepening her relationships with her extended family and her culture and passionately taking up yoga and meditation. She has been teaching yoga for about fifteen years and is currently training to become a yoga therapist. Perhaps one of the few South Asian yoga teachers in Marin County, Bhavana teaches yoga classes and Indian dance classes, shamelessly claiming her *Indian-ness*.

Natani Notah is an interdisciplinary artist, poet, and graphic designer. Inspired by acts of decolonization, environmental justice, Indigenous feminism, and Indigenous futurism, she explores contemporary Native American identity through the lens of Diné (Navajo) womanhood. She graduated in 2014 from Cornell University with a bachelor's degree in fine art and a minor in feminist, gender, and sexuality studies. Natani is currently a candidate for the master of fine arts degree in art practice at Stanford University, where she is also an art studio instructor and teaching assistant.

Leah Lakshmi Piepzna-Samarasinha is a queer, nonbinary, disabled femme writer, curator, and educator of Burgher/Tamil Sri Lankan and Irish/Roma ascent. The Lambda Award–winning author of *Dirty River, Bodymap, Love Cake,* and *Consensual Genocide* and co-editor of *The Revolution Starts at Home,* she cofounded and codirected the QTPOC performance collective Mangos With Chili from 2005 to 2015. She is also a lead artist with the disability justice performance collective Sins Invalid and cofounded Toronto's Asian Arts Freedom School. Her new book of essays, *Care Work: Dreaming Disability Justice,* is forthcoming in the fall of 2018. Raised in Worcester, Massachusetts, she divides her time between Tkaronto and South Seattle.

Andrea L. Pino is the coauthor of *We Believe You: Survivors of Campus Sexual Assault Speak Out* and cofounder of the national survivor advocacy organization End Rape on Campus. She attended the

University of North Carolina at Chapel Hill as a first-generation college student and was among the first survivors of campus sexual assault to publicly file a federal Title IX complaint. Her activism and personal journey is prominently featured in the 2015 Sundance film *The Hunting Ground*, and she appeared alongside Lady Gaga and fifty other survivors at the 2016 Academy Awards.

Gwendolyn D. Pough is a professor and chair of graduate studies in the Women's and Gender Studies Department and Dean's Professor of the Humanities at Syracuse University. She is the author of *Check It While I Wreck It: Black Womanhood Hip-Hop Culture and the Public Sphere*. She is also the author of several hip-hop feminist romance novels under the pen name Gwyneth Bolton.

Sirena J. Riley was born in Columbus, Georgia, and raised in Prince George's County, Maryland, just outside of Washington, DC. After completing a bachelor's degree in women's studies at the University of Maryland, College Park, she worked for several feminist nonprofits in the nation's capital. Sirena is now a singer-songwriter and voiceover artist based in London. She is the voice of activist Assata Shakur in the audiobook version of Shakur's autobiography, *Assata*. For more information visit sirenariley.com.

Kiini Ibura Salaam is a writer, painter, and traveler from New Orleans, Louisiana. Her work is rooted in speculative events, women's perspectives, and personal freedom. She is the author of two short-story collections: *Ancient, Ancient*—winner of the 2012 James Tiptree Jr. Award—and *When the World Wounds*. Her fiction has been anthologized in such collections as *Dark Matter*, *Mojo: Conjure Stories*, and *Dark Eros*. Her essays have been published in *Essence*, *Utne Reader*, and *Ms*. She examines the writing life in her

Notes from the Trenches ebook series. Her writing and art are archived at kiiniibura.com.

Almas Sayeed is an antipoverty advocate, organizer, policy nerd, lawyer, and writer based in Los Angeles.

Tanmeet Sethi, MD, is an integrative medicine physician and fellowship director at Swedish Cherry Hill in Seattle, Washington, where she serves vulnerable populations and uses medicine as a vehicle for social justice. She serves as senior faculty for the Center for Mind Body Medicine in Washington, DC, and as an assistant professor at the University of Washington Medical School. She is a two-time TEDxSeattle speaker and has a gratitude blog on her website, www.tanmeetsethimd.com. When she isn't mothering her three children, fighting for food justice, writing, speaking, or teaching, she tries to remember that every act of compassion and love is a peaceful protest to the darkness in the world.

Taigi Smith has been a full-time journalist for more than two decades. She is an award-winning television producer, a writer, and a mother. Her career has taken her to cult compounds, murder trials, and movie sets, with the high point of her career being the time she spent in Thailand covering the deadly tsunami of 2004. Taigi is the editor of *Sometimes Rhythm, Sometimes Blues: Young African Americans on Love, Relationships, Sex, and the Search for Mr. Right*. Taigi was born in Newark, New Jersey, and raised in San Francisco. She attended Mills College in Oakland, California, where she received her bachelor's degree in communications. You can reach her @cgmTaigi.

Phoenix Soleil is an artist, activist, and teacher. She is passionate about the intersections of community, emotional intelligence, and trauma and has led trainings in communication, racial justice, and emotional resiliency for individuals, groups, and organizations such as Google, the Kellogg Foundation, the University of California, Berkeley, and the Search Inside Yourself Leadership Institute. Check out her website for upcoming trainings and for more information on her artistic endeavors (phoenixsoleil.com).

Amber Taylor is a soft black girl from Columbus, Ohio. She recently graduated from Miami University in Oxford, Ohio, where she studied creative writing and learned how to cook more than just scrambled eggs. When she isn't reading, she enjoys watching Korean dramas and cartoons for kids. You can find her nonfiction at *Crab Fat Magazine*, *The Blueshift Journal*, and *Rigorous*.

Cristina Tzintzún is a leading civil rights leader based in Texas. She was named "Hero of the New South" by *Southern Living* magazine in 2013 and her work has been featured on National Public Radio, MTV, Univision, and MSNBC's *Up Late with Alec Baldwin* as well as in the *New York Times* and *USA Today*, among others. She is a 2017 J.M.K. Innovation Prize winner through the J. M. Kaplan Fund and a 2018 Roddenberry Fellow. Today, Cristina is the founder and executive director of Jolt—a Texas organization that lifts up the voice, vote, and issues impacting Latinos. Previously, she founded and led the Workers Defense Project, a statewide workers' rights organization that was called "one of the most creative organizations for immigrant workers in the country" by the *New York Times*.

Lisa Weiner-Mahfuz is a queer, disabled, mixed-race Arab/Jew who has been a racial and gender justice organizer for the past twenty-five years. She has written extensively on the issues of mixed-race identity—particularly as it relates to the work light-skinned people of color must do to challenge and dismantle white supremacy. In 2012 she was a member of the first LGBTQ delegation to Palestine. Since the first edition of *Colonize This!*, she has worked across multiracial movements as a capacity builder and strategist. Currently she is the executive for program and strategic partnerships at the Religious Coalition for Reproductive Choice.

About the Editors

Daisy Hernández is the author of *A Cup of Water Under My Bed: A Memoir* and coeditor of *Colonize This! Young Women of Color on Today's Feminism*. A journalist and former editor of *ColorLines* magazine, Daisy has reported for the *Atlantic*, the *New York Times*, and *Slate*, and her writing has been aired on NPR's *All Things Considered*. Her essays and fiction have been published in *Aster(ix)*, *Brevity*, *Dogwood*, *Fourth Genre*, *Gulf Coast*, *Juked*, *Rumpus*, and *Tricycle: The Buddhist Review*, among others. She is an assistant professor in the Creative Writing Program at Miami University in Ohio.

Bushra Rehman is a poet, novelist, and teaching artist. Her novel *Corona*, a dark comedy about being South Asian American, was noted by *Poets & Writers* among the year's Best Debut Fiction. Her poetry collection *Marianna's Beauty Salon* has been described as a "love poem for Muslim girls, Queens, and immigrants." Her first YA novel, *Corona: Stories of a Queens Girlhood*, is forthcoming from Tor/Macmillan. Rehman is coeditor of *Colonize This! Young Women of Color on Today's Feminism* and creator of the community-based writing workshop "Two Truths and a Lie: Writing Memoir and Autobiographical Fiction."